Balthasar Hubmaier's
Doctrine of Salvation
in Dynamic and
Relational Perspective

Balthasar Hubmaier's Doctrine of Salvation in Dynamic and Relational Perspective

CHANGKYU KIM

With a foreword by Stuart Murray Williams

◠PICKWICK *Publications* · Eugene, Oregon

BALTHASAR HUBMAIER'S DOCTRINE OF SALVATION IN DYNAMIC AND RELATIONAL PERSPECTIVE

Copyright © 2013 Changkyu Kim. All rights reserved. Except for brief quotations in critical publications or reviews, no part of this book may be reproduced in any manner without prior written permission from the publisher. Write: Permissions, Wipf and Stock Publishers, 199 W. 8th Ave., Suite 3, Eugene, OR 97401.

Pickwick Publications
An Imprint of Wipf and Stock Publishers
199 W. 8th Ave., Suite 3
Eugene, OR 97401

www.wipfandstock.com

ISBN 13: 978-1-62032-119-5

Cataloguing-in-Publication data:

Kim, Changkyu.

    Balthasar Hubmaier's doctrine of salvation in dynamic and relational perspective / Changkyu Kim ; foreword by Stuart Murray Williams.

    xvi + 210 pp. ; 23 cm. Includes bibliographical references and index.

    ISBN 13: 978-1-62032-119-5

    1. Hubmaier, Balthasar, –1528. 2. Salvation. I. Murray, Stuart, 1956–. II. Title.

BX4946.H8 K49 2013

Manufactured in the U.S.A.

For My Mother, Ok-Ran Park

and

in Memory of My Father, Man-Ha Kim

"I may err, I am a human being—but a heretic I cannot be, for I constantly ask instruction in the Word of God."

"Die Warheit ist untödlich (Truth is Immortal)."

—Balthasar Hubmaier (ca. 1480–1528)

Contents

Foreword by Stuart Murray Williams   ix

Preface   xi

Acknowledgments   xiii

Abbreviations   xv

1. Introduction   1
2. Hubmaier's Doctrine of the Freedom of the Will   31
3. Hubmaier's Doctrine of Baptism (I)   69
4. Hubmaier's Doctrine of Baptism (II)   107
5. Hubmaier's Doctrine of the Lord's Supper   146
6. Conclusion: A Fresh Perspective on Hubmaier's Doctrine of Salvation   180

Bibliography   197

Index   203

Foreword

BALTHASAR HUBMAIER HAS LONG been regarded as an enigmatic figure among sixteenth-century reformers. As this fresh study of his writings recognizes, he is difficult to locate satisfactorily within either the magisterial or radical reform movements. There are Anabaptist, Reformed, and Catholic elements within his theology, blended together into a creative and nuanced approach to diverse ecclesial and ethical issues. His significance among his contemporaries is unquestionable, but his lasting contribution is less easy to identify.

One of the reasons for this, argues Kim Changkyu, is that too much attention has been paid to tracing the various influences upon his thinking and not enough to his writings themselves and the internal evidence for his passions and priorities. Deep concern for the proper reform of the church, the author insists, is the primary motivation behind all that Hubmaier writes, whatever the particular topic he is addressing.

Attempting to remedy this deficiency in previous studies of Hubmaier, Kim Changkyu embarks on an ambitious re-reading of significant sections of his writings, focusing especially on the meaning of "faith" and the understanding of "salvation" that undergird Hubmaier's theology and have all kinds of ecclesial outworkings. What emerges is a distinctive soteriology and redefinition of the phrase "justification by faith."

Kim Changkyu's chosen method of interpreting Hubmaier's writings draws on the seminal work of Martin Buber. Rejecting transactional and overly objective portrayals of Hubmaier's theology, he advocates and demonstrates the significance of viewing Hubmaier's writings through the lens of dialogical personalism. Through this lens the coherence of Hubmaier's perspectives on baptism, the Lord's Supper, the ban, free will, Christology and faith becomes increasingly clear: all are related to his understanding of salvation, viewed in dynamic and relational terms.

During the past three decades the contemporary significance of the Anabaptist tradition has been recognised by Christians in many different contexts. Anabaptist networks, centres and movements have emerged in

Foreword

nations with no historic Anabaptist heritage, including the United Kingdom in which the author studied and Korea from where he hails. Scholars in these contexts are coming to Anabaptists writings with fresh questions and offering new insights alongside more established North American and continental European scholars. This book represents a welcome addition to the literature on Balthasar Hubmaier and a significant contribution from a Korean Anabaptist scholar.

Not only does Kim Changkyu throw fresh light on how Hubmaier's writings are to be understood and his significance assessed in his sixteenth-century context. He also suggests ways in which his doctrine of salvation and its ecclesial implications might be resources for Anabaptists and others in the twenty-first century. Readers in Korea, the United Kingdom, Tanzania (where the author now teaches) and elsewhere will find in this book not only a detailed study of the theology and concerns of a fascinating and influential reformer but challenges to our own views and practices.

Stuart Murray Williams
April 2012

Preface

THE KOREAN CHURCH WAS evangelized tremendously in the twentieth century. The quantitative growth has been remarkable in growing the many mega-churches in Korea. The largest church in the world (Yoido Full Gospel Church with more than 830,000 members as of 2007) and four more out of the ten largest Protestant churches in the world were in Korea in 2007. However, in recent decades the Korean Christian population has been decreasing. There have been analyses of the cause of this decrease by Korean scholars and pastors. Abusive leadership and immorality of Christians are the most agreed upon causes for people to leave the church. These problems are not only in the Korean church but also in the third world countries. In other countries, too, some of which I have experienced, overly authoritative leadership, sexual immorality, and dishonesty are prevalent in the church. We could say that these are the causes of corruption and the diminishing reliability of Christianity.

Why has this happened in our churches today? I suggest that one of the reasons is misunderstanding or misusing the concept of salvation by faith. Although Scripture teaches us what salvation means and how we should live as Christians, many church-goers can easily conclude that the meaning of salvation by faith is to get a ticket that can lead to heaven after death or to provide a way of being blessed. For them, to be a Christian is about how to hold to certain faith statements rather than how their lives should be changed according to Scripture. This tendency has developed not simply because of individual church-goers, but because many churches have not focused sufficiently on the significance of the transformation of life in Christ.

This issue has been thought about critically not only in our own time, but by church leaders in the sixteenth century as well. Balthasar Hubmaier is one of the most representative Anabaptist theologians among the sixteenth-century reformers who considered this matter seriously. He was grieved over seeing those who emphasized the doctrine of "justification by faith" in ways that did not transform their immoral and corrupt lives.

Preface

In this context, Hubmaier wrote many treatises to help people understand what salvation and being a Christian mean. Through examining his writings on such issues as baptism, the Lord's Supper, the ban, freewill, and faith, therefore, we will see how Hubmaier understood the meaning of salvation and interpreted the reformation motto, "justification by faith." I hope that this work may lead us to rethink the meaning of salvation and its ecclesial implications for Christian life through Hubmaier's unique understanding of salvation in dynamic and relational perspective.

Acknowledgments

THIS BOOK IS A revision of a doctoral dissertation submitted to the University of Bristol in 2009. In writing my dissertation, I have contracted many debts. First of all, I am deeply indebted to my supervisor Rev. Dr. Ruth Gouldbourne, who enabled me to study Anabaptism and Balthasar Hubmaier. Without her patience, generosity, guidance, and encouragement this work would never have been completed. I would also like to express my sincere appreciation to my second supervisor, Dr. Stuart Murray Williams, who offered valuable suggestions on my thesis and the courage to carry on my research with confidence. I would like to thank both of them for their diligent supervision, perceptive criticism, and continuous encouragement over the period in which this dissertation was written. I am grateful to Dr. Ian Randall, who offered his time to read some of the chapters and gave insightful suggestions and encouragement. To the two examiners, Rev. Dr. John Colwell and Rev. Dr. James Steven, I record my gratitude for their critical comments and helpful suggestions on my work.

For me, it was a wonderful privilege to study at Trinity College, Bristol. I am grateful to the faculty and staff for their support in various ways I thank Su Brown, the Librarian of Trinity College, Bristol, for all her help in providing materials for my research, and Shirley Shire, the Librarian of Bristol Baptist College. I would like to give particular thanks to Mr. Andrew Lucas, the executive director of Trinity College, Bristol, for his concern and prayer. I am also grateful to my friends, Rev. Dr. Emma Ineson and Mrs. Jeannie Reid who proofread my thesis for errors and corrections.

My deepest gratitude goes to my family. My special thanks go to my beloved wife, Sora Lee, for her wholehearted and unfailing support, encouragement, and love. I owe her more than I can write here. I thank my mother, Ok-Ran Park, who brought me up in the Christian faith and showed me how to serve God and God's people throughout her life. To my mother I express my more than grateful recognition for her great encouragement and prayer for me not only during my research but also all my life. While I was in the final stages of writing this dissertation, there

Acknowledgments

was the significant distress of my father, Man-Ha Kim's sudden illness and death in September 2007. My father, to me, was the most important mentor, who showed me, through his own example, how to live as a Christian. I miss him very much. I look forward to seeing him in heaven. This book is dedicated, therefore, not only to my mother, Ok-Ran Park but also to the memory of my father, Man-Ha Kim, with my respect, love, and the deepest appreciation.

Abbreviations

ARG	*Archiv für Reformationsgeschichte*
ATR	*Anglican Theological Review*
CC	*Corpus Christianorum*
CSEL	C. F. Urba and J. Zycha, eds. *Corpus Scriptorum Ecclesiasticorum Latinorum*. Vienna: Tempsky, 1902–
EDT	Elwell, Walter A., ed. *Evangelical Dictionary of Theology*. Carlisle: Paternoster, 1984.
HS	*Balthasar Hubmaier Schriften*, QGT IX
LCC	*Library of Christian Classics*
LW	*Luther's Works*. 55vols. Philadelphia, PA: Muhlenberg, 1955–
ME	*Mennonite Encyclopedia*
MQR	*Mennonite Quarterly Review*
NIDOTTE	VanGemeren, W. A., ed. *New International Dictionary of Old Testament Theology and Exegesis*. 5 vols. Lancaster: Paternoster, 1997
PL	J. P. Migne, ed. *Patrologia Latina*. Paris, 1862–1865
SAMH	Studies in Anabaptist and Mennonite History Schornbaum, Quelle *Markgraftum Brandenburg*, QGT II
ST	*Summa Theologica*
QGT	*Quellen Zur Geschichte der Täufer*
vMS	Leonhard von Muralt and Water Schmidt, QGT I. Zürich 1952
WA	*D. Martin Luthers Werke*. Weimar: Böhlau, 1883–
YP	*Balthasar Hubmaier: Theologian of Anabaptism*

Abbreviations

Z	*Huldreich Zwingli Sämtliche Werke*, Band II. Leipzig Hensius, 1908
ZB	*Zwingli and Bullinger*
ZL	*The Latin Works of Hudlreich Zwingli*

1

Introduction

BALTHASAR HUBMAIER HAS BEEN recognized as one of the most creative writers of the early sixteenth-century Radical Reformation. Although his rejection of infant baptism and embrace of believers' baptism give sufficient grounds for classifying him as an Anabaptist,[1] there are still debates about his identity in the origin of the early Anabaptism movement. This is because distinctive theological features in his writings, such as tripartite anthropology, Christology, the Lord's Supper, and threefold baptism, appear peculiar from the point of view of other Anabaptists' theology. Previous researchers on Hubmaier's theology have tended to explain his theological characteristics by forming a link with some of the most influential sources of his theology. Although they have attempted to show possible influences resulting in the particular characteristics of Hubmaier's theology, there is a distinct lack of explanation of the detailed reasons why Hubmaier deemed it imperative to assert them, nor is there any consideration of the way in which these theological characteristics are related to his soteriology. Hubmaier's main motive in writing his theses on free will, baptism, and the Lord's Supper comes from the desire to clarify the meaning of salvation by faith to those using the term "justification by faith" to rationalize their immorality. This does not mean that Hubmaier denied the motto of the Reformation, "justification by faith," but rather that he reinforced the meaning of salvation within the same terms. Such a context means that the unique characteristics of Hubmaier's theology need to be understood within the milieu of his soteriological perspective. Thus, the aim of this study is to analyze and illumine Hubmaier's meaning of salvation as it appears in his theses.

1. MacGregor, *Radical and Magisterial Reform*, 35.

Balthasar Hubmaier's Doctrine of Salvation

The significance of Hubmaier's doctrine of salvation will be better understood when set against his biographical background. Therefore, in this chapter, I shall first summarize his life and examine the theological influences on him and his own contributions to the early Anabaptist movement. Second, I shall survey the trends in the studies thus far on Hubmaier and his theology. Such an exploration into the previous studies will aid readers in appreciating the significance of this study on Hubmaier's soteriology, for it will reveal the errors and failures of former researchers in basing their studies on incorrect methodology. To understand Hubmaier's doctrine of salvation, finally, I shall present a new methodology, one which enables the study not only of the doctrine of salvation but of Hubmaier's theology in its entirety.

1. Hubmaier's Career and His Theological Background

Balthasar Hubmaier was the only early Anabaptist leader who had a doctorate in theology and a public career as a Catholic priest. Although the period of his participation in the Anabaptist wing of the Reformation was less than three years,[2] he left a number of writings and had a well-earned reputation as the most gifted communicator among the Anabaptists.[3]

Hubmaier was born in Friedberg near Augsburg, in either 1480 or 1481,[4] but there is no evidence of the exact date of his birth or of his family. He seemed to have received good religious training at home from his mother who was devoutly Christian.[5] He attended the Latin school of Augsburg, and entered the University of Freiburg in 1503 where he studied under the great Catholic scholar John Eck, who was the opponent of Karlstadt and Luther at the Leipzig disputation and who had powerful influence over Hubmaier's theological studies.[6] After he received his master's degree in 1505 or 1506, Hubmaier taught as a school-teacher in Schaffhausen for a brief time because of a lack of funds.[7] He subsequently returned to the university and was ordained as a priest.[8]

---

2. He was baptized in Waldshut on Easter Saturday, April 15, 1525, and died at the stake in Vienna on March 10, 1528.
3. Pipkin and Yoder, *Balthasar Hubmaier*, 15. Hereafter cited as YP.
4. Vedder, *Balthasar Hübmaier*, 24.
5. Ibid., 25–26.
6. Williams, *Radical Reformation*, 149.
7. Loserth, "Stadt Waldshut," 143; Williams, *Radical Reformation*, 148.
8. YP 16.

Introduction

In 1512, Hubmaier followed John Eck to the University of Ingolstadt. Hubmaier earned a doctorate in theology there and then became a professor of theology. He was also appointed as university preacher and chaplain of the Church of the Virgin, the largest parish church in the city.[9] In January of 1516, he left Ingolstadt, accepting a call to become the Cathedral Preacher at Regensburg.[10] At that time, the people of Regensburg were involved in an anti-Jewish movement. Hubmaier incited the citizens against the Jews of the city and led to the expulsion of all Jews from the city.[11] The Jewish synagogue was destroyed and in its place was erected a Catholic chapel *"zur Schönen Maria"* (to the beauteous Mary).[12] Because of Hubmaier's preaching and the reputation for miracles at the statues of Mary in the chapel, a number of pilgrims visited the chapel, bringing economic benefits to the city. However, the offerings of pilgrims caused local monks to suffer from the loss of income and prestige, and they became jealous of Hubmaier and his chapel. Consequently, Hubmaier was caught between the city authorities and the Dominican monks, and at the end of 1520 he left Regensburg and went to Waldshut.[13] During his time at Regensburg, Hubmaier had a close relationship with Rychard, a humanist scholar who introduced him to the new thinking.[14] In June of 1522, this interest in humanism compelled him to go to Basel, where he made the acquaintance of Glareanus (Grebel's old teacher), Erasmus, and Pelikan.[15]

During his first year at Waldshut in 1521, Hubmaier remained a zealous Catholic and observed all the duties of a typical medieval parish priest but his thoughts began to change after studying the Scriptures, in particular the Pauline epistles. While studying the Pauline epistles, Hubmaier

---

9. Ibid.

10. Bergsten and Westin, *Schriften*, 12–13. Hereafter cited as HS.

11. At that time, Hubmaier believed that involvement in an anti-Jewish movement was being a good Catholic and he simply followed the teaching of Eck. See Sachsse, *Hubmaier Als Theologe*, 126–29.

12. Vedder, *Balthasar Hübmaier*, 44.

13. Estep, *Anabaptist Story*, 80–81.

14. Bergsten, *Balthasar Hubmaier*, 98. The meaning of humanism can be explained in the slogan *ad fontes*—return to the original sources. Humanist research on classical and original texts for their studies could help them to recover the intellectual and artistic glories of the classical period. The concept of humanism itself was based on the secular context but was applied to the study of Christianity in order to engage directly with original texts on the Bible. cf. McGrath, *Reformation Thought*, 39–65.

15. Bergsten, *Balthasar Hubmaier*, 73–74. These people were the Basel circle of humanists who influenced to Hubmaier's thought to be regarded as an "evangelical humanist."

journeyed to Basel and other Swiss cities where the Reformation was underway.[16] After he returned to Waldshut and became more immersed in the study of the Pauline epistles,[17] there was a new call from Regensburg in late 1522. However, given that Hubmaier's mind and attitude were now committed to the Reformation, he could stay in Regensburg for only a short time because the people there were not ready to accept the new theology. He was glad to return to Waldshut in the spring of 1523, where he then became interested in the Swiss reformers. Hubmaier went to Zurich to visit Zwingli, and on this visit, he also met Conrad Grebel and other Swiss reformers who would become the leaders of the Zurich Anabaptists.[18] After contacting Zwingli, he attended the second religious disputation in Zurich in October 1523 as an ally of the Swiss reformer.[19]

When he returned to Waldshut, committed to the work of reform, Hubmaier invited all the clergy of the district to a disputation, and presented *Achtzehn Schlußreden* (eighteen articles concerning the Christian life). This document was Hubmaier's first published work and was available in print by June 1524.[20] This was the document in which he argued for the introduction of the German service, banished pictures and images from the church, and abolished fasting regulations. Following the decision for reform, he married Elizabeth Hugline, the daughter of a citizen of Reichenau.[21] Hubmaier's endorsement of the Reformation disturbed the Austrian government which belonged to a Catholic territory. The Catholic party sent two commissioners with official letters dismissing Hubmaier from his positions at the chapel and as the senior priest of the city,

---

16. The Reformation is the name given to a series of religious renewals in Europe in the sixteenth century. There were two main streams of the Reformation for Hubmaier's period: the Lutheran Reformation and the Swiss Reformation. The Lutheran Reformation emerged within the German territories under Luther's leadership. This reformation was made famous by Luther's personal activities, such as his posting of the Ninety-five Theses (October 31, 1517) and the Leipzig Disputation (June–July 1519). But his program of reformation was much more conservative. On the other hand, the Swiss Reformation, which was led by Zwingli, seemed to seek more radical ways of reform. This way of reforming the church sought to reshape the morals and worship of the church according to a more biblical pattern. See McGrath, *Reformation Thought*, 6–9.

17. Vedder, *Balthasar Hübmaier*, 54.

18. Bergsten, *Balthasar Hubmaier*, 114.

19. Estep, *Anabaptist Story*, 81.

20. Vedder, *Balthasar Hübmaier*, 69–72.

21. Ibid., 83.

requiring that it be turned over to the bishop of Constance.[22] However, the city council and parishioners at Waldshut rejected the commissioners' request and protected Hubmaier. Nevertheless, the pressure to remove Hubmaier continued to mount from both the civil authorities and the bishop of Constance. In order to protect the community from the danger of armed intervention and to protect his reform initiatives, on September 1, 1524, Hubmaier left Waldshut for Swiss Schaffhausen, where he had been a teacher during his student days.[23]

As we move to the last few years of his life, we need to consider them in slightly more detail. In Schaffhausen, Hubmaier addressed three letters to the council asking for permission to abide peaceably in their town. Although Schaffhausen protected him from the Austrian government, his position was precarious; even so, during that time, he wrote several treatises. One of these, a pamphlet on religious liberty, was one of the most significant pieces of literature of the Reformation.[24] Entitled *Von Ketzern und ihren Verbrennern* (Concerning Heretics and Those Who Burn Them), it presented the concepts of freedom and the limitations of the magistrates' power, which the whole Anabaptist movement stressed. He defined the term "heretics" as those who deceitfully undermine the Holy Scriptures.[25] He insisted that, according to his understanding of the gospel, faith could not be forced. Therefore, he wrote, "to burn heretics is in appearance to profess Christ (Titus 1:10, 11), but in reality to deny him, and to be more monstrous than Jehoiakim, the king of Judah (Jer 36:23)."[26] He also wrote, "But a Turk or a heretic cannot be overcome by our doing, neither by sword nor by fire, but alone with patience and supplication, whereby we patiently await divine judgment."[27] From these citations, we can see that Hubmaier asserted that even the state did not have the right to use force against a person because of religious differences. Here, the Zurich radicals and Hubmaier shared the same opinion that the church itself should be governed only by the Word of God and God's Spirit, and not by the state's interference.[28] It is crucial, however, to recognize that the Zurich radicals and Hubmaier had a different view on the role of the state

22. Williams, *Radical Reformation*, 150.
23. Vedder, *Balthasar Hübmaier*, 78–81.
24. Ibid., 83–84.
25. Estep, *Anabaptist Story*, 85.
26. Vedder, *Balthasar Hübmaier*, 87.
27. HS 98; YP 62.
28. Snyder, "Swiss Anabaptism," 527.

in the church from that of Zwingli. In this treatise, Hubmaier penned the characteristic motto of all his writings: "*Die Warheit ist untödlich* (Truth is Immortal)."[29]

In October 1524, Hubmaier returned to Waldshut where he sharply criticized the practice of infant baptism. While Waldshut was involved in the South German Peasants' War, the city's political fate was uncertain, and during this time Conrad Grebel visited Hubmaier and his church officially announced that they were Anabaptists on April 15, 1525, the day before Easter Sunday.[30] Wilhelm Reublin, who had been deported from Zurich, sought refuge in Waldshut in early April 1525. Reublin baptized Hubmaier and about sixty others, and Hubmaier baptized over 300 men on Easter Sunday. The movement towards Anabaptism continued. On the Monday and Tuesday after Easter, Hubmaier baptized from seventy to eighty men.[31] On May 28, Zwingli's tract, *Von der Taufe, von der Wiedertaufe, und von der Kindertaufe* (On Baptism, Anabaptism, and Infant Baptism) was published, which challenged the Anabaptists' position on believer's baptism. Hubmaier answered by writing, *Von der christlichen Taufe der Gläubigen* (The Christian Baptism of Believers), in July.

His argument against Zwingli's doctrine of baptism resulted in his being seized and placed in the Wellenberg prison, known as the "Wasserturm."[32] While he was in prison, he was required to recant his assertion on baptism. His recantation satisfied Zwingli and he was released. Even though this recantation might be seen to demonstrate a weakness on the part of Hubmaier, it is not that he gave up seeking the truth of God. Rather, it became the motivation for Hubmaier to repent of his weakness, the more strongly to affirm his faith. In *Eine kurze Entschuldigung* (A Brief Apologia), he wrote:

> I may err, I am a human being—but a heretic I cannot be, for I constantly ask instruction in the Word of God.[33]

In 1526, after Hubmaier was discredited before Zwingli's followers and dishonored among the Anabaptists, he stole out of Zurich and made

---

29. Estep, *Anabaptist Story*, 86. The "*untödlich*" is translated in English as "immortal" by Estep and Pipkin, but as "unkillable" by Yoder. In his book, *Scholar, Pastor, Martyr*, Pipkin introduces the story of translating Hubmaier's epigram "*Die Warheit ist untödlich.*"

30. Estep, *Anabaptist Story*, 427.

31. Vedder, *Balthasar Hübmaier*, 111–12.

32. Estep, *Anabaptist Story*, 93.

33. YP 308.

Introduction

his way to Augsburg for a short time. He then went to Nikolsburg, which was one of the most tolerant cities in Europe under the jurisdiction of Moravian noblemen.[34] The Moravian evangelicals accepted Hubmaier and he became a guest in the home of Oswald Glaidt, who was the coadjutor of the chief evangelical preacher. Hubmaier converted church leaders and a Moravian baron, Leonhard von Liechtenstein, to Anabaptism. During the year at Nikolsburg, Hubmaier's ministries in preaching and teaching were successful, and approximately 6,000 people were baptized in the city. While Hubmaier was busy with his ministries in Nikolsburg, Froschauer, a printer from Zurich, became the publisher of Hubmaier's treatises.[35] There were at least sixteen pamphlets printed in just over two years between 1526 and 1527.[36] Most of Hubmaier's writings were produced as catechetical instruction for basic knowledge of Christianity and the obligation of believers at church.[37] But his two most significant treatises were about the freedom of the human will: *Von der Freiheit des Willens* and *Das andere Büchlein von der Freiwilligkeit des Menschen* (1527).

After the death of King Louis of Hungary, Moravia came under the jurisdiction of Ferdinand I, who tried to eradicate every trace of heresy in the region. A general edict was made to enforce strictly the decree of the Diet of Worms on August 28, 1527. Under this edict, Hubmaier and his wife were arrested and imprisoned in Kreuzenstein Castle. Hubmaier compromised on several points of his former position because of the pressures of ill health, the inevitable death sentence, and his characteristic openness to the truth. However, he refused to compromise on baptism, the Lord's Supper, and his previous denial of the existence of purgatory. Thus, on March 3, 1528, he was taken to Vienna and tortured. However, the Austrian authorities could not obtain a recantation. He also refused to confess to a priest and to receive the last rites of the church before his execution. On March 10, 1528, Hubmaier was burned at the stake in Vienna

---

34. Estep, *Anabaptist Story*, 94–95.

35. YP 426, 449.

36. Pipkin, *Scholar, Pastor, Martyr*, 82. Some of these treatises were written while Hubmaier was in Waldshut, or at least begun there. However, there were published later in Nikolsburg. Pipkin distinguished Hubmaier's writings during that time in four types: (1) controversies (largest set of six writings) (2) church development, sacramental and worship forms (five writings) (3) defense of personal faith, work and theology (three writings) (4) devotion and spirituality (two wrings).

37. Bergsten and Estep, *Theologian and Martyr*, 325–26. Hubmaier's major writings about baptism and the Lord's Supper were also included: *Eine Form zu taufen, Eine Form des Nachtmahls Christi, Eine christliche Lehrtafel*.

without recanting his faith. Three days later, his wife Elizabeth was also executed by drowning in the Danube with a stone tied around her neck.

From this brief account of Hubmaier's life, we can infer several significant points which will help us to understand Hubmaier's thought. First, Hubmaier's theology did not consist of one specific influence but of several, such as his high class Catholic education, the influence of contemporary reformers such as Luther and Zwingli, the connection of humanists such as Erasmus, and his relationship with the Swiss radicals. Second, as we will see in the next chapter, his views on free will are reflected in his recantation of his theology before his martyrdom. Though Hubmaier sometimes recanted his theology in order to save his life, the fact that he chose martyrdom in the end shows his regard for the significance of human will in terms of soteriology. Third, his main concern with respect to the Reformation was built on two major issues: the baptism of believers and the Lord's Supper. After he dedicated himself to reforming the church wherever he was, he never lost sight of the significance of the role of baptism and the Lord's Supper. His refusal to compromise on these points in his last recantation before his execution shows how central he considered their importance for church reform.

2. Balthasar Hubmaier in Recent Anabaptist Studies

From this account of Hubmaier's life and his theological background, we can see that his theology of church reform was influenced by various circumstances and environments. However, his identification as an Anabaptist who asserted the baptism of believers has been evaluated differently in various studies on the origins of early Anabaptist movements. For most of the four centuries since the Anabaptist movements emerged in the early sixteenth century, they were neglected or regarded as a fanatical sect and a heretical group separate from the mainstream Protestant Reformation.[38] During the twentieth century, however, a new perspective on the Anabaptist movement developed among various American Mennonite scholars and certain secular historians, as they realized the need to evaluate the Anabaptist movement in terms of its own merits. In this context, research on Hubmaier has evolved in conjunction with the general tendencies of Anabaptist research. In particular, there are questions about whether the Anabaptist movement emerged through *monogenesis* or *polygenesis*. The answer to this question influences evaluations of Hubmaier's identity.

38. Goertz, *Anabaptists*, 1.

Introduction

Before we move to consider Hubmaier's identification in the context of early Anabaptism, we need to understand these two views of the origin of Anabaptism: monogenesis and polygenesis. First, the theory of "monogenesis" argues that Anabaptism originated from one single source, the Swiss Brethren who were set firmly within the context of the Protestant Reformation. Secondly, the theory of "polygenesis" argues alternatively that early Anabaptism emerged not only from the Swiss Brethren but from various contexts and for various reasons.

Harold Bender was the most remarkable figure in the rehabilitation of Anabaptism from misrepresentation and negative views in the modern era. In his article, "The Anabaptist Vision," Bender challenged past prejudices and misrepresentations of the Anabaptists as revolutionaries or enthusiasts by asserting the characteristic features of Anabaptism as discipleship, the church as a brotherhood, and an ethic of love and non-resistance.[39] For him, the origin of "true Anabaptist movement" stemmed from the "evangelical Anabaptists" who emerged in Zurich from the Zwinglian reformation and spread into the Low Countries, later becoming the Mennonites.[40] In this monogenesis argument, the Swiss Brethren were regarded as the only authentic origin of the Anabaptist movement, and the Mennonites could thus be regarded as an authentic derivative. On the other hand, other groups such as the South Germans, Austrians, and Hutterites were excluded by this argument from classification as authentic Anabaptist groups and regarded rather as semi-authentic derivatives. However, Bender's theory of monogenesis has been criticized in many ways. Arnold Snyder summarizes several criticisms of monogenesis in his appendix, "A Review of Anabaptist Histography": for its lack of historical evidence for Swiss Brethren Anabaptist groups; no perfect unification of theology among the Swiss Brethren themselves; the development of other Anabaptist groups through different influences such as medieval spirituality or Protestant teachings; the existence of various Anabaptist groups in the contemporary context; and the obscurity of the definition of "true Anabaptism."[41] The alternative theory—"polygenesis"—is the theory that Anabaptist groups appeared in many places with varying characteristics.[42]

---

39. Bender, "Anabaptist Vision," 29–54.

40. Ibid., 52–53; cf. Murray, *Radical Christian*, 21.2–3.

41. Snyder, *History and Theology*, 397–408.

42. James M. Stayer, Werner O. Packull, and Klaus Deppermann attempted to trace all varieties of Anabaptism back through Zurich as "unhistorical theological abstractions" (Stayer et al., "From Monogenesis to Polygenesis," 87).

These two views posit contradictory opinions about the origin of the early Anabaptists and, therefore, have different influences on the evaluation of Hubmaier's identity.

There were two significant and classic biographies on Hubmaier dating from the late nineteenth and the early twentieth centuries before the beginning of the rediscovery of Anabaptism and the dispute about the origins. In 1893, Johann Loserth published a biography of Hubmaier, *Doctor Balthasar Hubmaier und die Anfange der Wiedertaufe in Mähren*. In this work he expressed that Hubmaier, even more than Zwingli, was the intelligent and well-trained theologian of the Swiss Anabaptist movement.[43] His positive view of Hubmaier, defending him from the criticisms of earlier historians, influenced later generations' research and evaluations of Hubmaier.[44] In 1905, Henry C. Vedder wrote *Balthasar Hubmaier, the Leader of Anabaptists*, which depended heavily upon Loserth's work but was focused more on the historical story. Vedder portrayed Hubmaier in a positive way as a person who constantly depended upon the Word of God to preserve the truth. He even insisted that Hubmaier's recantations can be reinterpreted in such a way that Hubmaier does not appear to have *really* recanted of any of his basic convictions.[45] These two early biographies influenced a positive approach regarding Hubmaier which is reflected in the works of later Anabaptist historians such as William R. Estep, Torsten Bergsten and Christof Windhorst.[46] However, although these two biographies presented Hubmaier as a significant person in the Anabaptist movement in the sixteenth century, early modern Anabaptist studies, which began with Bender, tended to regard him as not being an authentic Anabaptist.

a. Evaluation of Hubmaier's Identity in the Different Aspects about the Origin of Anabaptists

As we have already seen, Bender argued that "normative" and "true" Anabaptists originated with the Swiss Brethren who emerged in Zurich from the Zwinglian reformation.[47] This moved Anabaptist studies away from the

43. Loserth, *Balthasar Hubmaier*, 210; Mabry, *Faith*, viii.
44. Bergsten and Estep, *Theologian and Martyr*, 30–31.
45. Vedder, *Balthasar Hübmaier*, 235–38.
46. Mabry, *Faith*, viii. This will be discussed later.
47. Bender, "Anabaptist Vision," 42, suggested three major points of the Anabaptist vision: (1) a new conception of the essence of Christianity as discipleship; (2)

negative prejudice that viewed Anabaptists as "devilish enemies and destroyers of the Church of God," or "Schwärmer" (fanatics or enthusiasts),[48] and saw them as proto-socialist shock troops, an underground network of Müntzerite revolutionaries. By stressing the concept of non-resistance as a key characteristic of the Anabaptist vision (marking "true Anabaptism"), Hubmaier's position had to be distinguished from those whom Bender recognized as contemporary original and authentic Anabaptists such as Conrad Grebel, Pilgram Marpeck, Peter Riedemann, and Menno Simmons.[49] Bender's evaluation of Hubmaier seems to inspire mid-century Mennonite scholars who asserted the monogenesis interpretation of Anabaptism, which saw the Swiss Brethren and the Dutch Mennonites as authentic descendants. In this sense, John H. Yoder also argued that Hubmaier was never truly a real Anabaptist within the characteristic feature of his definition of the term.[50] He argued that Hubmaier's approval of the authority of the state to reform the church and the demand that Christians "disobey biblical injunctions (oath, armed defense, interest, defense of the property structure)" shows that he followed the magisterial Reformers rather than the Swiss Brethren.[51] It is clear that Yoder's research into, and evaluation of, Hubmaier is based on Bender's definition of "authentic Anabaptism." The mid-twentieth century studies of Hubmaier focused on the historical context of Hubmaier's place within the larger Reformation and the Anabaptist movement, rather than on Hubmaier's theological thought itself. With their distinguishing of Hubmaier from the Swiss Brethren it seems that both Bender and Yoder were overly anxious to minimize a possible connection to Müntzer and the revolutionary radicals, which could be plausible if they accepted Hubmaier (who supported the sword and the oath) as an authentic Swiss Brethren Anabaptist.

However, Bender and Yoder's evaluation of Hubmaier was challenged by Torsten Bergsten's biography, *Balthasar Hubmaier. Seine Stellung Zu Reformation Und Täufertum, 1521–1528*, which was published in 1961.[52] Using a significant number of previously unknown sources, Bergsten

---

a new conception of the church as a brotherhood; and (3) a new ethic of love and non-resistance.

48. Luther called them *Schwärmer*, which, translated, means enthusiasts. Estep, *Anabaptist Story*, 4; cf. Williams, "Sanctification," 5–25. Williams deals with Luther's conception of sanctification in the context of the controversy with the Schwärmer.

49. Bender, "Anabaptist Vision," 51.

50. Yoder, "Swiss Anabaptism," 5; Chatfield, "Clarity of Scripture," 17.

51. Yoder, "Swiss Anabaptism," 17.

52. Bergsten, *Balthasar Hubmaier*.

investigated and shed more light on the life and theology of Hubmaier. Bergsten pointed out Yoder's narrow definition of Anabaptism, and suggested a broader definition which allowed him to regard Hubmaier as an authentic Anabaptist.[53] Later, G. H. Williams in his revised massive work *The Radical Reformation* clearly affirmed that Hubmaier was a representative of "normative evangelical Anabaptism."[54] In particular, Bergsten's contribution with Westin, *Balthasar Hubmaier, Schriften*, is regarded as the definitive critical edition of Hubmaier's writings and includes a major corpus of Hubmaier's primary works with commentary, allowing greater textual research into Hubmaier's thought. In 1989 this German edition was translated into English, *Balthasar Hubmaier: Theologian of Anabaptism*, and included supplementary items of Hubmaier's writing, as well as some comments and related bibliographies.[55]

The issue of Hubmaier's identification as an authentic Anabaptist who followed non-resistance and pacifism entered a new phase with the polygenesis theory of the origin of the Anabaptist movement. Even though Friedmann subscribed to the monogenesis model of Anabaptism, he pointed out that "the differentiating elements of the Anabaptist groups have never been clearly analyzed in a general history of Anabaptist ideas" and that "Anabaptism in South Germany, Switzerland and Austria was by no means a uniform movement. There was even less uniformity in Central Germany or the Netherlands."[56] In this context, there can be two different ways of interpreting the origins of Anabaptism. First, that the Swiss Brethren were the only authentic Anabaptists and other groups of Anabaptism were malformed. Second, that there is ambiguity with regard to what are "true" or "authentic Anabaptists" and whether they could truly be limited to any particular expression of Anabaptism in the sixteenth century. James M. Stayer took the latter point of view and expanded the definition of Anabaptism to include those who are members of groups practicing believers' baptism.[57] He further argued that non-resistance and pacifism, which were based on the monogenesis theory's definition of normative Anabaptism, were not generally shown in the early Anabaptist movement but only in a small group of Anabaptists until about 1560.[58] Stayer, with

---

53. Ibid., 53–54.
54. Williams, *Radical Reformation*, 1253.
55. Pipkin and Yoder, *Theologian of Anabaptism*.
56. Friedmann, "Peter Riedemann," 38–39.
57. Stayer, *Sword*, 20.
58. Ibid., 328.

Introduction

Packull and Deppermann, suggested that there were three independent origins of Anabaptism rather than a monogenetic origin in the sixteenth century: the Swiss Brethren, South German and Austrian Anabaptists, and the Central-German and Dutch Anabaptists.[59] In this view, Stayer argued that Hubmaier can be identified as one of the leaders and founders of the upper German Anabaptists with Denck and Hut.[60] The polygenesis theory is significant in allowing the identification of Hubmaier as a leader of Anabaptists and encourages a more positive evaluation of him.

Beyond the monogenesis and polygenesis debate about Anabaptist origins, Snyder's recent research on "The Birth and Evolution of Swiss Anabaptism" argued that any evaluation of Hubmaier's identity as a true Anabaptist pacifist cannot depend solely on his position on government and the sword.[61] Snyder asserted that Hubmaier's views on government and the sword were indicative of the trend among early Swiss Anabaptists, although it differed from the Schleitheim's Confession which insisted on the separation of Christians from the sword of government for non-resistant separatists in 1527.[62] Rather, he argued, there were two circles in the early Swiss Anabaptists groups: the circle around Felix Mantz who emphasized non-resistant separatism, and Grebel's circle which was not a committed non-resistant separatist.[63] In this context, the influence of Hubmaier's writings on Grebel's circle before the Schleitheim Confession was published, is potential evidence that Hubmaier was one of the significant Anabaptists in the Swiss Radical movement. Accordingly, we can say that the traditional tendency of scholars such as Bender, to evaluate Hubmaier's identity as an inauthentic Anabaptist, because of his position on government and the sword, is erroneous, given the existence of two different views on the role of government among the early Swiss Anabaptist before the Schleitheim Confession.

In 2008, one of the recent biographies on Hubmaier, *Scholar, Pastor, Martyr: The Life and Ministry of Balthasar Hubmaier (ca 1480–1528)* was produced by H. W. W. Pipkin. As already mentioned, Pipkin who with Yoder translated the German primary texts of Hubmaier into English has massive knowledge in Hubmaier's studies. As a church historian, Pipkin has explored Hubmaier's life and ministry in order to trace and interpret

59. Stayer et al., "Polygenesis," 83–86.
60. Stayer, *Sword*, 141.
61. Snyder, "Swiss Anabaptism," 579–80.
62. Ibid., 563–64.
63. Ibid., 558.

the sources and historical events carefully. His detailed chronological explanation of Hubmaier's life shows the process by which Hubmaier's thoughts were influenced and changed by his teacher, friends, and other colleagues for reformation, and how he drove forward his reformation in church ministry. Pipkin's emphasis on the significance of tracing historical events in Hubmaier's studies helps us to understand more fully the background from which Hubmaier developed his theology, and how he applied it to his church ministry. In his final chapter, Pipkin showed the relationship between Hubmaier's writings and ministry in Nikolsburg and a baptist congregation and its theology.[64] Consequently, Pipkin concluded that Hubmaier was a minister of a baptist congregation at least while he was working in Nikolsburg.

b. Research on Hubmaier's Theology

As well as the great attention given to the question of Hubmaier's position among Anabaptists up until the mid-twentieth century, there have been some scholars who were interested in Hubmaier's theology. In the early twentieth century, C. Sachsse wrote two theological books about Hubmaier—*Dr Balthasar Hubmaiers Anschauungen von der Kirche, den Sakramenten und der Obrigkeit* (1913), and *D. Balthasar Hubmaier als Theologe* (1914).[65] Sachsse's work on Hubmaier, in comparison with Loserth and Vedder, focuses much more on Hubmaier's theology than on historical events. In *D. Balthasar Hubmaier als Theologe*, Sachsse discussed Hubmaier's *schriften*, carefully summarizing Hubmaier's thinking on various subjects such as salvation, church, sacraments, and the sword—all major issues during the Reformation. Beginning in the nineteenth century, Ludwig Keller led the study of the theological influences on Hubmaier in the light of the relationship between the radical Protestant theology of the sixteenth century and late medieval mysticism.[66] However, these works are out of date and in need of revision in light of current research on the shape of late medieval scholasticism.

---

64. McClendon, *Ethics*, 20–46 notes that Pipkin used the term "baptist" to refer to a church that is neither Protestant nor Catholic, and that is much wider than the historic Anabaptist or Baptist movement.

65. Sachsse, *Hubmaiers Anschauungen*; Sachsse, *Hubmaier Als Theologe*.

66. Keller, *Geschichte Der Wiedertäufer*; *Ein Apostel Der Wiedertäufer*; *Johann Von Staupitz*. Cf. Steinmetz, "Scholasticism," 123.

Introduction

i. Concerning Free Will

Studies of Hubmaier's theology tend to lead to questions about who or what influenced him. In particular, researchers seem to be interested in the influential sources on Hubmaier's doctrine of free will. In his article *Possibilities of Erasmian Influence on Denck and Hubmaier in Their Views on the Freedom of the Will*, Thor Hall, who focused on the issue of the freedom of the will in early sixteenth century, shows how Erasmus and humanistic thought was influential on such men as Hans Denck and Balthasar Hubmaier.[67] Nevertheless, Hall did not intend to provide evidence of a direct connection between Denck and Hubmaier and Erasmus. It is sufficient for him to show that their views on free will are so close that Erasmus probably had some degree of influence on the two Anabaptist leaders. In conclusion, Hall argued that Hubmaier's thoughts on the freedom of the will and salvation, as influenced by Erasmus, can be understood as closer to Catholic doctrine than to reformist doctrine.

Further concern on the relationship between Hubmaier's theology and Catholicism has been researched by other theologians. In the 1970s, Steinmetz explored how medieval nominalism had a significant part to play in the theology of Hubmaier as well as that of Luther, Zwingli, and Erasmus.[68] Even though Hubmaier's view of baptism and of the voluntary church were different from contemporary Catholics and reformers, in defending the freedom of human will and grace he stood for conservative theological motifs in late medieval nominalism, as opposed to the theological insights of Luther. Steinmetz showed that the influence of late medieval nominalism introduced the possibility of the problem of *meritum de congruo* (merit of congruity) to Hubmaier's theology.[69] Further, Steinmetz affirmed that Hubmaier's concepts of good works within the order of salvation and of *gratia gratis data* (preparatory grace) suggest that he

---

67. Hall, "Erasmian Influence," 170.

68. Steinmetz, "Scholasticism," 123–44.

69. Cf. Muller, *Latin and Greek*, 191–92. In late medieval scholastic theology, there was a distinction between a *meritum de condigno* (a merit of condignity or full merit), in which one deserves grace, and a *meritum de congruo* (a half merit or act not truly deserving of grace), in which one receives grace on the basis of the divine generosity. The former means that "the work of Holy Spirit in the individual is absolutely good and is the ground of a truly and justly deserved salvation." But the latter means that "no human act can justly deserve the reward of human salvation though the half merit can be viewed as receiving a proportionate reward in the gift of salvation" (ibid.). The concept of a *meritum de congruo* allowed late medieval scholastics to argue that a minimal act might be performed and, because of it, first grace conferred.

can be regarded as a Semi-Pelagian from the perspective of Reformation theology.[70] In his article "Catholic Teacher and Anabaptist Pupil,"[71] Moore took further the idea of Catholic influence on Hubmaier's thought, by showing the connection between Hubmaier and his mentor Eck, who was one of the best known Catholic theologians of the period. Moore affirmed that Hubmaier's understanding of free will argues for the possibility that fallen humankind could have continued as it was to salvation, without the need for any divine assistance, other than its own intrinsic freedom to choose between opposites. From this point of view, Hubmaier could be regarded as Pelagian or Semi-Pelagian.[72]

Another way of exploring influences is shown by Kenneth Davis. In his study of the connection between late medieval theology and early Anabaptism, *Anabaptism and Asceticism*, Davis compared and contrasted early Anabaptism with monastic movements. Davis introduced Ritschl's theory which was the first to clearly show a third approach to Anabaptist origins, suggesting that Anabaptism was related to a late medieval, Catholic, ascetic, reform tradition.[73] While accepting Ritschl's observation, Davies pointed out that Erasmian version of *devotio moderna* in his humanism is a particularly important intellectual origin of Anabaptism in medieval asceticism.[74] He argued that the dominant motif in Evangelical Anabaptist theology is concerned with holiness, and that its expression parallels in a general way traditional ascetic ideals and practices.[75] He pointed out that Hubmaier provided the best source in which to find the essential features of early Anabaptism, and provided the clues to the reconciliation of the extreme conflicts[76] around whether Anabaptist theology is Pelagian,[77] or whether the Anabaptism position regarding salvation as

---

70. Steinmetz, "Scholasticism," 144. It appears in English as "Luther and Hubmaier on the Freedom of the Human Will" in *Luther in Context*. Here Steinmetz asserts that "Hubmaier understood himself to be following a middle way between the Pelagianism of the late scholastics and what he regarded as the Stoicism of Luther, retaining the best features of each and avoiding the mistakes of both" (*Luther in Context*, 70).

71. Moore, "Anabaptist Pupil," 91–94.

72. MacGregor, *Radical and Magisterial Reform*, 15.

73. Ritschl, *Pietismus*, 1–37; Davis, *Asceticism*, 29–31. However, Davis points to "Ritschl's lack of documentation, since Ritschl's theory was only introductory to a larger work, which subsequently led to a general dismissal of his theory."

74. Davis, *Asceticism*, 30.

75. Ibid., 129–217.

76. Davis, *Asceticism*, 150.

77. Lüdemann, *Refomation*, 86.

dependent on grace alone was in accord with the Reformers' position on justification by faith and grace alone.[78] Davis appeared to depend heavily on Hubmaier's thinking on faith, on grace, and on free will, to prove the connection between Anabaptism and synergism.[79] In spite of his assertion that Hubmaier's theory on the combination of actual, relative, and inner perfection and imputed justification and perfection could be harmonized with the placing of both faith and works in salvation, he failed to show an escape from the accusation of Pelagianism.

In his book, *The Concept of Grace in the Radical Reformation*, Beachy argued that the concept of grace which prevailed in the magisterial Reformation could not be separated from the concept of double predestination and the bondage of the will. Radical reformers rejected this view because they thought it would describe God as the mediate or the immediate source of sin, and would therefore imply a lack of human responsibility for moral behavior.[80] Through a study on grace as understood by both the magisterial reformers and the radical reformers, Beachy suggested that the understanding of the concept of grace in radical thought was the key to understanding how their doctrines were linked to their ecclesiastical practices. In his appendix, Beachy accepted that the influence of the medieval mystic tradition on Hubmaier's anthropology could not be denied, but asserted that Hubmaier's anthropology with the tripartite model[81] was closer to the thought of Gerson than that of Tauler.[82] Although Hubmaier is described as one of several radical reformers investigated in his research, Beachy failed to show any consideration of Hubmaier's thought in one significant chapter, the "hermeneutics of grace."[83]

---

78. Wenger, *Even Unto Death*, 31–32.

79. Davis, *Asceticism*, 149–91. For the argument of "synergism" Davis concentrates on Hubmaier's *A Christian Catechism*, and *Freedom of the Will I, II*. Using the word "synergism" from Hubmaier's concept of faith and free will might not be satisfactory because it could give an impression that Hubmaier was a semi-Pelagian. "Synergism" can be defined as "the doctrine of divine and human cooperation in conversion"; it is regarded as the opposition of "monergism," which is "the position that the grace of God constitutes the only efficient cause in beginning and effecting conversion" (MacGregor, *Radical and Magisterial Reform*, 16).

80. Beachy, *Concept of Grace*.

81. Hubmaier's anthropology is "tripartite," in that the human being is constituted in three parts: spirit, soul, and body. This will be discussed in the next chapter.

82. Beachy, *Concept of Grace*, 129–52; cf. Williams, *Radical Reformation*, 273. Williams suggests that Hubmaier's trichotomic anthropology may have been indirectly inspired by one of Johannes Tauler's mystical sermons.

83. Chatfield, "Clarity of Scripture," 32.

In his recent article on "Hubmaier's concord of Predestination with Free Will," MacGregor showed that Hubmaier proposed a reconciliation between human will and God's predestination.[84] He asserted that Hubmaier's explanation of God's character as omniscience and omnipotence by use of the Scholastic dichotomy between *the voluntas absoluta* and *the voluntas ordinata* can solve the difficulty of answering the question of God's salvific anomalies in Scripture (for instance, Esau and other evildoers), without denying the significance of human will.[85] As MacGregor rightly pointed out in his introduction, Hubmaier's motive in attempting to engage with the relationship between foreknowledge and predestination was based on his pastoral concerns over a misunderstanding of the meaning of *sola fide* for salvation. From this point of view of Hubmaier's concept of the relationship between predestination and free will, MacGregor concluded that Hubmaier was a significant theologian who emphasized human will in order to codify the teachings of the earlier reformers with Scholastic methodology.[86] His conclusion that Hubmaier's ideas on human will were developed through the combination of two different concepts shows us that the character of Hubmaier's theology cannot be distinguished within one specific category.

ii. Concerning Baptism and the Lord's Supper

Scholarly concerns about Hubmaier's concept of free will are also related to research on his baptismal theology. In his book *Anabaptist Baptism: A Representative Study*, Rollin Armour regarded Hubmaier as a representative of Anabaptist leaders, and the one who was first to give a detailed defense of Anabaptist baptism.[87] The many tracts he authored on the topic are now understood to exemplify the basic Anabaptist position. Unfortunately, this account does not consider two areas which were crucial for the foundation and development of this position: the Swiss origins and Menno

---

84. MacGregor, "Predestination," 279–99.

85. Ibid. The *voluntas absoluta*, or "absolute will," of God comprises God's power to do whatever God chooses, unconstrained by any law above Godself, while the *voluntas ordinata*, or "ordained will," of God amounts for God's merciful choice to act toward humanity according to precepts God has freely instituted. See Williams, *Radical Reformation*, 336.

86. MacGregor, "Predestination," 295.

87. Armour, *Anabaptist Baptism*, 17.

Simons' baptismal doctrine.[88] Armour attempted not only to focus on the meaning of baptism but also to expand it to include other areas to which it is related for the church and the whole of Christian life. He believed that Hubmaier's thoughts were nearer to the Catholic view than the Protestant with regard to human will as means of receiving the gift of God's salvation, justification, and how humans attain a relative perfection.[89] This does not, however, mean that Hubmaier's thought fully depended on Catholic or Zwinglian Protestantism. Armour suggested in conclusion that Hubmaier "might best be classified as belonging to a third party, neither Protestant nor Catholic."[90]

Christof Windhorst published his book, *Täuferisches Taufverständnis. Balthasar Hubmaiers Lehre zwischen traditioneller und reformatorischer Theologie*, in 1976, one of the most significant studies on Hubmaier's baptismal theology.[91] This survey of contemporary research into, and analysis of, Hubmaier's theology is distinct from previous studies of Hubmaier's thought. Windhorst's comparison between Hubmaier and Catholicism and contemporary reformers and radical reformers concludes that there was some influence upon Hubmaier's theology from both his medieval theological background and from the thoughts of contemporary reformers. Windhorst insisted that even though Hubmaier's views on baptism and the Lord's Supper were influenced by his nominalist background, the radical content of his new teaching was influenced first by Luther and then more significantly Zwingli.[92] His conclusion, that Hubmaier's doctrine of baptism and his theology lies somewhere between traditional Catholic theology and the Reformation theology of the sixteenth century, acknowledges Anabaptism's intellectual origins in medieval Catholicism.[93] Windhorst traced the doctrine's development in the context of it being a meeting point between scholasticism, Augustinian spiritualism and Reformation interpretations of the Word.[94]

There are others who use sacramental theology as an entry point. Few studies of Hubmaier's doctrine of baptism have been shown before

---

88. Goertz, *Anabaptists*, 69.

89. Armour, *Anabaptist Baptism*, 33–34.

90. Ibid., 34.

91. Windhorst, *Täuferisches Taufverstädnis*.

92. Windhorst, "Theologie Hubmaiers," 148–68; Chatfield, "Clarity of Scripture," 31.

93. Windhorst, *Täuferisches Taufverstädnis*, 257.

94. Goertz, *Anabaptists*, 69.

or after the publication of Windhorst's book. In 1971, Steinmetz particularly asserted that Hubmaier's view of grace and free will were related to nominalist motifs from the late Middle Ages,[95] and he attempted to show the relationship of Hubmaier's thought on baptism to medieval thought. In contrast with Windhorst, who made a brief attempt to place the controversy between Hubmaier and Zwingli into the context of medieval theology, using only the teaching of Peter Lombard, Steinmetz preferred to cite Biel's teaching, which provides the context and background for the sixteenth century.[96] He concluded that Hubmaier's sharp division between the baptism of John and of Jesus shows that his thinking on baptism still remained closer to Catholic roots.

Pipkin also explored Hubmaier's baptismal theology but concentrated on the historical context. In his article, *The baptismal theology of Balthasar Hubmaier*, he gave a brief summary of the contents of Hubmaier's writings on baptism, and noted the major concerns which appear from Hubmaier's writings, but the discussion lacks critical analysis.[97] His study on Hubmaier's baptismal theology seems to search for the meaning of baptism in the biblical text itself rather than considering the intellectual origin of Hubmaier's thought. In conclusion, Pipkin asserted that the significance of baptism in Hubmaier's theology needs to be understood in terms of his ecclesiology which is related to his views on discipleship.

Todd E. Johnson's attempt to examine both the theology and rite of baptism in light of Hubmaier's doctrine of church and his understanding of believers' baptism argued that the apostolic calling to preach Christ to the world was not for the cleric alone, but for all those who were baptized.[98] Johnson insisted that Hubmaier's reinterpretation of "the laying on of hands" is a commissioning of the neophyte into the priesthood of all believers. His emphasis on the meaning of the laying on of hands in the rite after baptism is important in understanding the relationship between Hubmaier's ecclesiology and his baptismal theology.

A greater concentration on the Lord's Supper in Hubmaier's theology was presented by Rempel. His book, *The Lord's Supper in Anabaptism*, is one of the most representative works about Hubmaier's understanding of the Lord's Supper, along with the views of two other Anabaptists' (Pilgram

---

95. Steinmetz, "Scholasticism," 123–44.
96. Steinmetz, "Baptism of John," 170–73.
97. Pipkin, "Baptismal Theology," 51–52.
98. Johnson, "Initiation or Ordination?," 82–85.

Introduction

Marpeck and Dirk Philips) on the doctrine of the Lord's Supper.[99] His main concern was to explore the theology of the Lord's Supper and the Christology of each man. He asserted that Hubmaier, along with Marpeck and Philips, understood the Lord's Supper as the human response of faith and love in contrast to thinking of Catholicism and the Magisterial Reformation in which the definitive characteristic of a sacrament was God's initiative.[100] Rempel asserted that the meaning of the Supper in Hubmaier's thought can be understood as the sign of a present reality for the pledge of love.[101] His careful analysis of Hubmaier's biblical material on the Supper shows that Hubmaier's work stands apart from Zwingli.[102] His attempt to interpret Hubmaier's concept of the Supper in Christological perspective leads us to realize the significance for Hubmaier of the relationship between Christ and his members.

One of the recent works on Hubmaier's theology is *A Central European Synthesis of Radical and Magisterial Reform: The Sacramental Theology of Balthasar Hubmaier* a monograph by Kirk R. MacGregor.[103] MacGregor demonstrated that aspects Hubmaier's theology such as anthropology, sacramental theology, and ecclesiology, were influenced by Bernard of Clairvaux. He attempted to show how much Hubmaier's theology depended on Bernard's materials by comparing their writings on the issue of the freedom of the will. Given the similarities between them, MacGregor was convinced that Hubmaier's theology follows the sacramental perspective of medieval Catholicism. Here, Hubmaier's doctrine of baptism and the Eucharist are regarded as grace-imparting sacraments instead of ordinances without salvific power. In particular, he argued that Hubmaier accepted that the participants of a Eucharist were consubstantiated with the physical body of Christ through the Eucharist.[104] In his analysis of Hubmaier's theology as sacramental, MacGregor suggested that it should be regarded as a bridge between the Radical and Magisterial branches of the Reformation. His attempt to show the literary dependence

99. Rempel, *Lord's Supper*.
100. Ibid., 26.
101. Ibid., 63.
102. Ibid., 85.
103. MacGregor, *Radical and Magisterial Reform*.
104. Ibid., 197–98. The term of consubstantiation used to refer to the theory of the real presence, particularly with Luther's concept of the Supper. Luther asserted that the substance of the bread and wine for the Lord's Supper are given together within the substance of the body and blood of Christ. See McGrath, *Christian Theology*, 513. This issue will be discussed later in the chapter on the Lord's Supper.

of Hubmaier upon Bernard of Clairvaux is a new resource to support the position that Hubmaier's theology was much closer to Catholicism. His close reading of the primary texts helps to defend his assertion that the main purpose of Hubmaier's writings is sacramental theology. However, his over-zealous assertion that Hubmaier's theology was strongly linked to sacramental theology, means that he sometimes changed or omitted some significant words from the original texts to support his argument.[105] Although MacGregor provided a substantial amount of good material which supports his understanding of Hubmaier's theology, his partial misuse of the primary texts undermined the credibility of his argument.

In his work on Hubmaier's theology, *Wounds That Heal: The Importance of Church Discipline within Balthasar Hubmaier's Theology*, Simon Victor Goncharenko showed that Hubmaier's doctrine of church discipline appeared in his major concern for theological issues such as anthropology, soteriology and ecclesiology with sacramental theology. He argued that church discipline is one of the significant unifying factors for the whole of Hubmaier's theology. In chapter three, particularly, Goncharenko demonstrated that Hubmaier's understanding of salvation should not be understood as "either the works-based justification of the Catholic Church or the incomplete understanding of salvation of the Magisterial Reformers."[106] He did not, however, clearly show how Hubmaier understood the meaning of salvation.

Another recent work on Hubmaier's sacramental theology is Brian C. Brewer's *A Pledge of Love: The Anabaptist Sacramental Theology of Balthasar Hubmaier*. Similarly to MacGregor, Brewer demonstrated that the influence of Catholic thought provided and developed Hubmaier's mature Anabaptist sacramental theology on the Lord's Supper, baptism, and other church practices. In order to understand Hubmaier's sacramental theology, Brewer argued that Hubmaier insisted the significance of "pledge" as "a believer's response to God's grace" in his Eucharistic and baptismal liturgy.[107] He, moreover, carefully analyses the way that Hubmaier's sacramental thought contributed not only to Anabaptist worship in his own time but also influenced later generations of Christians.

Finally, Mabry's work, *Balthasar Hubmaier's Doctrine of the Church*, deals with Hubmaier's understanding of the basic nature of the church, which is related to the doctrine of baptism and the Lord's Supper, and

---

105. The evidence will be shown later in the chapter on baptism.
106. Goncharenko, *Wounds That Heal*, 81.
107. Brewer, *Pledge of Love*, 141.

soteriology.[108] The main purpose of this work is to rediscover the character of Anabaptism, especially as it pertains to Hubmaier's thoughts. Unlike most previous studies on Hubmaier and his theology, Mabry attempted to analyze and explore Hubmaier's doctrine of the church from his own texts in sixteenth century German. The direct translation of Hubmaier's own writings from sixteenth century German indicates Mabry's intention to provide a valuable resource for studies of Hubmaier and Anabaptism. In his second study of Hubmaier's theology, *Balthasar Hubmaier's Understanding of Faith*,[109] Mabry asserted that for Hubmaier, as for the reformers in the sixteenth century, the doctrine of faith was at the heart of the disputation about the nature of the Christian life and of the church. In other words, through exploration and definition of what faith actually meant in his writings, Hubmaier's thoughts about contemporary issues such as the doctrine of baptism, the Lord's Supper, and salvation, could be clarified.

However, the methodology of Mabry's studies on Hubmaier, which depends on the primary writings, can be evaluated in two contrary ways. First, expanding the interpretation of Hubmaier's theology using his primary sources is significant in examining Hubmaier's theology itself without interpretation through other scholars. Mabry's attention to analysis of the primary texts helps to trace Hubmaier's intention to emphasize the significance of the relation of faith to Christian life. However, although Mabry concentrated on the primary sources, he did not sufficiently explain why this is an appropriate method. When he does engage with secondary sources, he does not appear to be aware of the modern critical debates. For a solid foundation in making clear Hubmaier's thoughts, Mabry needs to explore in detail more recent works on Hubmaier, and to show his clear purpose and views in approaching studies of Hubmaier. Although Mabry's methodology of researching Hubmaier's thoughts, focusing on the primary sources themselves, is valuable, his efforts leave something to be desired.

As this survey shows, the scholarly studies of Hubmaier can be categorized into three main areas of enquiry: first, whether Hubmaier could be regarded as a true Anabaptist; second, what constituted the influences on Hubmaier's theology; and, third, what were the meanings of Hubmaier's theology concerning free will, baptism, and the Lord's Supper. However, there is little research into Hubmaier's doctrine of salvation (although his writings on theological issues such as human will, baptism and the Lord's

---

108. Mabry, *Church*.
109. Mabry, *Faith*.

Supper are related to his understanding of salvation). Accordingly, I intend to explore the meaning of salvation in Hubmaier's theology through the issues which were discussed in his writings.

3. Methodology for the Understanding of Hubmaier's Doctrine of Salvation

In light of these directions of research on Hubmaier and his theology, the mainstream methodology has been either to identify his career from the Anabaptist perspective or to identify other influences on his thought, such as his educational background or his teachers or colleagues. Hubmaier has been regarded, not as an authentic Anabaptist, but as a Catholic or even a Magisterial Anabaptist. But these labels for Hubmaier may not fairly represent his theological character, because his theological uniqueness had no one single influence. Hubmaier's thought was influenced by various sources and cannot be explained on the basis of the influence of one specific group, be it magisterial reformers, radical reformers or Catholic reformers. Given this difficulty, studies on Hubmaier until the mid-twentieth century have been more concerned with identifying whether or not he was an authentic Anabaptist.

However, as we have seen, by Bender's delineation of what constitutes an authentic Anabaptist, Hubmaier could not be regarded as authentic, since he acknowledged the role of government. The studies on Hubmaier have tended to center around the question of what elements influenced Hubmaier's thought or which characteristic features Hubmaier incorporated into his theology. In distinguishing Hubmaier's identity from that of an authentic Anabaptist, as already mentioned, some scholars (such as Bender and Yoder)[110] have attempted to show differences between Hubmaier and the Swiss Brethren. If they were to acknowledge Hubmaier as an authentic Anabaptist, this would undermine the positive view of Anabaptists as pacifists. Hubmaier's understanding of the role of government in his work of reformation is different from that of the Swiss Brethren and the Mennonites, who are regarded as authentic Anabaptist groups. Thus, using this approach, Hubmaier's identity tends to be regarded as a magisterial reformer rather than an authentic Anabaptist.

Although Hubmaier's understanding of the role of government is nearer to the position of magisterial reformers, his insistence on the significance of baptism and the Lord's Supper reflects the influence of

110. See Bender, "Anabaptist Vision"; Yoder, "Swiss Anabaptism."

Introduction

Catholicism. Some scholars (for instance, McClendon, Moor, Steinmetz and MacGregor)[111] asserted that the Catholic tradition (although they differ as to which Catholic tradition) was a major influence on Hubmaier's theology. From this perspective, Hubmaier could be labeled as a Catholic Anabaptist. In particular, this approach evaluates Hubmaier as an heir of the Catholic tradition, given his understanding of human will and his stress on the rite of baptism and of the Lord's Supper. Many scholars who have attempted to determine the main influence on Hubmaier's thinking on human will, confirm the Catholic background in which he was educated under Eck, who was one of the most famous Catholic scholars, or from his contemporary theologians and colleagues, such as Erasmus and Denck. Although scholars have not agreed as to the exact influence on Hubmaier's understanding of human will, it is sufficient to say that Hubmaier's thoughts on human will are much closer to Catholicism than to the magisterial reformers.

However, Moore argued that there seems to be no one specific source for Hubmaier's idea of free will, although Hubmaier could have been influenced by his teacher Eck.[112] Mabry also pointed out that Hubmaier and Erasmus held different presuppositions in their understanding of grace and free will, so that there seem to be other possible influences on Hubmaier's idea of free will.[113] Here, MacGregor attempted to find out the degree to which Hubmaier's theology was influenced by Bernard of Clairvaux (1090–1153), by showing the similarity of two theologians' writings about human will. However, it still appears to be difficult to identify one single reason as the original influence on Hubmaier's thoughts, although much has been said to demonstrate the possibility of various influences. Rather, it is better to say that Hubmaier's doctrine of human will had a number of influences. Hubmaier developed his doctrine of free will for his soteriology. To do this, he borrowed ideas from different contexts. Therefore, we can suppose, he must have had some intention to mold them into his reformed theology in the light of pastoral concern over misunderstandings of salvation by faith.

A methodology that concentrates entirely on tracing influences will always be problematical. For example in the studies by Windhorst and Steinmetz, they are particularly concerned about interpreting Hubmaier's

---

111. Cf. McClendon, "Catholic Anabaptist," 20–33; Moore, "Anabaptist Pupil"; Steinmetz, "Scholasticism"; MacGregor, *Radical and Magisterial Reform*.

112. Moore, "Anabaptist Pupil," 80.

113. Mabry, *Church*, 26, 30.

doctrine of baptism in the context of Catholic tradition.[114] In particular, their methodologies focus on his distinctive term of two baptisms (baptism of John and baptism of Christ) which are based on interpretations from the medieval tradition. In his thesis about Hubmaier's doctrine of baptism, *Täuferisches Taufverständnis. Balthasar Hubmaiers Lehre zwischen traditioneller und reformatorischer Theologie*, Windhorst presented the similarity of the term of two baptisms between Hubmaier and Peter Lombard and suggested that Hubmaier's idea of baptism was influenced by medieval theology. Steinmetz agreed with Windhorst's view that medieval theology was the influential source of Hubmaier's perspective on baptism, but he also suggested the possibility Gabriel Biel.[115] Although both scholars tried to show that there was a Catholic influence in his thinking, by separating out a particular element of Hubmaier's baptismal theology, they did not seem to be able to explain why he needed this influence. Studies on the Lord's Supper in Hubmaier's theology also exhibit the same methodological tendency of focusing on the origin of the influences rather than Hubmaier's own explanation. Thus, attention is paid to Zwingli's concept of memorial or Catholic concept of sacrament rather than Hubmaier's own theology. Though both perspectives are evident in Hubmaier's writings, this does not mean that his thought can be classified as solely Zwinglian or Catholic or Anabaptist. Rather, we should be more concerned with what he wanted to articulate through the doctrine of the Lord's Supper in his writings.

It is true that recent research into Hubmaier's theology attempts to place him among the magisterial reformers and the radical reformers. However, it is clear that efforts to evaluate Hubmaier's character through examining the influential elements have a serious weakness in that they cannot classify his position into the one specific category, nor clearly show how his theology was molded. There is a need for a paradigm shift in how Hubmaier's theology is analyzed. An analogy for the need of paradigm shift required could be in comparing the difference between physical reaction and chemical reaction. In a physical reaction there are no fundamental changes in the components of matter and the forces between them, although the shape of the product looks different. In other words, to understand the character of each component of matter is to explain the characteristic features of the final product. In a chemical reaction, one

---

114. Cf. Mabry, *Church*; Steinmetz, "Scholasticism."

115. The possibility of Gabriel Biel's influence on Hubmaier's baptism will be discussed in chapter 3.

Introduction

or more substances react to form one or more different products, which are different from the previous substances. Therefore, the quality of the final product of a chemical reaction cannot necessarily be explained by the characteristic feature of each substance before the chemical reaction. The distinguishing feature of the final product of a chemical reaction is explained by observing the final product itself. According to the experimenter's intention as to what characteristic product he or she wants to produce, the substances for the chemical experiment are changed accordingly. Here, how to analyze the character of some products can be decided by whether it is formed by a physical reaction or a chemical reaction.

This analogy is useful in analyzing studies of Hubmaier's theology. If the uniqueness of Hubmaier's theology could be explained by distinguishing the influential sources from his theology like a case of physical reaction, studies on Hubmaier's theology should focus on exploring the singular influences upon him. If not, then we need to change our paradigm. However, as we have identified above, although many scholars have attempted to analyze the uniqueness of Hubmaier's theology from various sources, they have generally agreed that it is not possible to classify Hubmaier's theology according to one specific group of reformers. Consequently, the reality is that his theological developments had multiple influences, thereby producing a new theological character which transformed the original components. The question of what influenced Hubmaier's thinking does not fully explain the theology he produces. To understand Hubmaier's theology, one needs to analyze his writings themselves rather than *simply* considering external influences. His theology, though it developed from various sources, should not be understood as belonging to those sources. To understand Hubmaier's theology, one needs to focus on his motive and purpose through his theses directly, rather than look primarily at external influences. Hubmaier used various sources to build up and reinforce his theology, but they were not the final goal. Hubmaier's theology is best understood by interpreting his primary writings themselves, which support each other for the purpose of his theses.

Therefore, my approach to understanding Hubmaier's theology in this thesis focuses much more on the interpretation of his primary theses themselves rather than tracing his theological backgrounds. The origin of influences on Hubmaier's thoughts does not explain what Hubmaier said through his writing to contemporary readers in his day. To focus on the influences on Hubmaier's thoughts could run the risk of not seeing what Hubmaier exactly wanted to tell his readers. Hubmaier's concern as a pastor was that his readers at church would easily be able to understand his message. Thus, simply to explore or research the origin of the influences upon his theology cannot provide an exact answer to the question of what he was saying through his writings. When I point out some sources of influence upon Hubmaier's theology, it does not necessarily mean that his theology depended on these influences, but he imported these influences to bolster his arguments.

To use this methodology we need to explore Hubmaier's motive and purpose for his teaching. During the Reformation, though Hubmaier was influenced by, and accepted, reformation doctrines, such as justification by faith, he nevertheless questioned the effect of these doctrines. His consideration on this matter is clearly shown in his thesis, *Von der Freiheit des Willens*.

> . . . I, nevertheless, unfortunately, find many people who to this point have learned and grasped no more than two pieces from all the preaching. First, one says: "We believe; faith saves us." Second, "We can do nothing good. God works in us the desire and the doing. We have no free will." Now, however, such remarks are only half-truths from which one can conclude no more than half-judgments. Whoever makes a whole judgment and does not lay the counter-Scriptures on the same scale next to it, to him a half-truth is more damaging than a whole lie.[116]

From this, we can see that Hubmaier's main intention in writing was not to show that he had a different slogan of soteriology, "justification by faith," but that he had a different understanding of that motto. His main concern was how we should understand the meaning of the faith which saves us. His reconsideration of the meaning of salvation by faith, which was spread by the Protestant reformation, meant that the main motive and purpose of his writings was to argue against both traditional theology and the mainline reformers. For Hubmaier, other contemporary theologians appear to understand salvation by faith primarily from the point of view of cause and effect. This understanding creates an objective and static perspective on soteriology. Such a view is dangerous because of its inherent antinomianism. Hubmaier's emphasis on the necessity of good Christian life for salvation, though he continued to maintain the slogan "justification by faith," is explained in his dynamic and relational perspective for soteriology. At the heart of the understanding of Hubmaier's soteriology, I wish to put forward a contrast between the static and transactional, and the dynamic

116. HS 381; YP 427–28.

and relational perspective, on the doctrine of salvation. Most of his theses focus on one of three subjects: the freedom of the will, baptism and the Lord's Supper.[117] For Hubmaier, these subjects were sufficient to explain his understanding of salvation by faith. In his theses, the issue of human will is a fundamental question by which we understand the meaning of faith for salvation. From the right understanding of faith, for Hubmaier, the practice of baptism and the Lord's Supper become an obligation for those who believe in Christ. Hubmaier clearly showed in his theology how significant baptism and the Lord's Supper are for the salvific life of Christians. In *Eine Form des Nachtmahls Christi* (A Form for Christ's Supper), Hubmaier wrote:

> If now one had no other word or Scripture, but only the correct understanding of water baptism and the Supper of Christ, one would have God and all his creatures, faith and love, the law and all the prophets.[118]

In this case, the proper understanding of baptism and the Lord's Supper are regarded as essential elements for Christian salvation. To know the truth of salvation in Christianity, one cannot ignore the correct understanding of baptism and the Lord's Supper. Consequently, for Hubmaier, these three subjects—the freedom of the will, baptism and the Lord's Supper—are the main emphases to explain the meaning of salvation in order to understand the concept of justification by faith. In order to demonstrate this, I shall examine the three topics, the freedom of the will, baptism and the Lord's Supper, looking at Hubmaier's writings on each, and demonstrating the differences between his theology, and that of others. In the following chapter, as his main concern is the meaning of faith for salvation, I shall first look at Hubmaier's understanding of free will which is directly related to the concept of faith. I shall examine the theological features of his doctrine of salvation as a dynamic and relational perspective in his doctrine of free will. Second, I shall demonstrate how the concept of faith in dynamic and relational perspective relates to the meaning of baptism

---

117. The lists of Hubmaier's representative writings in these three categories are as follows: (1) Freedom of the Will—*Von der Freiheit des Willens* (1527) and *Das andere Büchlein von der Freiwilligkeit des Menschen* (1527) (2) Baptism—*Von der christlichen Taufe der Gläubigen* (1525), *Ein Gespräch auf Zwinglis Taufbüchlein* (1525–1526) and *Der uralten und gar neuen Lehrer Urteil (Ausgabe I und II)* (1525–1526) (3) Lord's Supper—*Etliche Schlußreden vom Unterricht der Messe* (1525), *Ein einfältiger Unterricht* (1526), and *Eine Form des Nachtmahls Christi* (1526–1527). *Eine christliche Lehrtafel* includes three subjects together.

118. HS 359; YP 399.

in the perspective of salvation. I shall show why Hubmaier had to accentuate the necessity of baptism for his soteriology. In the final chapter, I shall examine the way in which Hubmaier's doctrine of the Lord's Supper continued to be developed using a concept of faith understood in dynamic and relational perspective. From these three chapters, we will discover that Hubmaier's motif of the meaning of salvation produced a new perspective on the doctrine of salvation as a dynamic and relational perspective on soteriology. Particularly, in conclusion, for the account of his unique approach to faith in dynamic and relational perspectives, I shall draw upon the concept of Martin Buber's dialogical personalism to help provide a deeper understanding of the concept of dynamic and relational perspectives within Hubmaier's doctrine of salvation. We will also understand why Hubmaier had to emphasize these three issues for his soteriology.

2

Hubmaier's Doctrine of the Freedom of the Will

Introduction

As mentioned in the previous chapter, Hubmaier's consideration of the way the meaning of faith is directly related to the doctrine of salvation was the most significant element of his theology. His theology deals with the main slogan of the Reformation: "justification by faith." In this context, the nature of the Christian doctrine of justification could be regarded as a *hot potato* among the scholars in the Reformation era, whether they were Protestant or Catholic. For the reformers in particular, justification by faith was concerned not only with the question of what a person must do to enter into a "relationship with God through Christ," but also with establishing the doctrine's "presuppositions and consequences."[1] These particular differences between presupposition and consequence in the doctrine of justification are, especially, shown in the differences between mainstream reformers and Anabaptists. Both believed that a person is saved by God's grace which operates through faith and not through any merits of the person. However, Anabaptists seemed to equally emphasize human ability to choose, so much so that they rejected the main reformers' doctrine of the "bondage of the will" and "predestination."[2]

Since both these communities believed a person is saved only by faith, why then did they come to this conclusion in different ways? One

1. McGrath, *Iustitia Dei*, 1.
2. Klaassen, *Anabaptism in Outline*, 41.

approach to understanding the different conclusions is to consider the different definitions of faith. Using this approach, I shall analyze Balthasar Hubmaier's understanding of faith through his perspective on the doctrine of salvation. To analyze his understanding of faith, I shall first examine and analyze Hubmaier's description of faith in his theses. This will demonstrate that his understanding of faith is related to the concept of human will, which was itself a controversial issue during the Reformation era. Therefore, I shall briefly survey different views of the human will among the contemporary scholars of his time, which will help us to understand the context of Hubmaier's day: why he emphasized the freedom of the will. Third, I shall examine Hubmaier's methodology in defending the doctrine of free will against the doctrine of the bondage of the will among mainline reformers by looking at his explanations of the freedom of the human will. To explore these features of Hubmaier's theology, I shall draw on the concept of the freedom of the will using a dynamic and relational perspective, which will help us to better understand his soteriology.

1. The Definition of Faith in Hubmaier's Theology

Hubmaier's first definition of faith appears in his earliest public writing, *Achtzehn schlußreden*, in April or May 1524.[3] Here, the initial three theses show Hubmaier's understanding of faith:[4]

> 1. Faith alone makes us righteous before God.

> 2. This faith is the knowledge of God's mercy, which he has shown us by offering his only begotten Son. Here fail those who are Christian in appearance [only], who have only an historical faith in God.

> 3. Such Faith cannot be idle, but must break forth in gratitude toward God and in all sorts of works of brotherly love toward others.

---

3. HS 71–74; YP 30–34.
4. HS 72; YP 32. Cf. the German text from *Schriften*: "1. Der eynig glaub macht vns frumm vor Gott. 2. Diser glaub ist die erkantnyß der barmhertzigkeyt Gottes, so er vns in der darstreckung seyns eingebornen suns erzeygt hat. Da niderligen alle scheynende Christen, die nichts dann ein Historischen glauben von Gott haben. 3. Solcher glaub mag nit müssig geen, sunder muß außbrechen gegen Gott in dancksagung vnd gegen den menschen in allerley werck brudcrlicher liebe. Hie werden alle butzenwerck nider gestossen als kertzen, palmen vnd weyhwasser."

Hubmaier's Doctrine of the Freedom of the Will

In the first two theses Hubmaier seems to follow the same definition of faith as the mainstream Reformation.[5] Does Hubmaier, then, emphasize the same concept of "justification by faith alone," which was the motto of Luther's reformation?

In the first thesis, Hubmaier asserted that we can be righteous before God only by faith, which did indeed sound very like Luther.[6] However, as we look closer, we discover that there are differences between Luther and Hubmaier's understandings of the doctrine of justification by faith. In the first thesis of *Achtzehn schlußreden*, Hubmaier used the word *"fromm,"* here translated as "righteous."[7] This is in contrast to the term "justified." Vedder argued that Hubmaier intentionally omitted the word "justification" from his writings in order to distinguish himself from Luther's concept of this principle.[8] Moreover, Mabry showed how Hubmaier used a different word from Luther.[9] Luther generally used the word *"Rechtifertigung,"* which means "justified," or "justification," for his doctrine of justification by faith. As this writing shows, Hubmaier instead used the word *"fromm,"* which can mean "pious," "devout," or "religious."[10] He used the word *"fromm"* or *"Frombmachung"* for justification or righteousness not only in his treatises but also in the various translations from the Vulgate text—for example, 1 Tim 1:15.[11] For Hubmaier, Luther's concept of forensic justification needed to be refuted. Hubmaier recognized that if he used the same vocabulary as Luther for his theses, then people would understand his arguments in the same way as that of the mainstream reformers. It is clear that Hubmaier believed that a forensic concept of justification could bring many problems to the Christian life. As we have seen in the previous chapter, Hubmaier's intention to avoid using the forensic concept of justification by faith is clearly shown in the introduction of his later thesis, *Von der Freiheit des Willens*. In writing about the freedom of human will,

---

5. For instance, Martin Luther's emphasis on faith appeared in the doctrine of justification by faith, *sola fide*.

6. See the Preface to WA 54:185.12–186.21.

7. The word *"fromm"* is sometimes appeared as *"frumm"* in Hubmaier's writings. The *"frumm"* seems to be a dialect in the sixteenth century.

8. Vedder, *Balthasar Hübmaier*, 200–201.

9. Mabry, *Church*, 103.

10. Ibid.

11. Ibid. Cf. the Vulgate text of 1 Tim 1:15: "quod Christus Jesus venit in hunc mundum *peccatores salvos facere*." Hubmaier translates this phrase as "der kommen ist in dise welt, *den sünder gerecht und fromb zemachen*" (who has come into this world *to make the sinner just and righteous*), HS 111; YP 84.

Balthasar Hubmaier's Doctrine of Salvation

Hubmaier's main concern was to guide people whom he believed were in danger of misunderstanding the term "justification by faith." Here, Vedder and Mabry demonstrated persuasively that Hubmaier's use of the term "*fromm*" or "*Frombmachung*" is his attempt to disassociate his concept of "justification" from that of other reformers such as Luther.

The second thesis on faith also seems to be similar to that of Luther. Both Luther and Hubmaier focused on the personal recognition of God but they rejected a simple belief in historical details. They believed that faith is a recognition or knowledge of the truth of the gospel, which includes acceptance of it.[12] However, there are some differences in emphasis. Bernhard Lohse argued that Luther regarded the awareness of one's sinfulness as of central importance to Christian faith and all theology.[13] Hubmaier, however, seems to focus more on the recognition of God's mercy and human acceptance of it. Hubmaier showed this more clearly in his writing *Von der christlichen Taufer der Gläubigen*, (December 10, 1526) where he posited:

> Leonhart: What is faith?
>
> Hans: Faith is the realization of the unspeakable mercy of God, his gracious favor and goodwill, which he bears to us through his most beloved Son Jesus Christ, whom he did not spare and delivered him to death for our sakes that sin might be paid for, and we might be reconciled to him and with the assurance of our hearts cry to him: Abba, Father, our Father who are in heaven.[14]

For Hubmaier, faith is not only recognition in the sense of acknowledgement, but also in the sense that one comes to understand and accept the unspeakable mercies of God, expressed in the gift of God.[15] This concept of faith continues to be explored in Hubmaier's third thesis on faith.

Hubmaier continued to show his concern with Luther's formulation, as is seen in his other works. In the third thesis he demonstrated his concept of faith, which is distinct from that of the mainstream reformers. He insisted that faith must be active rather than passive, as opposed to Luther's emphasis.[16]

---

12. Mabry, *Church*, 130. Cf. McGrath, *Christian Theology*, 155.
13. Lohse, *Luther's Theology*, 248.
14. HS 313; YP 348.
15. Mabry, *Church*, 130.
16. LW 25:368–69; WA 56:379.1–15.

Hubmaier's Doctrine of the Freedom of the Will

Mabry showed how Hubmaier's concept of faith can be distinguished into two kinds: initial faith as belief and saving faith.[17] Initial faith arises out of human capacity. It is the intellectual capacity of humans to believe what the gospel says when it is heard. In other words, the individual himself or herself can understand and act. We will look further at this concept of active human behavior as a key issue in Hubmaier's theology. Hubmaier claimed that faith must include active human behavior, not only toward God, but also to others. Why did Hubmaier emphasize active human behavior to explain faith? What significance did this have in his theology? For the answer to these questions, we are required to look at some of the controversies concerning the issue of human will among scholars in Hubmaier's day. This will help us to understand why Hubmaier emphasized the freedom of the will in the doctrine of salvation.

2. Background of the Controversy on Free Will

Hubmaier's concept of the freedom of the will as active human behavior appears in the context of his disagreement with the Lutheran doctrines of predestination and bondage of the will.[18] Before his writings on the freedom of the will, there already existed controversy over this issue between Erasmus and Luther. An examination of the general argument between Erasmus and Luther will be valuable in helping us understand more of Hubmaier's purpose and intention in emphasizing free will.

a. Erasmus's Diatribe *De Libero Arbitrio*

In the discussion between Erasmus and Luther which took place between 1524 and 1525, the issues are clearly laid out. Erasmus seems to have believed that Luther's theology, which emphasized only the Providence of God, led to permission for human immorality and malice. He pointed out the weakness and danger of Luther's theology in supposing that if whatever is done by us is done not by free choice but by sheer necessity, there would be no way for an evildoer to correct his life.[19] His consideration of this matter led him to insist on the freedom of the human will. Through his reinvigoration of Christianity from the Sermon on the Mount, Eras-

---

17. Mabry, *Faith*, 19–55.
18. Beachy, *Concept of Grace*, 201.
19. Rupp and Watson, *Luther and Erasmus*, 41. Hereafter cited as LCC 17.

mus believed that the significance for Christianity is not dependent upon the abundance of ecclesiastical norms and regulation, but rather upon humility and discipleship.[20] Therefore, Erasmus insisted that people must have freedom of will. However, he did not regard the issue of free will as a philosophical matter, but as an ethical matter.[21] In other words, he thought that the concept of free will was necessary to improve Christians' morality and discipleship. Erasmus wrote: "By free choice in this place we mean a power of the human will by which a man can apply himself to the things which lead to eternal salvation, or turn away from them."[22] Erasmus understood free will as the power or force of the will that can turn to, or turn away from, something. For Erasmus, a devout person should attempt to seek out and to follow the will of God, and to turn away from sin. Even though this person may willingly give praise that his or her goodness is achieved by God's grace, he or she actually needs to strive for it.[23] Erasmus's primary concern about free will is that human beings have a totally free choice of action, so that they can be held responsible for their sin. In spite of his stress on the freedom of human will, he never asserted that a person can himself or herself achieve salvation without the grace of God. So Erasmus wrote:

> In man the will was so upright and free that, apart from new grace, he could continue in innocence but, apart from the help of new grace, he could not attain the happiness of eternal life which the Lord Jesus promised to his followers.[24]

This different concept of free will, which is in contrast to Pelagianism, shows that Erasmus, at least, understood the danger that he might be regarded as a kind of Pelagian if he asserted the significance of free will. Thus, he attempted both to hold on to the necessity of free will as a moral choice, and emphasized its limits, even presenting it as a gift of God:

---

20. Lohse, *Luther's Theology*, 161.

21. Ibid.

22. LCC 17:47. Cf. *De libero arbitrio* 1b.10 (36): "liberum arbitrium hoc loco sentimus vim humanae voluntatis, qua se posit homo applicare ad ea, quae perducunt ad aeternam salutem, aut abiisdem avertere." According to Rupp, "this is a key passage, for it shows that *arbitrium* involves the action of *voluntas*, and therefore cannot simply be translated 'will.'" Parenthetical numbers in the Erasmus citations from *De libero arbitrio* refer to the page numbers from the Lesowsky critical edition. See Erasmus, *De libero arbitrio*.

23. Brecht, *Shaping and Defining*, 220.

24. LCC 17:48.

> Here we can placate those who cannot bear that man can achieve any good work which he does not owe to God, when we say that it is nevertheless true that the whole work is due to God, without whom we do nothing; that the contribution of free choice is extremely small, and that this itself is part of the divine gift, that we can turn our souls to those things pertaining to salvation, or work together (*synergein*) with grace.[25]

As Brecht pointed out, Erasmus's contribution on free will is that he found it in a combination of human will and divine grace, because he wanted to argue against Luther's view that a person is an unfree sinner and therefore incapable of doing any good.[26] His theory, that the grace of God is more dominant than the freedom of human will for salvation, created confusion about the exact significance and role of the human will for salvation.[27] Nevertheless, Erasmus believed in the necessity to stress free will for the Christian life, and in his character as a Skeptic, put himself forward to be criticized:

> And, in fact, so far am I from delighting in "assertions" that I would readily take refuge in the opinion of the Skeptics, wherever this is allowed by the inviolable authority of the Holy Scriptures and by the decrees of the Church, to which I everywhere willingly submit my personal feelings, whether I grasp what it prescribes or not.[28]

b. Luther's Response in *De Servo Arbitrio*

Luther's response to Erasmus's treatise on free will began with a criticism of Erasmus's Skeptic. According to Luther, if someone takes no delight in the assertion of his or her faith, he or she cannot be truly a

---

25. LCC 17:89-90. *De libero arbitrio* 4.7 (170).

26. Brecht, *Shaping and Defining*, 222.

27. LCC 17:90. *De libero arbitrio* 4.8 (172). Erasmus said: "For since there are three stages in all things—beginning, progress, and end—they attribute the first and last to grace, and only in progress say that free choice achieves anything, yet in such wise that in each individual action two causes come together, the grace is the principal cause and the will secondary, which can do nothing apart from the principal cause, since the principal is sufficient in itself" (ibid.).

28. LCC 17:37. *De libero arbitrio* 1a.4 (6): "Et adeo non delector assertionibus, ut facile in Scepticorum pedibus discessurus sim, ubicumque per divinarum scripturarum inviolabilem auctoritatem et ecelesiae decreta liceat, quibus meurn sensum ubique libens submitto, sive assequor, quod praescribit, sive non assequor."

Balthasar Hubmaier's Doctrine of Salvation

Christian.[29] He defined "assertion" in this context in the following way: "And by assertion—in order that we may not be misled by words—I mean a constant adhering, affirming, confessing, maintaining, and an invincible persevering."[30] Luther's theology depends on his presupposition that this assertion of faith is essential for Christian life.[31] For Luther, the clarity of the Scriptures and the central theme of the Bible are a focus on Christ, our Savior.[32] Scripture clearly sets forth truths such as the divine and human natures in Christ, Jesus Christ the Son of God, and the Trinity of God.[33] In other words, these truths in Scripture are clearly sufficient to show the way of salvation for Christian faith.

Luther's presuppositions on both the assertion of faith and the clarity of the Scripture could support his idea of the bondage of the will. He argued that Christian assertion and the clarity of the Scripture will lead to the acknowledgement of the sovereignty and Providence of God. Luther's doctrine of the bondage of the will needs to be understood in the context of his insistence on the Providence of God and the transcendence of God. He asserted that the relationship between God and a human being is controlled by God's total initiative, with the individual contributing nothing. He wrote:

> God must therefore be left to himself in his own majesty, for in this regard we have nothing to do with him, nor has he willed that we should have anything to do with him. But we have something to do with him insofar as he is clothed and set forth in his Word, though which he offers himself to us.[34]

Luther asserted that we are free only in the limited area where things are beneath us, but not in respect of that which is above us.[35] Thus, while we are free to choose what we eat or buy, we are not able to choose to be justified. Moreover, his stress on the Providence of God and human creatureliness stemmed from his argument about the soteriological bondage of the human will. Luther's emphasis is that everything happens in

---

29. LW 33:19–20; WA 18:603–5.
30. LW 33:20; WA 18:603–5.
31. Lohse, *Luther's Theology*, 164.
32. Ibid.
33. LW 33:28; WA 18:606.
34. LW 33:139; WA 18:685.
35. Lohse, *Luther's Theology*, 167.

relation to salvation is necessarily and immutably according to God's will.[36] Consequently, the accentuation of this concept of human will means that Luther had a deterministic view that there is no human freedom of life because God has the entire initiative in terms of salvation.

In his writing *De Servo Arbitrio*, therefore, Luther comes to the following conclusions about human will:

> For if we believe it to be true that God foreknows and predestines all things, that he can neither be mistaken in his foreknowledge nor hindered in his predestination, and that nothing takes place but as he wills it (as reason itself is forced to admit), then on the testimony of reason itself there cannot be any free choice in man or angel or any creature.[37]

c. Summary

From the controversy between Luther and Erasmus over the nature of free will, we see that their different motivations led to different interpretations of the role of human will. For Erasmus, Luther's inordinate stress on the Providence of God for human salvation could be considered as fatalistic determination that could endanger people's moral motivation.[38] He wanted rather to emphasize the necessity of free will to do good according to an ethical perspective, rather than a soteriological perspective. However, for Luther the acceptance of free will within the perspective of salvation ran the risk of reducing and denying the fact that God alone works for our salvation and humans do nothing for it. Here, faith, that essential element for salvation as stipulated by the tenets of the Reformation, cannot depend on human will but only on the Providence of God. These different views on human will show how important the issue of free will was for the concept of faith during the Reformation. In this circumstance, though Hubmaier did not deny the motto "justification by faith," he could have bucked this trend of the issue of human will for soteriology. That is the reason why Hubmaier was so concerned with the issue of free will. Surveying how the concept of free will appears in his writings will help us to understand how Hubmaier approached this issue.

---

36. Brecht, *Shaping and Defining*, 228.
37. LW 33:293; WA 18:786.
38. Brecht, *Shaping and Defining*, 229.

3. Appearance of Free Will in Hubmaier's Writings

Like Erasmus, Hubmaier believed that human choice is effective. In this, he was opposed to Luther. However, whereas Erasmus concentrated on free will with regard to ethical behavior, Hubmaier was concerned with the question of having saving faith.

a. *Eine christliche Lehrtafel*

Hubmaier first discussed this issue in *Eine christliche Lehrtafel*, (A Christian Catechism) written on December 10, 1526.[39] The catechism, which usually consists of questions and answers, is a popular manual of Christian doctrine used for religious instruction.[40] A catechism aimed to help readers simply and coherently understand the true doctrine according to the author. In other words, a catechism contained its author's thoughts and doctrine. It is a fair assumption then, that Hubmaier included in *Eine christliche Lehrtafel* the thought and doctrine that he wanted to emphasize. He described it as "a Christian Catechism that every person before he is baptized in water should previously know, in the form of a dialogue."[41] An examination of the catechism will illustrate his intended position.

In his consideration of his readers, who were generally new believers, Hubmaier focused primarily on how to live as a Christian. Here, the meaning of "new believers" needs to be considered in the context of Hubmaier's period of activity. The words "new believer" might have seemed anachronistic at that time, as everyone was baptized in infancy, thus becoming officially "Christian" automatically. For Hubmaier, however, without the experience of conversion, such a person could not be classified as a believer.[42] Thus, Hubmaier could well hold a concept of "new believers" and a reason to write this catechism for them.

---

39. YP 426. The preface was begun on December 10, 1526; printing was completed early in 1527.

40. McGrath, *Reformation Thought*, 239–41. "With its considerable emphasis upon religious education, the Reformation saw the appearance of a number of major catechisms, most notably Luther's Lesser Catechism (1529) and the celebrated Heidelberg Catechism (1563)" (ibid., 280).

41. HS 311; YP 345.

42. The "experience of conversion" does not mean a charismatic experience of conversion. For Hubmaier, conversion means one's confession of faith in God with his or her commitment to God.

Even though he began by explaining the nature of humanity, and of God, he spent more space and time explaining not only the nature of sin but also the way in which we repent and overcome sin in a practical way. He also insisted on the relationship between faith and baptism.

> Leonhart: After faith what do you desire?
>
> Hans: Water baptism.[43]

The confession of faith should lead to the desire for water baptism. Here, Hubmaier stressed the significance of baptism and why it is necessary for Christian life. For him, the confessions of faith, baptism and church could not be separated from each other. Hubmaier also attempted to explain to believers why the doctrines of Roman Catholicism are wrong and does so through teaching the meaning of church ceremonies. For example, he taught that the Lord's Supper, which is interpreted as a sacrament in Roman teaching, should rather be understood as a memorial symbol of Christ's suffering and death for the forgiveness of our sins. For believers, according Hubmaier, the Lord's Supper should also function in their lives as a sign of the obligation that one believer has toward another.[44] In this context, as Bergsten rightly pointed out it was Hubmaier's pastoral concern that caused him to address the issue.[45] We will look in more detail at this issue below.

In spite of this stress on practical and pastoral concerns, Hubmaier put specific weight on the issue of free will in the later part of the catechism:

> ... In sum: First God made us good and free in soul, body, and spirit. This goodness and freedom were through Adam's disobedience taken captive in our spirit, wounded in our soul, and completely corrupted in our flesh; therefore we are all conceived and born in sin and are by nature the children of wrath . . . But now God has given birth to us of his own will, as James writes, James 1:18, and Peter, 1 Pet. 1:3, by the word of his power in which we are really made whole and free again . . . Yes, to the present day through the Word God sent, our souls are just as free in themselves to will good and evil as was Adam's soul in Paradise.[46]

---

43. HS 313-14; YP 349–50.

44. HS 317; YP 354.

45. HS 379. The pastoral concern of Hubmaier's theology will be presented later, as will the theologies of baptism and the Lord's Supper.

46. HS 322–23; YP 361.

Hubmaier never lost sight of his important argument in support of the freedom of the will. His arguments can also be seen in minute detail in the first treatise of *Von der Freiheit des Willens* (April 1, 1527) as I will go on to demonstrate. For Hubmaier, the understanding of free will is one of the most significant motives for life as a Christian.

b. *Von der Freiheit des Willens*

After his *Eine christliche Lehrtafel*, Hubmaier wrote another two treatises on the freedom of human will. As we have seen, the catechism is a guide book for new believers, but these two treatises are more systematic and theological, for more advanced readers. In this, he was dealing with the issue of human will as the Lehrtafel, although in more detail. As well as the more systematic approach, his writing style changed because of the different readership. His first treatise *Von der Freiheit des Willens* (April 1, 1527) was dedicated to Count George of Brandenburg-Ansbach, a follower of Luther. Count George of Brandenburg-Ansbach was probably influenced by Luther's theology of the human will, the view that even in the external aspects of life, humans have no freedom but are controlled by God.[47] In essence, Hubmaier wrote this treatise specifically to argue against Luther's view of the bondage of the human will.[48] The systematic approach of Luther's argument provokes an equally systematic response in Hubmaier. These systematic theological abilities are particularly evident in this writing. His unique approach to human nature through trichotomism[49] is clear, as he insists on the freedom of the will. In this treatise, Hubmaier attempted to prove the significance of human will at the same time without denying the significant role of God's grace in his understanding of salvation.[50]

c. *Das andere Büchlein von der Freiwilligkeit des Menschen*

The writing style of *Das andere Büchlein von der Freiwilligkeit des Menschen* is very different from the systematic approach of *Von der Freiheit*

---

47. Lohse, *Luther's Theology*, 167.

48. See Hubmaier's prologue of *Von der Freiheit des Willens* in HS 381; YP 427–29.

49. This concept will be explained later, but this basically means that a human being consists of three elements: body, spirit, and soul.

50. YP 426.

des Willens. It was dedicated to Duke Friedrich II of Liegnitz, Brieg, and Wohlau, in Silesia on May 20, 1527. Even though Duke Friedrich II provided a place of refuge for many Anabaptists, he was actually influenced by Caspar Schwenckfeld, who was a representative of the spiritualists. Schwenckfeld's thought was characterized by the conviction that the "inner word," the spirit, is more important than the "external word," the letter of Scripture.[51] As Rothenberger said:

> For Schwenckfeld, literalism was the way of bondage and death to Christianity . . . He always remembered that the actual event comes before anything is written about the event.[52]

Anyone considering spiritualists as readers, therefore, might think that one of the strongest challenges to spiritualists in an argument is to appeal to their feelings or emotion through inspired messages from the Holy Spirit, rather than depending on Biblical texts. For spiritualists, revelation or prophecy by the Holy Spirit is much more meaningful than the written Bible. In this second treatise, however, Hubmaier expanded on the freedom of the will through citing or interpreting Bible texts, which support his argument. For example:

> Philippians 2:13:
>
> "It is God who works in you the willing and the doing according to good will."
>
> Listen: Paul says, "God works in you the willing and the doing." He does not say God wants and does in you, though both sayings are also true if you regard the problem as a whole.[53]

Here we see that Hubmaier's method of arguing his position with regards to free will seems to contradict the emphasis of the Spiritualists. Hubmaier quoted and interpreted biblical texts to support his argument. But if he knew the character of the spiritualists, why did he use Biblical literalism to defend his theory? Does it mean that he was oblivious to who the reader

---

51. Pearse, *Great Restoration*, 151–52. Pearse presented Schwenckfeld's thought as a spiritualist in at least four senses. First, Schwenckfeld emphasizes the "inner word," *the spirit*, more than the "external word," *the Bible*. Second, he accepts the doctrine of the "invisible church" as a mystical body of all those who have true faith, regardless of denominational affiliation. Third, his Christology is somewhat Platonic. Fourth, he denies the Eucharist is a sacrament.

52. Rothenberger, *Caspar Schwenckfeld*, 54, 57–58.

53. HS 409; YP 462.

was at this time? I do not believe so. Rather, it is more likely that he did indeed adapt his writing to his readers, as is evident in his conclusion:

> Accordingly, I beseech you to go forth and henceforth to be at peace with God, so that you do not sadden his Spirit, for I, unworthy servant of God, will henceforth give you little answer.[54]

In this treatise, Hubmaier's presupposition concerning the freedom of the will is that in order to understand God's will, proper exegesis of the Bible is much more significant, and proper than depending on the "inner word." However, Hubmaier recognized the spiritualists' priorities in their faith. He, therefore, concluded that if one refuses the biblical proof of free will, he or she will sadden the Spirit, a point that is likely to contain the most powerful challenge to spiritualists regarding free will, as their beliefs are based on the Holy Spirit.

d. Summary

These three representative writings help us identify most of Hubmaier's convictions about the freedom of the will. First, Hubmaier's concern for his readers produced a different way of writing about the issue of free will. His theses about free will were different because they were not only *for* those who were new believers but *against* the Lutheran theology of the bondage of the will and the doctrine of predestination. Moreover, Hubmaier appealed to the spiritualists to obtain a better understanding of free will among the radical reformers. Second, despite a varied audience, Hubmaier never changed nor was shaken from his central theme: the freedom of the will. For Hubmaier, the issue of free will is not only a controversial subject, but is also an element essential for understanding Christian life. In other words, the doctrine of free will in Hubmaier's theology cannot be separated from his other theological concerns such as baptism and the Lord's Supper. Therefore, understanding Hubmaier's doctrine of free will is the first step towards looking at other aspects of his theology. So, why was the issue of free will so significant for Hubmaier in his theology?

---

54. HS 431; YP 491.

4. Hubmaier's Methodology in Defending the Doctrine of Free Will

a. The Reason Why Hubmaier Stressed Free Will

As already mentioned in the previous chapter, in his prologue of *Von der Freiheit des Willens*, Hubmaier did not say that the reformers' soteriology itself was unbiblical.[55] Rather, he criticized deficiencies in their theory by saying that their doctrine is half-truth. However, for him, half-truth cannot be a truth. Rather it is an obstacle to revealing the whole truth.

Hubmaier's understanding of soteriology seems to deny the strong connection between the first statement (We believe that faith saves us) as a reason and the second statement (We can do nothing good. God works in us the desire and the doing. We have no free will) as its result. For Hubmaier, the statement that we are saved *only* by faith itself is right, but it does *not* mean that we have no free will to do good, because God works in us both the desire and the doing. The two statements (We believe that faith saves us and we can do nothing good. God works in us the desire and the doing. We have no free will.), brought together could possibly suggest that God permits human beings to sin. It might, furthermore, bring a fatalistic belief that all false human behavior depends on the Providence and decision of God. Even if we have sinned, it would not be our fault, but God's plan for us.

To solve these problems, Hubmaier stressed *active* human behavior. If a human being has the free will to choose good or evil, our license is our own fault, not God's.

b. Hubmaier's Presuppositions about Free Will

i. Trichotomism

The premise of Hubmaier's first treatise "Freedom of the Will" is that the human being has three elements: spirit, soul, and body:

> The human being is a corporal and rational creature, created by God as body, spirit, and soul, Gen. 2:7. These three elements are found essentially and in varying ways in every human being, as the Scripture thoroughly proves.[56]

55. HS 381; YP 427–28.
56. HS 382; YP 429.

Balthasar Hubmaier's Doctrine of Salvation

Hubmaier did not consider it necessary to define these concepts. Rather, he simply explained these three elements through the meaning of the Hebrew language terms, like this:

> First, the flesh or the body is made out of the earth, which clod of earth or lump of clay, *aphar* and *erets* in the Hebrew, is translated in German as "dust," "ashes," or "mud taken from the earth." Second, notice the living breath, *neshamah* in the Hebrew, translated as "blowing on," "breathing on," "blowing upon," or "spirit." Third, the soul, called *nephesh*, is expressed separately; it is that which makes the body alive.[57]

Hubmaier depended a great deal on particular biblical texts to support his idea of three elements in human beings. He attempted to prove his argument for trichotomism by using 1 Thess 5:23 and Heb 4:12. Furthermore, he expanded his conviction that each of these three essential substances has its own will, by defining them thus:

> Now since with scriptural authority no one can deny these three essential things, substances, or essences, it follows that one must confess also three kinds of will in human beings, namely, the will of the flesh, the will of the soul, and the will of the spirit.[58]

Hubmaier asserted that the individual will of each of the three essential elements of human nature is able to act to some extent separately and independently of the others, and can freely choose according to its own will:

> Since free will in the human being is nothing other than a power, force, energy, or adroitness of the soul to will or not will something, to choose or flee, to accept or to reject good or evil, according to the will of God, or according to the will of the flesh, which fleshly will and potentiality should more exactly be called an impotence rather than a power or energy.[59]

For Hubmaier, following the will of God means suffering willingly in order to do God's will. In distinguishing between the three wills, he explored different aspects of this willing commitment. He argued that each component—body, mind and spirit—has a separate will that is committed in different degrees to following God. Thus, the will of the spirit wants to obey the will of God totally, and the will of the flesh does not want to

---

57. HS 382; YP 429–30.
58. HS 383; YP 430.
59. HS 393; YP 443.

follow the will of God at all. However, the will of the soul seems to stand between them:

> However, so that I might teach in clear writing the different divisions of these three wills, the Spirit of God speaks in John 1:13 of the will of the flesh, which does not want to suffer; the will of the soul, willing to suffer, but due to the flesh seeks not to; and the will of the spirit which strongly desires to suffer (cf. John 1:13).[60]

So, the differences between the wills of spirit, soul, and flesh depend on how each responds to and obeys the will of God. If the wills respond differently to the will of God, why is this? Were the characters of each will within human nature in existence since the beginning of creation?

Here we might ask a question about the definition of free will. When Hubmaier is discussing the issue of free will in the arguments about justification, does he mean all three wills or only one? And if one, which one? To make concrete this argument about trichotomism in terms of free will, Hubmaier attempted a new analysis of the story about the tree of the knowledge of good and evil. The three essential elements of human being—spirit, soul and flesh—change in their status in accordance with the three steps: before the fall of Adam, after the fall of Adam and after the restoration by Christ.

His discussion about three elements within a human being begins with the conviction that each will was perfectly free to choose good or evil on its own before Adam's Fall:

> The three substances were also wholly free to choose good or evil, life or death, heaven or hell. Thus they were originally made good and free also in the recognition, in the capability, and performance of good and evil by God . . .[61]

This statement builds on the argument that human beings are made in the image of God (Gen 1:31). The Fall of Adam, that is when Adam disobeyed the commandment of God, affected a fundamental change in each aspect of human substance. It brought two main effects on the will of the flesh:

> Thus the flesh has irretrievably lost its goodness and freedom through the Fall of Adam and has become entirely and wholly worthless and hopeless unto death. It is not able or capable of

60. HS 383; YP 430–31.
61. HS 385; YP 432.

anything other than sin, striving against God and being the enemy of his commandments.[62]

One effect of Adam's transgression is that the flesh of all human beings has irreparably lost its own freedom of the will to choose whatever it wants to do. The flesh could do nothing except sin against the commandments of God. There is no way for the flesh to be restored to its condition before the Fall. Another result of Adam's disobedience to God was that not only had Adam himself fallen, but also all of his descendants must carry the guilt of their forefather's sin against God. Humans are thus conceived and born in sin. Hubmaier cited Gen 2:17 "on the same day you eat of the tree of the knowledge of good and evil you will die," and provided further examples from Job, Jeremiah, and King David.[63] For Hubmaier, therefore, the sinful nature of the flesh is inherited by all humans. Because of sin, the flesh, a part of human nature, must be ruined and die. Here we can see that Hubmaier has a concept of original sin, at least for the flesh of human beings.

However, as we have seen above, Hubmaier drew a contrast between the flesh and the spirit. His premise is that the will of the spirit, unlike that of the flesh, was not affected by the Fall of Adam:

> The spirit of the human being, however, has before, during, and after the Fall remained upright, whole, and good.[64]

The will of the spirit could maintain its purity of freedom and goodness because it never participated in either the will to disobey God's commandment, or in allowing the flesh to eat the forbidden fruit.[65] For the biblical proof of the purity of the spirit, Hubmaier interpreted the meaning of 1 Thess 5:23: "and may your whole spirit and soul and body be held blameless until the coming of our Lord Jesus Christ." His interpretation on 1 Thess 5:23 raises several problems that will be discussed later, but as he wrote:

> Here you note again, dear Christian, the wholeness of the spirit in the human being which rightly judges all things and the wounds of the soul, which in itself is of no value for judging. Both flesh and soul are damaged and seriously wounded. Only

---

62. HS 385; YP 433.
63. HS 386; YP 434.
64. Ibid.
65. Ibid.

the spirit has retained its original righteousness in which it was first created.[66]

For Hubmaier the position of soul seems to be more neutral. Before the Fall, the will of the soul had the ability to choose good or evil, but as the result of the Fall it could no longer distinguish between good and evil:

> However, the soul, the third part of the human being, has through this disobedience of Adam been wounded in the will in such a way and become sick unto death so that it can on its own choose nothing good.[67]

Following the Fall, the soul could not do anything without the body because the body, the instrument of soul, is not able to do any good. The weakened soul cannot control the body, and so is incapable of doing good, or choosing good, even if the soul wants it.[68] For the nature of human will after Adam's Fall Hubmaier preferred to use the words "lost," "wounded," or "damaged" rather than "destroyed." These terms such as "lost," "wounded," and "damaged" reflect Hubmaier's conviction that human will is only wounded (or corrupted) rather than completely lost by the Fall and, therefore, it can be restored by a new action and the gift of God's grace in the soul.[69] Even though the will of the soul lost its knowledge of good and evil, it was restored through the Word of God and thus able to distinguish between good and evil:

> However, since it has been awakened by the heavenly Father through words of comfort, threats, promises, good things, punishment, and in other ways prodded, admonished, and drawn, as well as made whole by his dear Son, and enlightened by the Holy Spirit—as the three main articles of our Christian faith concerning God the Father and the Son and the Holy Spirit show—by this the soul now again knows what is good and evil.[70]

Consequently, before the Fall the will of each human element—the body, the soul and the spirit—was perfectly free to know and to choose good and evil. After the Fall, the body and the soul were seriously wounded. The wound to the will of the flesh was irreparable and even deadly. However,

66. HS 389; YP 438.
67. HS 386; YP 435.
68. HS 386–87; YP 435.
69. Mabry, *Faith*, 60.
70. HS 390; YP 439.

Balthasar Hubmaier's Doctrine of Salvation

the will of the soul is reparable through the Word of God. The will of the spirit was not affected by the Fall, so it has maintained its purity.

Hubmaier also distinguished between the different statuses of human substance after Christ's restoration. The flesh still remains wholly ruined and good for nothing. The spirit remains ready and willing to do good.

> The soul, sad and troubled, standing between the spirit and the flesh, knowing not what to do, is in its natural powers blind and ignorant of heavenly things.[71]

Even after the restoration of human substances, the soul still stands between flesh and spirit without knowing what to do. The will of the soul is ambivalent because it has been blinded and left ignorant of heavenly things. Through the illumination provided by the Holy Spirit, the soul now knows what is good and evil. Even though the soul is free after restoration, it does not necessarily mean that the soul will abstain from evil. The soul can will evil and perform evil like a useful instrument of the flesh.

Hubmaier, however, never lost his determination to insist on the significant role of the soul's will, which is restored and made healthy and truly free through the Word of God. As such, the soul can follow the will of God and control the flesh to obey God's will even against the flesh's own inclinations:

> Now it can will and do good, as much as depends on it, for it can command the flesh in such as way that it tames and masters it, so that against its own inclination it must go into the fire with the spirit and with the soul on account of the name of Christ.[72]

What does "go into the fire" mean? In Hubmaier's time, the Anabaptist witnesses faced persecution and even death. Persecution methods such as drowning, sword, and stake were all used to exterminate them.[73] Thus, martyrdom became a symbol of Anabaptism.[74] In this context, the meaning of "go into the fire" could be related to process of martyrdom.[75] According to Walter Klaassen, Hubmaier believed that suffering for Christ's sake is identified as the "nearest, most direct way of gaining eternal life."[76]

---

71. Ibid.
72. HS 391; YP 441.
73. Estep, *Anabaptist Story*, 29.
74. Ibid., 57.
75. Williams and Megal, *Anabaptist Writers*, 126.
76. Klaasen, *Anabaptism in Outline*, 85.

Hubmaier's Doctrine of the Freedom of the Will

Why does Hubmaier emphasize physical suffering as a symbol of obedience to God? Is it because the flesh will suffer more in the fire than non-physical aspects? Hubmaier never said that physical suffering (in the fire) is more painful or harder than other suffering. Rather, he asserted that complete obedience to the will of God needs to include the submission of the will of the flesh to God's will even against its own inclination, which is still good for naught. For Hubmaier, therefore, the will of the soul, which is restored by the Word of God, is very significant, because it means that the will of the flesh may be able to follow the will of God.

Consequently, free will in a human being is focused on the will of the soul. Hubmaier emphasized this concept as follows:

> Accordingly, henceforth every soul that sins will bear its sin itself since it is willingly responsible for its own sin and not Adam, not Eve, not the flesh, sin, death or the devil, for all these things are already captured, bound, and overcome in Christ.[77]

In spite of Hubmaier's assertion that the three different elements of the human being have their own wills, in this argument, he ultimately focused on the capacity of the will of the soul. However, as Mabry rightly pointed out, in this context when Hubmaier talked about the natural capacity of human beings, he meant human beings as *restored* through the death and resurrection of Christ, rather than human nature as *created* before the Fall.[78]

ii. Ambiguity in Hubmaier's Doctrine of Free Will

Several questions arise regarding Hubmaier's logic in relation to the condition of free will. The first is whether the premise of his doctrine of human nature is based on correct exegesis. Because of his assertion that biblical proofs are the most important and authorized, Hubmaier particularly emphasized two verses, Gen 2:7 and 1 Thess 5:23, to prove his theory of trichotomism. However, his exegesis of 1 Thess 5:23 raises a problem. Hubmaier used this verse to support the proof not only of trichotomism but also of the purity of the spirit. But, this text cannot be used as a prooftext for his understanding of human nature. He wrote:

> "And may your whole spirit and soul and body be held blameless until the coming of our Lord Jesus Christ," 1 Thess. 5:23. He

---

77. HS 396; YP 446.
78. Mabry, *Faith*, 22.

says, "Your whole spirit" and not "your whole soul," or "your whole body." For what has once disintegrated and been shattered is no longer whole.[79]

The fact that Hubmaier generally quoted and used texts from the Vulgate version of the Bible is important for understanding why he, in fact, bases his argument on a misinterpretation. The verse, 1 Thess 5:23 in the Vulgate is as follows: *ut integer spiritus vester et anima et corpus sine querela in adventu Domini nostri Jesu Christi servetur*. This Latin text was initially translated by Hubmaier into his native language, *Vnd eüer gantzer geyst vnd seel vnd leib muesse behalten werden vnnstrefflich auff die zukunfft vnsers herren Jesu Christi*, which would be translated into English, "And may your whole spirit and soul and body be held blameless until the coming of our Lord Jesus Christ." Hubmaier believed here that the word "whole" as an adjective modifies only spirit, but not soul nor body. The reason that Paul did not mention the other elements for "whole" here, according to Hubmaier, is that what was once wounded and broken cannot be made whole anymore.[80]

However, as Vedder rightly pointed out, this verse from the Greek, καὶ ὁλόκληρον ὑμῶν τὸ πνεῦμα καὶ ἡ ψυχὴ καὶ τὸ σῶμα ἀμέμπτως ἐν τῇ παρουσίᾳ τοῦ κυρίου ἡμῶν Ἰησοῦ Χριστοῦ τηρηθείη, should be translated as "and may your spirit and soul and body be preserved whole, without blame, at the coming of our Lord Jesus Christ."[81] The word "whole" modifies all the elements of human being rather than only the spirit. Accordingly, Hubmaier's assertion that the spirit in human nature has kept its purity, regardless of the Fall, is incorrect. Therefore, there is no guarantee that Hubmaier's assumption about the purity of the spirit in human nature even after the Fall by using 1 Thess 5:23 is right.

Moreover, Hubmaier's use of Gen 2:7, which he used to explain his understanding of flesh, spirit and soul, seems to be a poor example to support trichotomism as shown here:

> When the Lord God made the human being out of the dust from the earth, he blew a living breath into his face and thus the human being became a living soul, Gen. 2:7.[82]

---

79. HS 386; YP 434.
80. Mabry, *Faith*, 62.
81. Vedder, *Balthasar Hübmaier*, 191.
82. HS 382; YP 429.

For Hubmaier, the terms "dust" (*staub*), "living breath" (*lebendigen attemb*), and "living soul" (*lebendige seel*) are related to the human substances of flesh, spirit, and soul. That means, therefore, that he believed the Bible itself proves the existence of three human substances. However, Mabry rightly argued that when the Hebrew word *nephes* is translated into German as *seel* (soul), it does not necessarily mean a specific element of human being as soul.[83] Rather, it becomes a synecdoche, representing the whole personality of human beings; a composite of body and spirit.[84] Therefore, Hubmaier's interpretation of Gen 2:7 fails to demonstrate convincingly the trichotomous concept of human nature. Nevertheless, this remains the basis from which he works.

The second question is whether Hubmaier's convictions about the freedom of the will meant that he could conceive of the possibility that Adam was free not to fall. He explained simply that a human being's disobedience of God produced this fall. However, considering his premise about free will, the question remains. Hubmaier said that all three substances in the human being were absolutely free to choose either good or evil, life or death, heaven or hell. Furthermore, he insisted that the human being had enough knowledge of good or evil before the Fall as shown here:

> But the soul, through the eating of the forbidden tree lost the recognition of good and evil in the sight of God, which knowledge it certainly had before the Fall, as far as it was necessary and sufficient for a human creature to know.[85]

Hubmaier, however, pointed out that as a result of the Fall, Adam lost his ability to recognize good or bad because he ate the forbidden fruit. So, how does Hubmaier define the purpose of God's creation? He wrote:

> Before the human being are life and death, good and evil; whatever pleases him (yes, him) is given to him.[86]

Hubmaier explained that the main role of a human being is to please God. In order to please God, it is necessary to obey God's commands. From the above two premises on free will—that the first human being before the Fall had enough knowledge of good or evil and that the main purpose of a human being is to please God—we may see the problem in explaining the cause of the human Fall. If a human being has sufficient knowledge of

83. Mabry, *Faith*, 31.
84. *NIDOTTE*, 133.
85. HS 393; YP 443.
86. HS 385; YP 433.

good or evil, and knows how to please God, why, then does the human fall by his disobedience to God's commandment? In Hubmaier's two premises about free will, the first human being, Adam, should not disobey the command of God which forbids him from eating the fruit of tree of knowledge of good and evil. But Hubmaier did not make clear exactly why Adam fell, even though he had knowledge of good and evil and knew he could please God through obedience to God's command.[87]

Finally Hubmaier's stress on the freedom of the human will leads to the historically controversial issue of who has the initiative for human salvation. It is quite clear that Hubmaier is arguing strongly against Luther's theology, which he sees as diminishing the importance of human behavior. Hubmaier argued that doing good, or having the will to do good, matters. Such an emphasis on free will raises the possibility that Hubmaier is best regarded as a Pelagian according to the traditional understanding. However, despite his emphasis on free will, Hubmaier also emphasized the importance of God's grace as central to the understanding of salvation by justification through faith, just as the other mainline reformers did. Consequently, it is difficult to regard him as either a Pelagian or an Augustinian in the traditional view. Rather he seemed to hold onto the significance of human free will according to his own understanding of soteriology, within the doctrine of justification by faith, as constructed by the contemporary reformers' doctrine of salvation. Is his attempt to hold both of these together at the same time possible within the traditional view of soteriology?

5. Is Hubmaier a Pelagian or a Semi-Pelagian?

Hubmaier's strong emphasis on the freedom of the human will to choose salvation lies in the fact that he believed that Luther's theology (that we are saved only by faith) would lead to human license and immorality. However, his emphasis on free will as opposed to Luther's theology, could be regarded as a traditional Pelagian view, with the main purpose of vindicating the freedom and responsibility of the human will.[88] The controversy

---

87. This particular issue did not receive much attention from theologians during or after the Reformation era.

88. I will attempt to avoid making a judgment about who has the correct understanding of the human will, either Augustine or Pelagius. The main point of this example is to show the importance of the issue of the understanding of free will for the doctrine of salvation. This issue of the free will in the stream of the Pelagian controversy is still debated. Although Augustine's view seems to be dominant in the

had its origins in the fifth century in a debate between the two theologians, Augustine of Hippo and Pelagius. The controversy focused around several issues concerning how God justifies human being.[89]

One of the major concerns in this controversy is how properly to understand the freedom of the human will to choose salvation. Augustine stressed that although the first human being Adam had free will in his life, his will and actions were the inherent limitations imposed by human nature because free will is sufficient for evil but is too little for good.[90] Since Adam sinned, his nature was corrupted. As a result, his sinful nature was handed down to his descendants. In other words, Adam was created blameless and without any sin but the human nature which everyone inherited from Adam, is not healthy.[91] We have real freedom of action in a number of spheres of our lives because we are responsible for our own actions, but this does not mean that human beings have total freedom in every area of their existence. Augustine argued that even though human free will really exists in sinners, it is compromised by sin.[92] Humanity cannot properly use its free will because as a result of the Fall its propensity is toward evil. Augustine's concept of free will may be clarified further when it is related to the understanding of sin as a hostile power within us, and of grace, which is able to liberate free will from this tendency towards sin. Augustine stressed the significant insight that God's grace is both necessary and sufficient to overcome the negative effects of sin. His theory of free will, therefore, in spite of his emphasis on the existence of free will in human beings, comes to the conclusion that human free will is incapable of leading to humanity's justification unless it is first liberated by grace.[93] He believed that humanity itself cannot break and overcome its sinful character, except by the grace of God, which is a special gift that cannot be merited.[94] Consequently, humanity itself cannot do good without the

---

traditional environment, new evaluations of Pelagius have appeared. See, e.g., Phipps, "Pelagius or Augustine?," 124–33; Ferguson, *Pelagius*; Brown, "Pelagius and his Supporters," 93–114; Bonner, *Pelagianism*; Wright, "Pelagius the Twice-Born," 6–15.

89. The main issues in understanding the doctrine of salvation in the Pelagian controversy can be summarized in four main points: the understanding of the "freedom of the will," "sin," "grace," and the grounds of "justification." See McGrath, *Christian Theology*, 427.

90. Augustine, *de correptione et gratia*, 12.31.

91. Augustine, *de natura et gratia*, 3.3.

92. Augustine, *de diversibus quaestionibus ad Simplicianum*, 1.2.12.

93. Augustine, *de diversibus quaestionibus ad Simplicianum*, 1.2. 7.

94. Augustine, *de spiritu et littera*, 5.

grace of God. However, as has been pointed out, his theology of sin and grace is profoundly determined by his inter, spiritual experience.

On the other hand, it appears that Pelagius argued that Augustine's view of total dependence on divine grace is nonsense, because it appears to deny human responsibility and the need for human effort in becoming holy.[95] Pelagius rejected Augustine's view that we are all born in and with original sin as result of Adam's fall, but asserted that human nature is essentially free and uncompromised by any influence of sin.[96] According to Pelagius, humanity possesses total freedom of the will and is, therefore, entirely responsible for its own sins.[97] In other words, any imperfection in a human being would be a negative reflection upon the goodness of God, because if God influences human decision to act in any direct way, it is equivalent to compromising human integrity.[98] God created humanity and knows precisely what it is capable of doing. Therefore, all of God's commands are capable of being obeyed.[99] In this point of view, Pelagius asserted that "since perfection is possible for humanity, it is obligatory."[100]

Given the traditional views of the Pelagian controversy, we see that Augustine and Pelagius have different views on the role of free will for human salvation.[101] Augustine insisted that the human will is not free to do anything for its own merit unless it is helped by the grace of God. Human salvation, therefore, depends on the grace of God, which cannot be merited. Yet God, in his unlimited wisdom, chooses some to be saved and grants graces that will lead to salvation.[102] However, Pelagius argued that a person is elected for salvation by his or her own merit through obeying God's commandments according to his or her free will, a will perfectly

---

95. Augustine cites passages from Pelagius's writings, which are now lost, in order to argue against Pelagius' view. For this reason, these passages as they appear in Augustine's writings cannot be regarded as totally reliable. See McGrath, *Reader*, 222.

96. Pelagius, *pro libero arbitrio*, as reported by Augustine, *de peccato originale*, 13.14.

97. Pelagius, *pro libero arbitrio*, as reported by Augustine, *de gratia Christi*, 4.5.

98. Pelagius, *Letter to Demetrias*, 16.

99. McGrath, *Christian Theology*, 428.

100. Ibid.

101. A significant aspect of this difference is in their conception of the nature of sin. For Augustine, sin is a force outside of humans and, therefore, outside of human control, which can only be overcome by the power and grace of God and from which humans are freed through baptism. For Pelagius, on the other hand, sin is the willful act of human disobedience that is chosen.

102. Kyle, "Semi-Pelagianism," 1000.

free to choose good or evil. Consequently, Augustine's view of salvation insists on God's initiative which grants His grace to a human being according to His will alone. Alternatively, Pelagius emphasized the initiative of human nature for salvation through free will, which is capable of obeying all God's commandments. The main point of this controversy can be summarized as follows: how we understand free will can lead to different conclusions about soteriology. Thus, the understanding of the nature of humanity determines how the relationship between God and the believer is understood.

We have seen how Hubmaier linked the freedom of the will to the doctrine of salvation. Does this mean that Hubmaier was arguing that a human has the initiative for his or her salvation? Wray argued that Hubmaier acknowledged the sinful nature of human beings, but went on to say that the original freedom of the will has been restored through divine grace, even if imperfectly.[103] In other words, Hubmaier's concern was how best to develop the importance of both the grace of God and the freedom of the will for his soteriology, without losing their significance:

> Whether now such a power for willing what is right and good is in us, it is not in us as if it were from us, for it is originally from God and his image, in which he created us originally, 2 Cor. 3:18; Gen. 1:27 . . .[104]

When Hubmaier explained the nature of humanity after the Fall, he focused on the condition of the human substances and how they have changed. He asserted that the freedom of the will is the most significant aspect in following the will of God. But he also insisted that the ability of willing to do good according to God's will does not come from us but from God. Human nature itself can do nothing good without God. Even though man can choose good or evil by his own will, the origin of doing good belongs to God. In this context, it is quite clear that Hubmaier's understanding of free will is distinct from Pelagian thought, which has traditionally interpreted the role of human will, as achieving salvation by itself. This citation from Hubmaier's second treatise of *Free Will* illustrates his argument:

> As the eyes are ours and yet are not made by us, so is the work of willing and working the good also ours, but not from us. As the eye of the human being has the ability to see the light and

---

103. Wray, "Free Will with the Anabaptists," 367–69.
104. HS 389; YP 437–38.

> yet cannot see unless the light enters beforehand into the eye, so does the human being have the ability to see the light of faith through the Word of God, which he cannot see unless the light enters beforehand into his soul by heavenly illumination.[105]

Hubmaier believed that the theology of the mainstream reformers itself was not wrong, rather that it needed to be supplied and restored with another part of the truth, which had been lost or weakened by the mainstream reformers. This is the heart of the argument about free will. Hubmaier's attempt to balance the significance of God's work and human will is shown more clearly in his accentuation of God's grace and the merit of Jesus Christ for salvation, which seems to be part of the theology of the mainstream reformers. He wrote:

> Therefore this recognition and power of knowledge, willing, and working must happen and be attained by a new grace and drawing of the heavenly Father, who now looks at humanity anew by the merit of Jesus Christ our Lord, blesses and draws him with his life-giving Word which he speaks into the heart of a person.[106]

Thus, we need to reconsider carefully what Hubmaier's core intention is in arguing about the doctrine of free will. Even though he insisted on the freedom of the will, an argument which is used as an instrument to overcome the weakness of the mainstream reformers' soteriology, he still held on to the significance of a new grace, which comes from God. This may mean that Hubmaier recognized that he was in danger of being regarded as a Pelagian if he overly emphasized the freedom of the will for human salvation. As such, he must keep the significance of God's work in his theology.

Hubmaier's view of the nature of human will, therefore, is positioned between that of Augustine and Pelagius. Pelagius' concentration on the role of free will is focused on an increased human responsibility for salvation. Augustine's view on free will, however, shows an opposite understanding. Human free will, with its tendency toward evil, cannot contribute anything towards salvation. Hubmaier argued not only for the importance of the existence of human will, but also for the necessity of God's work for human salvation:

> Therefore there must be true health and freedom in humanity again after the restoration, for God works always in us the

---

105. HS 412; YP 466.
106. HS 394; YP 444.

> willing and the doing, according to the good resolution of the heart, Phil. 2:13. Although the flesh does not afterward want to do so, it must against its own will do what the soul, which is united with the spirit, wants.[107]

Here, Hubmaier's understanding of free will after restoration by Christ is apparently based on Augustine's doctrine of grace. Augustine believed that the freedom of the human will needs to be restored by the grace of God. It may then be improved by doing good works. Hubmaier understood that if the will of the soul is united with the spirit following restoration by the grace of God, it can overcome the will of the flesh, which tends toward evil. There are, however, different understandings of free will between Augustine and Hubmaier. Hubmaier regarded that the human will restored by God's grace is more positively able to follow the will of God, but Augustine supposed that there is still a limit to free will even if it is restored by the grace of God. Hubmaier's attempt to maintain the significance of *both* the grace of God *and* human free will for salvation may be the reason that he is regarded as a Semi-Pelagian.

What is Semi-Pelagianism? Semi-Pelagianism rejects the absolute views of both Pelagius and Augustine.[108] It rejects a number of points in the Augustinian doctrines of sin and grace; in particular, the assertion of the total bondage of the will, the priority and irresistibility of grace, and rigid predestination.[109] Adherents of Semi-Pelagianism agree with Augustine about the seriousness of sin, but they do not accept his doctrine of predestination, as it makes all human efforts superfluous. Although free will exists, it is weak and cannot be exercised for salvation without the aid of grace. Moreover, Semi-Pelagianism asserts that salvation is accomplished through the co-operation of human will and divine grace, and predestination is merely God's foreknowledge of what a person has freely decided.[110]

In sum, there are some similarities between Hubmaier's doctrine and Semi-Pelagianism. Both Hubmaier and the Semi-Pelagians emphasize the existence of free will since the Fall, although it has not worked perfectly.

---

107. HS 390: YP 439–40.

108. Weaver, *Divine Grace*, 40. The semi-Pelagian controversy began in a monastery at Hadrumetum (Sousse, Tunisia) in North Africa in 426, and later spread to southern Gaul. In 529, this position was condemned by the Council of Orange in southern Gaul.

109. Erickson, *Christian Theology*, 911.

110. Kyle, "Semi-Pelagianism," 1000.

They both attempt to reinforce the significance of free will for salvation, without losing the necessity of divine grace.

However, the Semi-Pelagians' doctrine of predestination faces the criticism that it does not deal with the fundamental question of who has the initiative for human salvation: God or human beings. Predestination, for Semi-Pelagians, does not mean that God chooses or elects a chosen group by His will for salvation, as Augustine argued. Rather it means that God knows a person's intention and what they are going to do, and He will select for salvation or damnation on that basis. The Semi-Pelagian doctrine of predestination seems to suggest that God does not take the initiative for human salvation, but rather that the human will is the first cause of election by God. Therefore, humans have a greater initiative for salvation than God.

In this traditional question as to whether God or humanity has the initiative for human salvation, what is Hubmaier's answer? The stress on God's initiative in salvation would mean that the plan of human salvation is accomplished by God's work and Providence without any human efforts. There is no need for human will or effort for salvation. Alternatively, if a person's work is required for salvation, even though it might be an extremely small amount, it means that God cannot save humans being without human effort. People hold the initiative for salvation. In spite of the Semi-Pelagian attempt to avoid these extremes, and to secure the middle ground, ultimately the work of salvation must belong to either God's or human initiative.

Therefore, either of these traditional approaches to soteriology will lead an extreme either/or conclusion. If Hubmaier's conclusions about free will mean that humanity has the initiative for human salvation, he should be regarded as a Semi-Pelagian. But if this is not his position, why does he emphasize the freedom of the will to explain human salvation? Why does he insist upon the doctrine of free will?

6. Hubmaier's Unique Intention in Discussing Free Will

Although Hubmaier emphasized the freedom of the will for human salvation, it is, as we have seen, difficult simply to regard him as a Pelagian or Semi-Pelagian. He clearly asserted that the human will has a place in attaining salvation, because his statements about the Providence of God and the freedom of the will for human salvation coexist in his treatise of

Hubmaier's Doctrine of the Freedom of the Will

Von der Freiheit des Willens. It is obvious that he intended to balance the two. Hubmaier simply described free will as the freedom of the soul to choose good or evil.[111] This simplification of the concept of free will may suggest that Hubmaier insisted on free will for human initiative in salvation. In this context, the concept of free will may mean that a human being can choose to do whatever he or she wants. However, the main reason Hubmaier emphasized the freedom of the will actually appears to lie in his attempt to overcome dangerous fatalism and compromising immorality among believers through the concept of justification by faith alone. Hubmaier did not assert free will to prove or defend the human initiative for salvation. Rather, he understood the role of free will differently in order to regard it as an instrument of connection—a concept to do with relationship.

a. Free Will Needs to Be Interpreted in the Context of Present Perspective

Hubmaier asserted that human free will has the ability to freely choose good or evil when it has been restored by God's grace. Even though human will can choose whatever it wants, it has to be responsible for its choice. In considering the responsibility of the will to choose, Hubmaier seems to focus on the present tense of the event by using language such as "here" and "now" when he presents examples defending the responsibility of the will. The most important reason for considering free will, for Hubmaier, is what we should do when we face particular issues. Hubmaier was not concerned with a past event and its result (with what a person did) to explain free will, nor with a future event. Rather he insisted on the freedom of the will as presented in the present time: "here" and "now."

Hubmaier put the restored will of the soul in the context of the present moment, and stresses the significance of its decision. This restored free will is in flux, choosing whatever it wants moment by moment. The soul can follow either the spirit or the flesh by its own will. Hubmaier described this restored will of the soul thus:

> The soul stands between the spirit and the flesh, as Adam stood between God, who tells him he should not eat of the tree of the knowledge of good and evil, and his Eve, who tells him he should eat of the tree, Gen. 2:3. The soul is now free and may follow the spirit or the flesh. However, if it follows Eve, that is,

---

111. HS 393; YP 443.

> the flesh, then it becomes an Eve and flesh. If it is obedient to the spirit, then it becomes a spirit.[112]

Here, Hubmaier argued that the restored soul should follow the will of the spirit, the will of God. To hear the voice of God and to obey His commandments are not an issue in the past or the future. For Hubmaier, obedience to God's commandments has to do with how much a human being commits himself or herself to Him *in the present context*. To illustrate the emphasis on the present context of free will, Hubmaier cited and interpreted the Bible here:

> Therefore David says, "I have hurried and neglected nothing to hold to your commandments," Ps. 119:4. And in another place: "If you today hear the voice of the Lord, do not stop your ears," Ps. 95:7f. "Today," he says, "Not *Cras, cras*, tomorrow, tomorrow, as the ravens cry."[113]

The word "today" can be seen to stress the significance of the present context, because Hubmaier focused on the necessity of understanding free will in context. The question is whether or not a person follows the will of God *now*. Hubmaier's emphasis on the present tense in understanding free will is clearly shown in his interpretation of the story of the rich young man to whom Jesus talks (Matt 19:17ff.):

> Thus, he says to the young man who asks what good things he should do in order to inherit eternal life: "He answers him: 'If you want to enter into life, then keep the commandments.'" Willing and keeping must have been in the power of the young man, for he said: "I have kept them from youth on," Matt. 19:17ff. Without doubt he spoke the truth. For Jesus looked at him and loved him, Mark 10:21. He does not, however, love liars. Nevertheless, Christ shows him his inborn imperfection, which is in every person, and tells him to sell everything that he has and give it to poor people. Therefore he was moved with sadness.[114]

There are questions that arise from this story. Why did the young man fail to follow Jesus in the final stage? Was he able to follow Jesus although he was rich? The answers to these questions will be different depending on the perspective of the person answering them. Thus, in the traditional perspective of Augustinian predestination, the young man was predestined to

---

112. HS 391; YP 440.
113. Ibid.
114. HS 392; YP 441.

Hubmaier's Doctrine of the Freedom of the Will

be unable to follow Jesus. In spite of keeping all of God's commandments, he failed to follow Jesus because he was not elected to follow Him. Alternatively, according to the tenets of Pelagianism the reason that the young man did not follow Jesus might be because of his own decision to keep his possessions rather than follow. The responsibility of what happened to him lay entirely with the young man himself. Semi-Pelagians, however, might assert that God foreknew that this young man would not give up his possessions for Jesus, and therefore chose him not to be a follower of Jesus.

So then, how does Hubmaier answer these questions? What interpretation does he follow? He said, directly following from the previous quotation:

> However, the same is unharmful to him, for it is fulfilled through Christ, who is the Alpha and Omega, the beginning and the end of the fulfillment of divine commandments. In him is our perfection.[115]

Hubmaier seems to avoid taking an approach, which would have focused on the reason for the young man's decision being made either according to his own will or the Providence of God. Rather Hubmaier is more interested in exploring what would happen if the young man were fulfilled through Christ. For Hubmaier, the young man's status as a rich man is not the most significant thing he must give up to follow Jesus Christ. Instead, he pointed to the state of the young man at that moment when he refused Jesus's proposal. Hubmaier supposed that if the young man were filled with Christ, in whom is our perfection, he would not refuse to follow Jesus. If Hubmaier wanted to use this story to explain free will according to a Pelagian perspective (that a human has an initiative to choose for salvation), he would have concluded that the young man chose not to be a follower of Jesus because of his decision to hold on to his possessions.

Hubmaier understood this issue as facing the young man in the present moment, not in the past. For Hubmaier, this event, which happened two thousand years ago, is also the present issue that faces us now. Thus, he explained this event in the subjunctive present tense rather than the subjunctive past tense, moving and transferring the story into the present moment although it is in the past. This way of interpreting the Scripture is explored through McClendon's notion of the "baptist vision." The "baptist vision," according to McClendon, has two mottoes: first, "This is that"; and, second, "Then is now."[116] He used this as a way of reading the Scrip-

---

115. Ibid.
116. McClendon, *Ethics*, 31–33.

ture that does not simply accept it as historical records of the past, but encounters it as a disclosure of the meaning and significance of the present. In this sense, the story of the New Testament period which happen two thousands years ago becomes the story of our own century. However, this is not to deny either the historicity of the New Testament stories or their significance, while asserting the historic significance of "this present time" in the life of Christians and, by implication, of every other present time in their life.[117] Likewise, the meaning of free will in the theology of Hubmaier has significance in the context of a present perspective. For Hubmaier, the concept of free will helps us to focus on our lives in the present time.

It is here that we can identify the crucial difference between theologians such as Augustine and Pelagius on the one hand, and Hubmaier on the other. Augustine and Pelagius, and those who follow them (on both sides of the debate) explored the question of salvation from the point of view of cause and effect. They were concerned with identifying the initiator of salvation, and the process by which it is appropriated. Salvation is an external state into which an individual must enter. This could be called a transactional and objective understanding. Hubmaier, on the other hand, refused to engage with the question that separated Augustine and Pelagius. He understood salvation as being a state of dynamic relationship between the individual and God. He was convinced that salvation is a present experience rather than a future destination. Such an understanding can be identified as relational and subjective. It has a dynamic character which is expressed in the very moment of life. To understand this, we need to look further at Hubmaier's relational perspective on free will.

b. Free Will as an Instrument for "Personal Relationship with God"

Hubmaier's understanding of free will in the perspective of the present can also be associated with the meaning of free will as an instrument for the personal relationship between God and humans. What is the meaning of "personal relationship with God" in the present perspective for the freedom of the will? Hubmaier explained it by two interlinked concepts of "relational" and "personal." First, he asserted the significance of free will as a connection which makes possible a relationship between God and man. His stress on the relational concept within the freedom of the will is shown as follows:

117. Ibid., 31.

> To summarize: The spirit is whole also after the restoration. The flesh can do nothing at all. The soul, however, can sin or not sin. But the soul which sins will die, Ezek. 18:20. Accordingly, it can will and rightfully say, *propter me orta est haec tempestas*, that is, "it has to do with me." The flesh has received its judgment. The spirit keeps its wholeness. If I now will, then I will be saved by the grace of God; if I do not will, then I will be damned, and that on the basis of my own obstinacy and willfulness. Thus speaks the Spirit of God through Hosea: "The condemnation is yours, Israel; only in me is your salvation," Hos. 13:9.[118]

Hubmaier believed that the general concept of an event is meaningless unless I allow it to affect who I am. For instance, there is sin, but if it is not related to me, then it will not harm anything in me. In spite of Jesus' death for us, if I do not believe Him now, I will not be saved, because the event of Jesus' death is not related to me. This relational concept of free will includes the significant meaning of a "subject"; that is, someone who is active to do something.[119] Hubmaier did not so much concentrate on the past or future events of the sinful flesh or the pure spirit, but considered rather the individual present relationship of the subjective will. Therefore, his concept of free will is not related to the meaning of human initiative in salvation. Rather it is focused on the issue of the formation of a relationship through it.

A meeting between two individual subjects can exist only when they esteem each other. If one subject forces the other subject into the relationship, it means that there is no personal relationship. The concept of unforced relationship is, therefore, important for a personal relationship to be vital. Hubmaier showed this significant point of unforced relation in his interpretation of the Bible with regards to free will in this citation:

> But whoever does not want to come, like Jerusalem and those who have bought oxen and houses and have taken wives—these he leaves out as unworthy of this Supper. He wants to have uncoerced, willing, and joyous guests and donors; these he loves. For God does not force anyone except through the sending and calling of his Word, as also the two disciples at Emmaus did not force Christ to remain with them otherwise than by request and good words, Luke 24:29. In the same way Lot was not compelled by the two angels in Sodom, Gen. 19:2f. For divine Word is so powerful, authoritative, and strong in the believers that the

---

118. HS 392; YP 442.
119. McGrath, *Justification by Faith*, 99.

> person (though not the godless one) can will and do everything that said Word commands him to want and to do.[120]

Here, Hubmaier did not say that there is the possibility that humans can be saved by free will, nor that God cannot save humans by His Providence. His real intention in this passage was to insist that God wants to treat humanity as a precious and personal subject. So Hubmaier said that:

> ... we are already helped, John 1:35ff. That is called his facing and drawing will with which he wants and draws all people so that they be saved. Nevertheless, the choice lies with them for God wants them, unpressed, unforced, and without coercion.[121]

7. Conclusion

We have seen that Hubmaier's understanding of faith, which is the key to understanding the doctrine of salvation, is different from other reformers of his time. Generally, other reformers insisted on the meaning of faith as a passive gift, but Hubmaier placed more stress on the active side of faith. In order to emphasize the active side of faith he used and stressed the concept of the freedom of the will.

During the Reformation, Erasmus was one of the theologians who emphasized free will. Hubmaier insisted on and developed Erasmus's concept of the freedom of the human will, but in a different dimension. In particular, Hubmaier's theological ability appeared in the Treatises of *Von der Freiheit des Willens* (April 1, 1527), where he delineated his unique theories and interpretations of the Bible, such as trichotomism and the story of the tree of the knowledge of good and evil, and so on. Here, he defended the necessity of free will through the explanation that the will of the soul is equal to the human will. However, there were some weak points in trichotomism as we have seen.

There is a tendency for the stress on free will in soteriology to be regarded as Pelagian or Semi-Pelagian. In other words, the emphasis on the freedom of the will is interpreted as the human initiative for salvation. Is Hubmaier's doctrine of free will in some regards in alignment with the Pelagians? Although Hubmaier emphasized the significance of free will for salvation, he never denied the motto of contemporary reformers that we are "saved only by faith." His attempt to balance the significance of

120. HS 394; YP 444.
121. HS 418; YP 475.

the Providence of God and human will was unusual, given the traditional concepts of the Pelagian controversy. His understanding of faith and of the concept of free will needs to be interpreted in a different dimension.

Hubmaier's intention in his doctrine of free will is not easily understood through a transactional and objective perspective, interested primarily in cause and effect. Using such a perspective to examine Hubmaier's theology will not facilitate a full understanding of what he meant. For Hubmaier, the emphasis on the Providence of God may lead to the compromise of human license and even antinomianism, but the weakening of the grace of God may contain the danger of suggesting that humanity can achieve salvation by itself. Even though he attempted to emphasize both the human will and the grace of God, an approach which chooses one of them as an initiator, is insufficient to understand his intention in this discussion. However, if we attempt to see Hubmaier's intention in this discussion from a dynamic and relational perspective, free will may be understood in a different way. In this view, to have human will means having the capability to commit ourselves to and obey God in the present moment rather than focus on whether humanity can achieve salvation by itself.

For Hubmaier, therefore, the stress on the freedom of the will is not about the initiator of human salvation, but the present obligation of human beings to respond to the will of God. Accordingly, in his thinking, the stress on the significance of the freedom of the will in the concept of faith should not be understood as a transactional question—whether or not a human has the initiative for salvation through the will. Rather, through his use of the concept of free will in his soteriology, he sustains the motto of the Reformation that we are saved by faith but he also attempts to clarify the meaning of salvation by faith. In his understanding of faith for salvation, Hubmaier insisted on the importance of the relational dimension—that those who believe in God should examine what relationship they themselves have with God in the present time. In other words, Hubmaier's concept of faith in his soteriology can be regarded as an attempt to transfer the meaning of salvation, which was interpreted with a transactional and objective approach by the contemporary reformers, to a relational and subjective perspective.

Although his understanding of faith was not the same as Pelagians or Semi-Pelagians, given his perspective, it is clear that his concept of free will connected with human active behavior. From this point of view, Hubmaier argued that one who has faith in God may show outwardly his or her confession of faith through the practice of baptism, in order to demonstrate his or her obedience to the command of Christ before the congregation of believers. In order to show the connection between faith and baptism, I shall examine more thoroughly the meaning of baptism for the understanding of Hubmaier's soteriology.

3

Hubmaier's Doctrine of Baptism (I)

Introduction

THE DOCTRINES OF FAITH and the nature of human will are very significant elements for understanding Hubmaier's theology. As we argued in the last chapter, in understanding Hubmaier's intention with regard to the relationship between faith and free will, a dynamic and subjective approach to a perspective on the relationship between God and human beings is more helpful than a transactional objective interpretation concerned with who has the initiative for salvation. This view of Hubmaier's theology can enable a new understanding of his soteriology that focuses on the relational perspective. However, it is important to note that the majority of his writing is not about free will but about baptism, despite the fact that Hubmaier's understanding of free will is the basic building block for developing his doctrine of salvation. Naturally, his writings on baptism are the most extensive—they comprise more than two-thirds of his published works. For that reason, we will divide our consideration of these into two main chapters. In the first we will examine the context and Hubmaier's consideration of the relationship between the baptisms of Jesus and John. In the next chapter we will focus on his understanding of baptism as threefold, and its practice and impact. For Hubmaier, faith is intimately linked with baptism, and his soteriology must be interpreted in light of his view of baptism. In addition, the fact that the majority of his writings are about baptism reflects just how important Hubmaier regarded it to be.

Balthasar Hubmaier's Doctrine of Salvation

What then is the meaning of baptism and its significance in the theology of Hubmaier? What role does his doctrine of baptism play in his perspective of salvation? In order to answer these questions, I shall survey the background controversy about baptism through the three representative approaches in his day—Catholic, Lutheran, and Zwinglian—in order to illuminate the reasons for Hubmaier's concern. An appreciation of the historical background will aid us in making a more reasonable interpretation of Hubmaier's theology. However, this exercise will only serve to offer a general understanding of his thought. Therefore, I shall concentrate on the interpretation of the primary texts themselves, in order to trace the meaning of baptism within his soteriology. In addition, this attempt to explore the primary texts on baptism will uncover not only the significance of baptism for Hubmaier, but also a proposal for another perspective on interpreting his writings about baptism which will help us to understand *why* there is such an emphasis on baptism in his soteriology.

1. Background of Controversy on Baptism

Why did Hubmaier put so much emphasis on the doctrine of baptism in his writings? Armour suggested that the insistence on baptism may have begun with Hubmaier's new understanding of salvation through faith, which was influenced by Luther's doctrine of *sola fide*.[1] Mabry pointed out that Hubmaier's doctrine of baptism was derived from Luther's assertion about how the sacrament could be efficacious.[2] However, Armour and Mabry both insisted that Hubmaier never depended absolutely upon Luther's idea of "justification by faith" but rather created his own theology using it. Although Luther and Hubmaier used the same language regarding the doctrine of salvation, *sola fide*, their different interpretations of faith caused further controversy concerning the issues of baptism, which in turn is strongly linked with the issue of faith.

---

1. Armour, *Anabaptist Baptism*, 24.
2. Mabry, *Church*, 133.

2. Appearance of Baptism in Hubmaier's Writings

a. Early Writings before His Believers' Baptism

i. Achtzehn Schlußreden

In his first published work, *Achtzehn Schlußreden* (Eighteen Theses Concerning the Christian life, April or May 1524), Hubmaier seemed to propose some basic guidelines for believers when serious faith matters arise. He focused on fundamental issues such as definition of faith, and contemporary issues such as abusing the mass, images, and other Catholic traditions. Here, Yoder and Pipkin argued that *Achtzehn Schlußreden* did not contain any specific meaning of the term "Anabaptist," because Hubmaier did not appear to address believers' baptism directly.[3] However, the eighth thesis shows his basic understanding of the doctrine of baptism even though he was not much concerned at this point with the issue of believers' baptism:

> 8. Since every Christian believes and is baptized for himself everyone should see and should judge by Scripture, whether he is being rightly fed and watered by his shepherd.[4]

In this thesis, as Yoder and Pipkin pointed out, Hubmaier never mentioned a negative opinion on infant baptism or believers' baptism, which he would later strongly defend. Rather, this thesis more likely suggests the significance of Scripture for Christian life. His basis for disputation is that a Christian's instruction should be on the grounds of the Bible, not on human teachings or human opinions and fancies.[5] The premise of this principle, however, is only required of those who believe for themselves and are baptized. In other words, baptized believers should use Scripture to judge whether their own Christian ways of life are right or wrong.

For Hubmaier, the definition of faith in his first three theses could also endorse the principle of using Scripture for the believers' life in the context of people who believe and are baptized first. Although he did not directly argue for the necessity of believers' baptism, the idea of believers' baptism was implicit in his writing from the time his concept of salvation by faith

---

3. YP 30.
4. HS 73; YP 33.
5. HS 72; YP 32.

developed. Here, we can presume that the connection between faith and the doctrine of baptism in his thought might be expanded further.

ii. A Letter to Oecolampad

Hubmaier's position on the issue of baptism is more clearly shown in his *Letter to Oecolampad* (January 16, 1525),[6] which was written before the institution of believers' baptism in Zurich. Hubmaier's thoughts concerning baptism are built on the words of Christ in Matt 28:19: "As you go forth, teach all nations, baptizing them in the name of the Father and of the Son and of the Holy Spirit." Using this verse, he argued that baptism was instituted by Christ so that nobody may weaken or abuse this baptism. For Hubmaier, the practice of baptizing the very young is inappropriate, because baptism is only of value to the one who has faith and hopes for the resurrection to life eternal.[7] Hubmaier gave little detailed argument on baptism in this letter, but he alluded to the fact that his methodology for defending believers' baptism is based upon the correct interpretation of the Bible when he wrote as he did here:

> Only one thing remains, and please do not fall in this Service: Write to me whether the promise of Matthew 19:14, "Let the little children to come unto me, etc.," applies only to young children, or whether the Word of Christ supports me which says "for the kingdom of God is for such as them" (not for "them"), and also what the Strasbourg brothers think about this. I have written 22 theses on baptism, with 64 notes added—you will be seeing all of this very soon.[8]

b. Later Writings after His Believers' Baptism

i. Eine Summe eines ganzen christlichen Lebens

After Wilhelm Reublin baptized him in Waldshut on the Saturday before Easter (April 15, 1525), Hubmaier began to accelerate his defense of

---

6. YP 67–72. The first draft translation of this letter was provided graciously by Prof. William Hunt of the University of Notre Dame. Earlier translations: Hosek, "Life of Hubmaier," 516; a fragment is in Vedder, *Balthasar Hübmaier*, 108. Source: Staehelin, *Leben Oekolampads*, 238, 341–44.

7. YP 70.

8. YP 71.

believers' baptism in public. His first published writing as an Anabaptist, *Eine Summe eines ganzen christlichen Lebens* (Summa of the Entire Christian Life), dated July 1, 1525, focuses on the issues of infant baptism and the Lord's Supper. In his introduction to this treatise, however, Hubmaier expressed his deep regret for leading people in false teachings when he followed Catholic traditions.[9] Bergsten pointed out that the reason for Hubmaier's intention in dedicating this work to three cities—Friedberg, Regensburg, and Ingolstadt—is that he spent most of his time as a Catholic priest there.[10] As he knew, when a blind person leads another, both will fall into a ditch (Matt 15:14), so he might have felt guilty unless he led them in the right way as instructed by the Bible.[11] Yoder and Pipkin, moreover, suggested that this treatise could be Hubmaier's response to several people in Regensburg who wished to have better instruction on the issues of baptism and the Lord's Supper.[12] Even though Hubmaier publicly confessed his false teaching and criticized Catholicism in the preface, he did not seem to carry this matter into his argument. In the treatise, his account of the issue of infant baptism and the Lord's Supper is constructed on the grounds of understanding Christian faith, which is seen as a more active response to the commandment of God.[13] His further explanation on the significance of faith for baptism is more clearly shown in his next thesis, *Von der christlichen Taufe der Gläubigen* (On the Christian Baptism of Believers, 1525).

ii. Von der christlichen Taufe der Gläubigen

Although most of his writings are related to the issue of baptism, there are three separate treatises on baptism: *Von der christlichen Taufe der Gläubigen* (On the Christian Baptism of Believers, 1525), *Ein Gespräch auf Zwinglis Taufbüchlein* (Dialogue with Zwingli's Baptism Book, 1525–1526) and *Der uralten und gar neuen Lehrer Urteil (Ausgabe I und II)* (Old and New Teachers on Believers Baptism, 1525–1526). His first major writing on

---

9. HS 110; YP 83. Hubmaier minutely enumerates Catholic traditions as follows: infant baptism, vigils, anniversary masses, purgatory, masses, idols, bells, ringing, organs, piping, indulgences, pilgrimages, brotherhoods, sacrifices, singing, and mumbling.

10. Bergsten, *Balthasar Hubmaier*, 326.

11. HS 110; YP 83.

12. YP 82.

13. HS 113; YP 87–88.

baptism, *Von der christlichen Taufe der Gläubigen*, was written in specific response to Zwingli's work on baptism, *Von der Taufer, von der Wiedertaufe, und von der Kindertaufe*. Windhorst suggested that Hubmaier's motivation was to answer Zwingli's three accusations about Anabaptists: first, that Anabaptists would create factions and sects; second, that Anabaptists reject the government; and third, that Anabaptists boast they are able to sin no more after baptism.[14] In his preface, Hubmaier rebutted these accusations for three reasons: first, it is unjust to condemn them for creating sects or factions when they act in this matter according to the Word of God;[15] second, that Anabaptists must want to obey a government when it is not contrary to God; third, that Anabaptists never boast that they have not sinned and will not sin both either before or after baptism.[16] Chatfield, however, pointed out that Hubmaier had further motivation to argue against the defense of infant baptism as advocated by Zwingli,[17] beyond what Windhorst suggested.[18] In addition, Hubmaier may have been motivated to challenge Zwingli's suggestion that Anabaptists argue that infant baptism is no baptism at all.[19]

Whatever the motivation for this treatise, Hubmaier's main intention was to stress that believers' baptism is clear according to the Word of God, although he acknowledged the necessary help of the Hebrew and Greek texts of the Bible for interpretation. He believed that the necessity of using the language of Greek or Hebrew should only be applied to those texts that remain unclear, but not to the baptismal texts which are clear, bright, and plain to understand. In this treatise, Hubmaier showed his ability to construct and defend his doctrine of baptism through his careful analysis of the New Testament text, which demonstrates the apostolic basis for believers' baptism.[20] He seemed to have innovatively re-arranged Zwingli's themes and composed a genuinely independent and positive statement on the subject of baptism.

---

14. Windhorst, *Täuferisches Taufverstädnis*, 41. Cf. HS 119–20; YP 97–98.
15. HS 119; YP 97.
16. HS 120; YP 98.
17. Harder, *Sources of Swiss Anabaptism*, 368.
18. Chatfield, "Clarity of Scripture," 100.
19. HS 153; YP 137.
20. YP 95.

iii. Ein Gespräch auf Zwinglis Taufbüchlein

Hubmaier's second major book about baptism, *Ein Gespräch auf Zwinglis Taufbüchlein* shows another argument against infant baptism, which appears similar in style, format, and content to *Von der Kindertaufe*, 1525–1526. Here, Hubmaier does not seem to show as much of his own genuine ideas of baptism as in *Von der christlichen Taufe der Gläubigen*. Rather, he followed the structure of Zwingli's arguments and even the texts that Zwingli used in support of his view of infant baptism. Chatfield strongly argued that this book shows a lack of creativity and independence in Hubmaier's thought about baptism, given his apparent failure to deal with Zwingli's significant arguments on the issue of baptism.[21] Hubmaier's arguments might have remained underdeveloped in this treatise because of his circumstances at that time. According to Bergsten, Hubmaier's situation prevented him from participating in the third Zurich Disputation and caused him to respond to Zwingli's theory of baptism without having read Zwingli's answer to Hubmaier's *Von der christlichen Taufe der Gläubigen*.[22] In other words, Hubmaier argued repeatedly against infant baptism as posited in Zwingli's previous book, *Von der Taufer, von der Wiedertaufe, und von der Kindertaufe*, as he had no access to any updated version of Zwingli's theory on baptism. In this context, it would be unreasonable to expect any more creative and developed ideas from Hubmaier.

However, it is possible to argue that his polemical tone and style seem to be more aggressive and sharper, although the argument does not flow as well in this treatise as in the previous one. Hubmaier directly mentioned Zwingli's name as his opponent in contrast to the earlier one where he avoids mentioning Zwingli's name directly.[23] In contrast to the former treatise in which he attempted to unfold his theory of baptism to let readers understand it without detailed refutations concerning some gossip and questions, here Hubmaier linked the disputation directly to Zwingli's accusations and questions, and argued straightforwardly against them. For example, Hubmaier noted Zwingli's accusation about Anabaptists in the *Von der christlichen Taufe der Gläubigen* in this treatise, and rebutted it

---

21. Chatfield, "Clarity of Scripture," 117. Chatfield points out that Hubmaier failed to argue using certain biblical texts and example such as the meaning of John's baptism being the same as the baptism of Christ, the use of Mark 1:2–4 which gives the order of the events of baptism and preaching, and so on. This matter will be discussed in detail later.

22. Bergsten and Estep, *Theologian and Martyr*, 167.

23. Ibid., 270.

explicitly.[24] His purpose in this dialogue is clearly shown in the preface as follows:

> Those [the legal system] are the swords and pikes by which Zwinglen has overcome the rebaptizers (as he wrongly names them), although he boasts in his little book that he has done so with Scripture. But he has not brought any into the light of day. He has himself confessed and attested even in public print that he is wrong, that those who baptize children have no clear word in Scripture by which they are commanded to baptize them—this on section E, page two, of the little book on the rebellious spirits published in 1525. In addition to that, he permits himself to boast shamelessly that he has triumphed and been victorious with Scriptures, just as if the Germans had no brains so that they could judge writings in black and white against each other.[25]

As he regarded the correct application of Scripture as the most significant principle in defending believers' baptism in *Von der christlichen Taufe der Gläubigen*, this treatise also contains many references from Scripture arguing against infant baptism, including Zwingli's references, albeit with different interpretations.[26]

iv. Der uralten und gar neuen Lehrer Urteil (Ausgabe I und II)

In contrast to his two previous books on baptism, which focused on the interpretation of Scripture, in his third major book, *Der uralten und gar neuen Lehrer Urteil (Ausgabe I und II)* 1525–1526, Hubmaier made use of a testimony of the "old and new teachers" in defense of believers' baptism. In *Achtzehn Schlußreden*, he rejected the ancient church fathers and all teachings not directly derived from the Word of God, using only

---

24. Cf. HS 175; YP 179 and HS 187; YP 195.

25. HS 170; YP 173–74.

26. See Chatfield, "Clarity of Scripture," 127. Chatfield shows the statistics of Hubmaier's use of Scripture: "The raw statistics are as follows: Old Testament references with quotations, none; references with recognizable allusions, twenty eight; references alone, nineteen; allusions without references, eight; and quotations without references, three; a total of forty seven Scripture references supplied by Hubmaier and fifty eight identifiable Scripture references. For the New Testament the figures are forty eight, ninety, one hundred and five, twenty nine and six respectively, giving totals of two hundred and fifty three and two hundred and seventy seven respectively" (ibid., 126–27).

Scripture to defend his position on baptism.²⁷ Despite that central principle, this treatise is constructed with citations from the teachings of the ancient church fathers and contemporary theologians. While Hubmaier was debating the issue of baptism, he faced challenges against believers' baptism not only biblically but also in the statements of the Fathers.²⁸ In this context, Hubmaier felt that it would be essential and effective support for his argument for believers' baptism to show evidence from church fathers and even from contemporary reformers.²⁹ However, this does not mean that Hubmaier gave more authority to the church fathers' statements in defense of his argument than Scripture itself. Rather he only wanted to show that in the matter of baptism, the church fathers, together with himself and the other reformers, claimed to be no more than expositors of Scripture.³⁰ In *Von der Kindertaufe*, Hubmaier clearly showed that rooting his argument in a firm biblical foundation is superior to any other proof:

> Oecolampad: Now the Pelagians were also highly learned in the Scripture. Likewise, Cyprian and the Council of Carthage have not been able to reject infant baptism.
>
> Balthasar: I will trust Cyprian, councils, and other teachings just as far as they use the Holy Scripture, and not more. They themselves also desire nothing more than that from me. With this I let it lie.³¹

Even though Hubmaier seems to depend entirely on references from church fathers and other contemporary reformers in his treatise, *Der uralten und gar neuen Lehrer Urteil*, it is better understood as a counter-argument to those who oppose believers' baptism by relying on the church

---

27. HS 73; YP 33.

28. In *Ein Gespräch auf Zwinglis Taufbüchlein*, Hubmaier shows increasing number of references to the church fathers, as is also the case in *Von der Kindertaufer*. See HS 176, 177, 184, 206, 207, 261, 266.

29. HS 261; YP 280–81.

30. HS 261; YP 281.

31. HS 261; YP 280. "Oecolampad: I will show you a place in Tertullian where baptism is not a covenant. Balthasar: You speak to me much of Tertullian, Origen, Cyprian, Augustine, councils, histories, and old customs. I must somehow think that you lack the Scriptures, which do not want to come out of the quiver. Dear Ecolampad, set your Scriptures together on infant baptism as I have done Scriptures on the baptism of believers in my baptism book printed at Straßburg. Then we will both consider them against each other and will soon agree. Do it; do not forget" (HS 266; YP 290–91).

fathers and tradition. Rather, it is a temporary method which shows his capacity to argue against all the ways that infant baptism is defended.

v. Other Writings on Baptism

Hubmaier's concentration on baptism after his own baptism as a believer is evident not only in his three major treatises on baptism but also his other writings. Using a writing style similar to that of *Ein Gespräch auf Zwinglis Taufbüchlein*, Hubmaier wrote another dialogue treatise, *Von der Kindertaufe*, with Oecolampad, who was the Reformed pastor of Basel and also his friend. In this treatise, Hubmaier argued against the unjust character of infant baptism in a form of dialogue with Oecolampad, and vindicated the necessity of believers' baptism. Hubmaier's writing, *Eine kurze Entschuldigung* (A Brief Apologia), is a significant text for understanding his concept of threefold baptism. In his apologia, Hubmaier began to expand the concept of baptism with the life of suffering (or martyrdom), what he called blood baptism, which had not been shown in his previous treatises on baptism.[32] His experience of being in prison for his faith might be a reason to explore the meaning of baptism in its relationship with a Christian life that should follow Christ until death. He seems to regard this idea of the threefold baptism as a fundamental doctrine for the Christian life, as seen in his catechism, *Eine christliche Lehrtafel*.[33] His consideration of the importance of baptism as the essential element for Christian life and his ministerial experience also led him to publish a form of service for water baptism, *Eine Form zu taufen* (A Form for Water Baptism). With all these examples of Hubmaier's writings on baptism, we can see that Hubmaier's concerns with baptism are not only shown in his doctrinal disputes but also in his consideration for church members in practical ways. In other words, Hubmaier regarded the doctrine of baptism as one of the main issues for church reform. So, how did Hubmaier defend and expand his doctrine of believers' baptism?

---

32. HS 275; YP 301. The concept of threefold baptism will be discussed later.
33. HS 313–14; YP 349–50.

3. Hubmaier's Methodology in Defending the Doctrine of Believers' Baptism

Hubmaier's understanding of baptism seems to be different not only from Catholic and contemporary mainline reformers such as Luther and Zwingli, but also from radical reformers such as Schwenckfeld, who was not interested in the practice of rebaptism, though he rejected infant baptism.[34] For Hubmaier, the doctrine of baptism is not merely an answer to the question of whether infants can be baptized but how significant baptism is for a Christian life. That is, the theology of baptism is less to do with the rejection of infant baptism, and more about its essential nature in and effect on Christian life. Although the definition of baptism can be seen in his works such as *Christian Catechism*, in reality Hubmaier's attempt to argue for believers' baptism through his theses shapes and is shaped by his convictions about the nature of Christian life.

What did baptism mean for Hubmaier? How did Hubmaier develop the meaning of baptism? To answer these questions, I shall look at how Hubmaier interpreted the Bible in defending his doctrine of baptism. Furthermore, an examination of what he argued is necessary before baptism will be helpful in understanding what Hubmaier meant by the doctrine of baptism.

a. Biblical Interpretation for the Disputation on Baptism

As Hubmaier prepared the *Achtzehn Schlußreden* for a debate concerning the general Christian life, he proposed another public challenge for a theological disputation on infant baptism, *Öffentliche Erbietung an alle christgläubigen Menschen* (A Public Challenge to All Believers, February 2, 1525), following the institution of believers' baptism in Zurich on January 21, 1525. Although he had not yet been baptized by Reublin at that time, Hubmaier showed his full conviction that infant baptism is practiced without any basis in the Scripture. Although it is not clear whether this document was printed separately at that time,[35] it was printed with *Eine Summe eines ganzen christlichen Lebens* as an appendix to his *Von der*

---

34. Snyder, *History and Theology*, 36.

35. YP 78. See Hilerbrand, *Bibliography of Anabaptism*. Hilerbrand follows "earlier sources in locating several copies in libraries." On the other hand, Westin and Bergsten argue "the listing is incorrect, doubting that it was ever printed separately." See HS 105.

christlichen Taufe der Gläubigen around the same time in July.³⁶ From the *Öffentliche Erbietung*, we can discover some principles of his methodology in defending believers' baptism, which are further developed in his later writings on baptism:

> Whoever wishes to do so, let him prove that infants should be baptized, and do it with German, plain, clear, and unambiguous Scriptures that deal only with baptism, without any addition. Balthazar Fridberger offers in his turn to prove that the baptism of infants is a work without any basis in the divine Word, and this he will do with German, plain, clear, and unambiguous Scriptures that deal only with baptism, without any addition. Now let a Bible, fifty or one hundred years old, as the right, proper, and true arbiter be placed between these two positions. Let it be opened and read aloud with imploring, humble spirit, and then let this dispute be decided and once for all brought to a conclusion. Thus I shall be well content for I want always to give God the glory and to allow his Word to be the sole judge; to him I herewith desire to submit and subject myself and all my teachings.³⁷

Just like all the contemporary Reformers who insisted on the principle of *sola scripture*, Hubmaier adhered to the conviction that only the Bible should be regarded as the authority in matters of faith.³⁸ The controversial matter of infant baptism ought to be examined from the point of view of whether it is based on the Bible. He argued that the issue of baptism is not difficult to clarify and interpret in the light of the Bible. It is clear and simple to understand. Hubmaier believed that it would be an invalid defense of the issue if it were accomplished without any Scriptural basis. Furthermore, although the doctrine of infant baptism was supported by tradition, custom and the teaching of Fathers with such glossaries and additions, it is meaningless and shows their tracks and deceptions in interpreting Scripture.³⁹ Hubmaier's fundamental principle for his reformation supported by biblical instruction is shown in his argument against Zwingli, *Ein Gespräch auf Zwinglis Taufbüchlein* and cited here:

> Remember what you said against Faber and published in the Article 15, that all truth stands clear in the Word of God. If now

---

36. YP 78. Cf. HS 118.
37. HS 106-7; YP 80. Cf. HS 157-58; YP 143.
38. Klaassen, "Speaking in Simplicity," 140.
39. Ibid., 143. Cf. HS 120.

infant baptism is truth, then point it out in the clear Word of God. Show it to us, for God's sake.[40]

In this passage, Hubmaier's response to Zwingli's arguments about infant baptism through biblical evidence reflects Zwingli's disputation against Faber in Zurich, January 29, 1523.[41] In other words, Hubmaier believed that if Zwingli still held the Bible as the norm for judging any reformation issue, he would acknowledge the injustice of infant baptism.

In spite of his emphasis on the significance of Scripture for defending believers' baptism, Hubmaier did not require every believer to have a deeper theological knowledge and skill. For example, he stressed that the interpretation of the Bible using the original languages of the biblical text is not essential to prove that baptism should be performed on the basis of the Scripture. Even his stress on the necessity of using vernacular language to read the Bible properly shows that the issue of baptism is capable of being judged not only by theologians or priests but also by anyone who reads the Bible itself carefully, because he assumed that believers can easily recognize the true meaning of baptism when they read the Bible properly without any prejudice.

His insistence on the necessity of reading the Bible in one's native language (in this case, German) leads to two significant points. First, it shows that his principle of biblical interpretation is applied to the doctrine of the priesthood of all believers, a core tenet of the Reformation. However, his understanding of the priesthood of all believers seems to differ from Luther's. Luther's emphasis on the priesthood of all believers referred to the spiritual and soteriological sense that the salvation of each believer is not dependent on mediation through a particular priest.[42] He did not use the term of the priesthood of all believers for an office of ministry in church, which is clearly shown in his commentary on Psalm 82.

> It is true that all Christians are priests, but not all are pastors. To be a pastor one must be not only a Christian and a priest but must have an office and a field of work committed to him. This call and command make pastors and preachers.[43]

---

40. HS 175; YP 180.
41. YP 180.
42. Lohse, *Luther's Theology*, 289–91.
43. WA 31:1.211.17–20.

From this, we may say that Hubmaier's emphasis on entrusting believers to make judgments through their own interpretation of the Bible exemplifies his particular definition of the priesthood of all believers.

Second, this understanding of the universal priesthood of the believers in his principle of biblical interpretation can be understood as the feature of his ecclesiology; that the church is a community of believers that is able to interpret the Bible itself through the horizontal relationships among community members. In other words, his declaration that every believer can interpret the Bible is not only the foundation of his methodology for defending theological issues but also for the foundation of his theology. Here, his methodology for defending believers' baptism seems to hold more strongly to the principles of the contemporary mottos of the Reformation than other mainline reformers.

Consequently, through this public challenge Hubmaier declared that he was ready to demonstrate with clear words from the Bible that infant baptism is an activity without any basis in the divine Word. His methodology for a disputation of baptism, where the authority of Scripture is defended against all other claims to authority, is shown repeatedly in his major writing on baptism, *Von der christlichen Taufe der Gläubigen* (July 11, 1525):

> Although I also do not reject tongues or languages for the exposition of dark passages, still for un-clear words one needs neither tongues nor lungs. Herewith I beseech and admonish you that you lay hold on the Scripture for that. It will give witness to the truth even if I had not written anything. If, however, you want to read my simplicity, then do it without any respecting of persons, of high names, of old practices, of traditions, also without any feelings which would tend to lead you away from the truth. After that, judge in your minds and consciences according to the simple Word of God. Let the Word of God alone be peacemaker and judge. Then you will not err. Be commended herewith unto God.[44]

In this citation, Hubmaier seems to have at least two principles for defending believers' baptism. First, the Scripture itself has the highest authority over anything else in interpreting Christian life. The best way to understand the meaning of Scripture on issues of Christian living is to read the Bible plainly without any prejudice and to interpret Scripture as it is. If it is argued that matters of faith depend more on other methods

44. HS 120–21; YP 99.

Hubmaier's Doctrine of Baptism (I)

and authority than the Scripture, such assertions can lead people astray. However, Hubmaier clearly recognized that the principle he held was also open to abuse and absurdity. In his *Von der Kindertaufe* he wrote: "What is not commanded in Scripture is prohibited in those matters that concern the honor of God and the salvation of our souls." In matters central to the Christian faith this rule holds; in peripheral matters, there is more freedom. For Hubmaier, however, the issue of baptism is no peripheral matter but a significant command of Christ, which is based on his view of the church.[45]

Second, Hubmaier argued that baptism is not an issue that is difficult or vague to discover and understand; its practice and meaning are clear from the Bible. The subject of baptism can be proved from the Bible as self-interpreting. Therefore, the Scripture itself is a sufficient means for discerning the meaning of baptism.[46]

However, these two elements in proving believers' baptism need to be interrelated and to be understood in conjunction with his strong belief that: "every plant that God the heavenly Father has not planted will be pulled up by the roots" (Matt 15:13). This citation appears in every one of Hubmaier's major writings concerning the argument of baptism.[47] Hubmaier's reply to the question of whether infant baptism is forbidden in the Bible came from his principle that every institution of Christian life should be placed within the scope of God's commandments. In other words, if infant baptism is not clearly proven or evident in the Bible, it should not be practiced or supported by any other sources, as he argued here:

> The first question: Whether infant baptism is forbidden in the Word of God. Answer: Yes. For baptizing believers is commanded. So by this it is already forbidden to baptize those who do not yet believe. A comparison: Christ commanded his apostles to preach the gospel when he said, "Preach the gospel." By this, human teaching, laws, dreams, and legends are already forbidden. For every institution which God the heavenly Father has not

---

45. Klaassen, "Speaking in Simplicity," 146.
46. Murray, *Anabaptist Tradition*, 37.
47. See *Von der christlichen Taufe der Gläubigen* (1525), *Ein Gespräch auf Zwinglis Taufbüchlein*, (1525–1526), *Der uralten und gar neuen Lehrer Urteil (Ausgabe I und II)* (1525–1526), and *Von der Kindertaufe*, (1525–1526). See HS 151–52; YP 136, HS 178; YP 184, HS 232; YP 255, HS 261; YP 280.

implanted makes blind and should be uprooted, Isa. 29; Matt. 15:13.[48]

Accordingly, Hubmaier's methodology for arguing for believers' baptism is based on three principles. First, he asserted that the authority of Scripture for Christian life is higher than anything else, and so the matter of baptism must be proven by biblical evidence. Second, the matter of baptism is not an ambiguous issue which can be interpreted in different ways, but it is plain and clear. Therefore, it is easy for anyone who reads the Bible carefully to see and recognize what baptism means in Scripture. For Hubmaier, therefore, baptism should be performed only if directed by the Word of God and as such will be the baptism of believers. Third, his understanding of baptism is applied on the basis that every institution for believers which has not been planted by God must be pulled out. What God has not commanded is unlawful; in this instance, infant baptism. These three principles of baptism show that although Hubmaier had different views on government and the role of civil magistracy from other Anabaptists of the period, at least his thoughts on baptism were congruent with Anabaptist tradition.[49]

b. Hubmaier's Precondition for Baptism

Hubmaier held that the authority of Scripture is higher than any other claims for defending baptism as instituted by the order of Christ. According to Hubmaier's understanding of baptism from Scripture, there are two preconditions which are required before baptism. As we saw briefly in the previous chapter, Hubmaier argued that the performance of believers' baptism cannot be undertaken without the personal faith which comes from hearing the Word of God. In other words, the necessity of hearing the Word of God before baptism and how that is interrelated with faith, is significant in our understanding of Hubmaier's doctrine of baptism.

48. HS 151–52; YP 136.

49. For example, see Wenger, "Schleitheim Confession," 248, article 1: "*Observe concerning baptism*: Baptism shall be given to all those who have learned repentance and amendment of life, and who believe truly that their sins are taken away by Christ, and to all those who walk in the resurrection of Jesus Christ, and wish to be buried with Him in death, so that they may be resurrected with Him and to all those who with this significance request it (baptism) of us and demand it for themselves. This excludes all infant baptism, the highest and chief abomination of the Pope. In this you have the foundation and testimony of the apostles. Matt 28, Mark 16, Acts 2, 8, 16, 19. This we wish to hold simply, yet firmly and with assurance."

i. Hearing the Word of God

Hubmaier's first priority is to examine and institute in the Christian life only that which is dependent upon what God commands through the Scripture, one of such commands being that of baptism. When Hubmaier defined the meaning of baptism, he presupposed that the hearing of the Word of God is required before baptizing those who want to be baptized. Hubmaier's suggestion of five meanings of baptism in *Von der christlichen Taufe der Gläubigen* seems to parallel Zwingli's use of the word *baptism* in four different ways. Zwingli's four distinctions of the meaning of the word "baptism" in the Bible are as follows:

> First, it is used for the immersion in water whereby we are pledged individually to the Christian life. Second, it is used for the inward enlightenment and calling when we know God and cleave to him—that is the baptism of the Spirit. Third, it is used for the external teaching of salvation and external immersion in water. Finally, it is used for external baptism and internal faith, that is, for the Christian salvation and dispensation as a whole.[50]

However, Hubmaier's purpose in delineating five different kinds of baptism is to emphasize that the Word of God or teaching must precede the water baptism. Here, Hubmaier's intention is to use the expression, *water baptism*, for believers' baptism in order to make clear that the concept of baptism which is practiced outwardly among believers stems from the baptism of the Spirit which is an inward occurrence. For Hubmaier, the meanings of water baptism and Spirit baptism are clearly different but each requires hearing the Word of God before it can occur:

> From these descriptions of the kinds of baptism anyone can see and recognize that the Word or teaching should precede the outward baptism, along with the determination to change one's life by the help of God.[51]

In this passage, Hubmaier pointed to three important requirements for outer baptism: the Word or teaching, the determination to change one's life, and the help of God. Even though Hubmaier mentioned the necessity both of human will and of the grace of God before baptism, his intention was primarily to highlight the significance of preaching or teaching before baptism. Hearing the Gospel before baptism is absolutely essential

---

50. Z 4:219–20; ZB 132. See YP 99.
51. HS 122; YP 101.

for those who want to be baptized. For Hubmaier, water baptism can be given only to those who have changed their lives. Without hearing the correct Gospel, or teaching based on the Word of God, the baptism of water cannot be a real process and even if it is practiced, it is meaningless. Unless the person seeking baptism has heard the Word of God, he or she cannot recognize sin within himself or herself and believe the forgiveness of that sin by Christ.

In particular, Hubmaier's assertion concerning the difference between the baptisms of John and of Christ shows why preaching or teaching of the Word of God is necessary and how faith is related to hearing this Word of God.[52] In his explanation of John and Christ's respective baptisms in *Von der christlichen Taufe der Gläubigen*, Hubmaier divided various biblical passages into five categories: (1) Word, (2) hearing, (3) change of life (or recognition of sin) or faith, (4) baptism, (5) works.[53] When Hubmaier clarified the meaning of baptism for John and for Christ, his concern began with whether the Word of God is preached. Hubmaier's conviction of the necessity of preaching the Word of God is plainly shown in his citation of Romans chapter 10:

> The second article is faith. Therefore one preaches that people should believe and trust in God, Joel 2. Paul describes this point to the Romans in chapter 10 (10:13ff.) as follows: "Everyone who calls upon the name of the Lord will be saved. But how can they call upon him, in whom they do not believe? And how can they believe in him of whom they have heard nothing? And how can they hear without a preacher? And how can they preach if they are not sent? Thus it is written: 'How beautiful are the feet of those who proclaim peace, who proclaim good things, etc.'" So faith comes through preaching; preaching, however, through the Word of God. Therefore one preaches so that people believe, trust God, expect all good things from God our heavenly Father and believe that he is our gracious, good, gentle, benevolent, and merciful Father in heaven, who carries, protects, and shields us as a human being [shields] his child, or like a hen her chicks under her wings.[54]

Like other Anabaptists concerned with believers' baptism, Hubmaier also believed that baptism does not mean anything unless the baptizand has

---

52. Some arguments on the differences between the baptism of John and of Christ will be discussed later.

53. HS 127–28; YP 106.

54. HS 135; YP 116.

an individual faith. Such individual faith requires that somebody has proclaimed the Word of God to them. Therefore, Hubmaier's presupposition is that baptism begins with hearing the Word of God through preaching.

ii. Faith and Baptism

In spite of Hubmaier's emphasis on the necessity of hearing the Word of God before baptism, his concern with it as a precondition of baptism is actually to do with personal faith in God rather than just simply hearing of the Word of God for its own sake. Even so, the reason that hearing the Word of God is important for baptism is that personal faith can only come from hearing the Word of God through preaching. The relationship between hearing the Word of God and faith as prerequisite for outward baptism is that they cannot be separated from each other. Hearing the Word of God engenders personal faith through which one can believe and trust in God. However, individual faith without the Word of God is impossible.[55] This basic principle clearly shows why Hubmaier had to deny infant baptism in *Ein Gespräch auf Zwinglis Taufbüchlein*:

> Zwingli: Why do you differentiate between persons? Are children people or not? If they are persons or people, then you must let them be baptized.
>
> Balthasar: This far-out argument does as much for the Turkish as for the Christian children. Turks are also people. But we want to give you a short piece of information. Christ commands that one should baptize believing people. Now we call those people believing who testify to their faith outwardly with their mouth and with their works. However, how it stands with the heart we want to leave with God. Now faith comes from hearing through the Word of God, which is shown by the preacher in Romans 10:17. One cannot preach to the young children. Therefore, we cannot scripturally ascribe any faith to them.[56]

Hubmaier's understanding that hearing of the Word of God and faith are preconditions for baptism concludes with the position that infant baptism must not be practiced according to Scripture. Zwingli's inquiry as to whether infants can be regarded as human beings seems to imply that if young children are indeed regarded as human beings, then they can

---

55. HS 135–36; YP 116.
56. HS 200; YP 214.

be baptized. In other words, even though there is no instruction that an infant needs to be baptized in the Bible, it is right to baptize young children. Hubmaier's response to the question addressed a different issue, as his concerns about infant baptism are not derived from whether or not infants are people, but instead with whether they have individual faith. Turks, who are people but do not have Christian faith, cannot be baptized, he said, likewise, infants who do not have faith cannot be baptized. His rejection of infant baptism came from his conviction that baptism is for those who believe and trust in God, and has nothing to do with an argument about personhood. For Hubmaier, it is impossible for young children to understand when a preacher proclaims the gospel and therefore, to have personal faith as a result of the preaching. In his concept of personal faith, which can only come from hearing the Word of God, the administration of baptism is inappropriate for young children who cannot confess their own faith.

Zwingli's premise about invisible faith—that whether someone has faith or not cannot be judged by us but only by God—was the foundation for the argument that an infant can be baptized. His understanding of faith relied heavily on the belief that the sovereignty of God means that human salvation by faith belongs to God. Although Hubmaier did not deny that human salvation belongs to God, his understanding of faith does not imply simply an invisible feeling or emotion. Rather he insisted that faith also involves one's will which means that one is able to show his or her faith outwardly through spoken words and deeds. For Hubmaier, a true confession of faith should be shown in public before other believers, demonstrating a self-awareness of inner change. From this point of view, his concept of faith means that one's public testimony must link with the exercise of water baptism, also in public. Consequently, Hubmaier's understanding of faith which focused on the active side of human nature is a significant base not only for the necessity of believers' baptism but also for rejecting infant baptism. Here, Hubmaier's accentuation on the active and outward confession of faith is coincident with his earlier publication before his believers' baptism, *Achtzehn Schlußreden* (1524).[57] This faith must be the significant element in entering into the community of believers beyond one's confidence of his or her emotional convictions about God.[58] In order to support his understanding of faith which required both the inner realization of God's mercy and the outward confession where one testifies before

57. HS 72; YP 32.
58. HS 314–15; YP 349.

other believers, Hubmaier develops his concept of threefold baptism.[59] In other words, as his understanding of faith is connected with his doctrine of salvation, his concept of baptism which is practiced on the basis of faith becomes an essential element for his soteriology.

4. Hubmaier's Definition of Baptism

Thus for Hubmaier, the elements of hearing of God's Word, faith, and baptism cannot be separated from each other. However, in order to understand fully the theology we must acknowledge that his concept of baptism is much wider than water baptism. There are various ways to explain the concept of Hubmaier's baptism, largely because he developed his theology in different ways according to the different situations he faced. In his masterpiece on baptism, *Von der christlichen Taufe der Gläubigen*, he divided baptism into five types.[60] In his later writing, *Eine christiliche Lehrtafel*, he asserted that there are three types of baptism.[61]

Why did Hubmaier enumerate the various types of baptism under his definition rather than simply have one kind of water baptism? There are several reasons why he divided and explained the baptism in various ways. First, he was attempting to explore the holistic definition of baptism through the explanation of various baptisms. Despite the multiple expressions of baptism identified in *Von der christlichen Taufe der Gläubigen*, and although different kinds of baptism are presented in the Scriptures, Hubmaier showed that there is an essential element for baptism. He believed that anyone can see and recognize the significance of the Word of God which should precede water baptism.[62]

Second, he denied the validity of infant baptism by emphasizing the meaning of water baptism. In *Von der christlichen Taufe der Gläubigen*, Hubmaier spent the greater part of his writing from the second to the fifth chapters comparing the baptisms of John and Jesus. Again, in *Ein Gespräch auf Zwinglis Taufbüchlein*, he argued against the insistence that the meaning of John's and Christ's baptisms is the same. He insisted that justification for infant baptism cannot be supported through conflating

---

59. This will be discussed later.
60. HS 121–23; YP 99–101.
61. HS 313–14; YP 349–50.
62. HS 122; YP 101.

the meaning of the two respective baptisms, although both baptisms of John and of Christ were water baptisms.[63]

The third reason for dividing baptism into various types is this: Hubmaier's concept of baptism goes further than a simple baptism by water. In his Catechism, Hubmaier divided baptism into three different kinds, the baptism of Holy Spirit, the baptism of Water, and the baptism of Blood, each of which holds a significant meaning. Even though the explanation of water baptism occupied a much larger section of the Catechism than the others, he did not subordinate the meaning of three kinds of baptism to the meaning of water baptism. For Hubmaier, baptism cannot be wholly explained by the concept of water baptism. The meaning of baptism should be understood as the integration of three kinds of baptism.

His arguments are constructed to oppose infant baptism. However, it is clear that, for Hubmaier, baptism has a crucial meaning other than just a ceremony. We need to examine what baptism meant for Hubmaier, why he needed to emphasize this meaning and how this meaning related to his convictions about soteriology. To answer these questions, I shall first examine Hubmaier's intention in comparing the meaning of the baptism of John with that of Christ. As mentioned earlier about the necessity to divide the chapters, I shall focus on Hubmaier's interpretation of baptism as threefold baptism, and point out his uniqueness in this regard in the next chapter. Moreover, I shall explore why Hubmaier rejected infant baptism. Finally, I shall suggest a new way to interpret Hubmaier's doctrine of baptism in the context of his soteriological perspective.

a. The Baptism of John and the Baptism of Christ

Hubmaier's most significant writing on baptism is *Von der christlichen Taufe der Gläubigen*. In this treatise, he focused on the difference between the baptism of John and the baptism of Christ. The reason for such a focus is that this treatise was written in response to the Zwingli's writing on baptism, *Von der Taufe, von der Wiedertaufe, und von der Kindertaufe*. The question of the baptism of John and whether it is the same baptism as that of Christ became a fundamental point of disagreement between Hubmaier and Zwingli.[64] Zwingli defended the appropriateness of infant baptism on the basis of the baptism of John found within the concept of Christ's baptism. He insisted that the basis of baptism is not from the

---

63. HS 182; YP 189–90.
64. HS 182; YP 189.

great commission in Matthew 28.⁶⁵ Hubmaier, however, emphasized the distinction between the baptism of John and the baptism of Christ. For him, only the baptism of Christ after resurrection is the proper baptism. Why was this dispute about the baptism of John and the baptism of Christ between Zwingli and Hubmaier important? And, what was the meaning of this dispute? To understand this dispute over baptism, we need to situate it amongst the wider debates of the medieval theologians. That will allow us to see why Hubmaier and Zwingli needed to debate the meaning of baptism. It will also illustrate how their different theologies developed.

i. The Medieval Catholic Tradition

The argument about the difference between the baptisms of John and of Christ did not start with Hubmaier and Zwingli. It can be found in the ideas of Peter Lombard in the twelfth century and Gabriel Biel in the fifteenth century. However, their arguments are different from the issues between Hubmaier and Zwingli, although both concern John and Christ's baptisms. For Peter Lombard and Biel, the difference between the baptisms of John and of Christ becomes important in the development of the Catholic tradition of sacramental theology. In contrast, Hubmaier and Zwingli explored the interpretation of the baptism of John and Christ as a means of interpreting baptism differently from the Catholic tradition. Even though both Hubmaier and Zwingli argued against medieval Catholicism by reinterpreting the concept of baptism, it is quite clear that the issue of the baptism of John and Christ in medieval theology gave context and language to their own developing doctrines of baptism.

Peter Lombard, who lived in the first half of the twelfth century, was a significant theologian in the development of early medieval theology. He defined sacrament thus:

> What is properly called "sacrament." We therefore properly call "sacrament" that which is a sign of the grace of God and the form of invisible grace, in such a way as to carry its image and to be its cause. Therefore, the sacraments were instituted not only for the sake of signifying, but of sanctifying as well.⁶⁶

---

65. ZB 141–75.
66. Peter Lombard. *Sent.* 4. d. 1 c.1 n. 2: 233. Cited in Rosemann, *Peter Lombard*, 145.

Balthasar Hubmaier's Doctrine of Salvation

Peter Lombard disagreed with contemporary theologians such as Hugh of St. Victor whom, he argued, worked with too broad a notion of sacrament, defining it as anything manifesting God to humanity and anything helpful in humanity's restoration. Peter Lombard, therefore, attempted to distinguish between sacraments, properly understood, and the signs represented by Old Testament rites such as sacrifices, offerings, and circumcision. The sacraments of the Old Testament were simply signs of divine grace, not possessing any efficacy to justify. Peter Lombard asserted that: "the sacraments are different since the former (the rites of the Old Law) only signified, but they (the sacraments) confer grace."[67] He wanted to distinguish himself from other contemporary theologians (such as Hugh of St. Victor, Roland of Bologna) who place circumcision and also the baptism of John as sacraments efficacious in the remission of sin.[68] Hugh of St. Victor argued that "a sacrament is a physical or material element set before the external senses, representing by likeness, signifying by its institution, and containing by sanctification, some invisible and spiritual grace."[69] Such a definition left no place, for example, for penance, since this had no physical element. Peter Lombard solved this problem by omitting any reference to a "physical or material element" (such as bread, wine and water). It was Peter Lombard who developed the list of seven sacraments which became definitive for the medieval catholic tradition.[70]

Why did Peter Lombard try to draw the distinction between the baptism of John and the baptism of Christ? Colish argued that Peter Lombard's interest was: "what makes the sacrament valid, but largely from the perspective of the capacity of the valid sacrament to serve as an efficacious channel of God's grace to the recipient and as a condition of his fruitful reception of it."[71] For his understanding of sacraments, which derive all their power from Christ, therefore, Peter Lombard asserted that the baptism of John should be understood as purely preparatory in nature for the true baptism. The baptism of John could similarly be called a sacrament only in the limited sense in which other pre-Christian rites can be considered as such.[72] According to Peter Lombard, the function of the baptism of John was to call those who were baptized to repentance, as a preparation for the

---

67. Peter Lombard. *Sent*. 3. d. 40 c. 3. n. 1, 2: 229. Cf. Colish, *Peter Lombard*, 529.
68. Colish, *Peter Lombard*, 533.
69. Hugh of St. Victor, "De Sacramentis," 9.2.
70. McGrath, *Christian Theology*, 498–99.
71. Colish, *Peter Lombard*, 547.
72. Rosemann, *Peter Lombard*, 147.

baptism of Christ that would remit sin. However, John's baptism was itself incapable of remitting sin.[73] This being the case, he argued that we must question whether those who had been baptized with the baptism of John needed to be baptized again with the baptism of Christ, given that, according to this theology, the baptism of John was incapable of remitting sin. To answer this problem, Peter Lombard attempted to distinguish between two groups of those baptized by John.[74] He identified the first group in Acts 19, the ones who lacked any knowledge of the Trinity but put their hope for salvation in the baptism of John, as candidates who needed to be rebaptized in the name of the Trinity by the apostles. Yet, he argued that what he called the second group in Acts 8 did not have to be rebaptized, because they had the baptism of John in relation to Christ and shared with the apostles a common faith in the Trinity.[75] However, the groups distinguished by Peter Lombard, particularly the group in Acts 8, did not easily support his assertion about the role of the baptism of John. Although Peter Lombard suggested that the second group of people in Acts 8 had been baptized by John, there was no evidence to support his supposition from the text itself. Rather, verse 16 says that they were baptized in the name of the Lord Jesus, not John the Baptist. Furthermore, if this group in Acts 8 was baptized by John, these people should be rebaptized in the name of the Trinity (or Christ), because Peter Lombard asserted that the role of John's baptism, which would not remit sin, was to account for the need for the rebaptism of forgiveness of sin.

This distinction between the baptism of John and the baptism of Christ was developed further in the fifteenth century by Gabriel Biel, in his book *Collectorium*. His interpretation of the meanings of John and Christ's baptisms seems firmly to support the Catholic sacramental understanding that: "unless the proper form (the name of the Trinity) is joined to the proper matter (water), no sin is remitted *ex opere operato*."[76] Biel's sacramental theology concluded that the meaning of John's baptism cannot be regarded as the same as the baptism of Christ, which remits sins. If those who had been baptized by John in Acts 19 have to be baptized again, it means, for Biel, that John did not properly administer baptism.[77] In other words, the recipients of baptism by John need to be baptized again with

---

73. Peter Lombard, *Sent.* 4. d. 2 c. 2–6.
74. Biel, *IV Sent.* d. 2 q. 2 a.1 nota. 2, 109. Cf. Steinmetz, "Baptism of John," 170–73.
75. Steinmetz, "Baptism of John," 172.
76. Biel, *IV Sent.* d. 2 q. 2 a. 1 nota. 1. Steinmetz, "Baptism of John," 171.
77. Ibid.

the proper baptism of Christ. In contrast with Peter Lombard's assumption, Biel did not suppose that there were two groups among the recipients of baptism by John. For Biel, unlike Peter Lombard, the issue of whether the recipients who were baptized by John had true faith in Christ or not was unimportant for salvation, because it was the lack of a proper form of baptism that meant that it could not be an efficacious sign of grace.[78] In this context, Peter Lombard's method that distinguished the recipients of John's baptism into two classes could not be used to justify the difference between the baptism of John and of Christ.

Although he did not regard the baptism of John as the same as Christ's baptism, Biel did not seem to ignore the significant role of the "baptism of John" in the New Testament, "which prepared people for the grace offered in the baptism of Christ."[79] The principal role of John's baptism was to make a bridge between circumcision as the Old Testament rite and the baptism of Christ as the New Testament rite.[80] However, his strict sense of a sacramental theology of baptism that was efficacious, by joining it to the proper form, emphasized another difference between "rebaptize" and "baptized with a repeated baptism."[81] The primary soteriological significance of baptism in medieval theology was the removal of the guilt (*culpa*) of original sin although the tinderbox of concupiscence (*fomes peccati*) remained and would inevitably flare up into actual sins.[82] Thus, the distinction could be interpreted in two ways. First, the phrase "rebaptize" should necessarily apply to those who are baptized with an improper form of baptism such as John's baptism, because baptism without a proper form cannot be efficacious to remit sins.[83] Second, there was no need to repeat baptism for the recipients after Christ's baptism which would wash away sins, as the practice of a proper baptism is only required once. Consequently, Biel's interpretation of John's baptism and of Christ's baptism seems to be based on the form of baptism currently concerned to justify to validity of a sacrament.

As shown above, in spite of some differences between Peter Lombard and Biel's understandings of the baptisms of John and of Christ, their main aim was to draw a distinction between the baptisms of John and of Christ

78. Steinmetz, "Baptism of John," 172.
79. Biel, *IV Sent.* d. 2 q. 2 a. 3 dub. 1. Steinmetz, "Baptism of John," 172–73.
80. Steinmetz, " Baptism of John," 173.
81. Biel, *IV Sent.* d. 2 q. 2 a. 1 nota. 3. Steinmetz, "Baptism of John," 172.
82. George, "Zwingli's Baptismal Theology," 74.
83. Steinmetz, "Baptism of John," 172.

in order to justify the validity of the Catholic tradition of *ex opere operato*, as an understanding of sacraments applying to the rite of baptism, which must be exercised according to the proper form. However, their interpretations of John and Christ's baptisms raise the possibility that a person can ask (or be asked) to be rebaptized if he or she has not been baptized in proper form. Furthermore, if the phrase "a proper form" can be defined in more than one context, what will happen to the previous baptizands? If one (whether an infant or an adult) has been baptized with a proper form, can he or she be baptized again? Thus, the issue of the relationship between the baptisms of John and of Christ arose for reformers, particularly for Zwingli and Hubmaier, albeit for different reasons.

ii. Zwingli

Zwingli's interpretation of the baptisms of John and of Christ seems to have been developed in the course of his struggles with not only Catholic tradition but also with the Anabaptists. As we have seen above, the medieval Catholic tradition concerning baptism had argued that the significance of the sacramental form of baptism is justified by the distinction between the baptisms of John and of Christ. In this context, Zwingli believed that if he proved that there was no difference in meaning between the baptisms of John and of Christ, then he could attack the medieval scholastic thought concerning the sacrament of baptism, and under which proper form it could confer grace *ex opere operato*. However, in spite of Zwingli's denial of Catholic tradition's sacramental thought, his defense of infant baptism, together with Luther and Calvin, stemmed from his conflict with the Anabaptists, who justified rebaptism through their assertion of the difference between the baptisms of John and of Christ.[84] Accordingly, Zwingli had to reformulate his view of baptism as well as to develop his case for infant baptism. The issue, the understanding of the relationship between the baptisms of John and of Christ, seems to have been important for Zwingli.

Zwingli's arguments concerning the baptisms of John and of Christ are shown in his writings *Commentarius de vera et falsa religion* (Commentary on False Religion), and *Von der Taufe, von der Wiedertaufe und von der Kindertaufe* (1525). His first attack on the medieval scholasticism in *Commentarius de vera et falsa religione* is based on the view that there is no difference, as far as nature, reason and purpose are concerned, between

---

84. Here the word "rebaptism" by Zwingli was not actually acknowledged by Anabaptists, who believed that infant baptism is not baptism at all.

Balthasar Hubmaier's Doctrine of Salvation

the baptisms of John and of Christ, although some slight differences are found in procedure or form.[85] From his premise regarding baptism that nothing is affected through the practice of water baptism, Zwingli regarded John's baptism of water as the same as Christ's baptism of water.[86] If John's baptism had not satisfied Christ when He was baptized, Christ would have been baptized again by another baptism which would be more proper than John's. Furthermore, in Luke 7:29, if the baptism of John was not same as Christ's, those who had already heard Christ and had been justified by Him but were baptized with John's baptism, would have been rebaptized by the baptism of Christ.[87] In other words, there is no special effect from the baptism of Christ or the baptism of John from a sacramental perspective.

Second, Zwingli attempted to distinguish the character of both baptisms as "teaching" and as "the external baptism of water."[88] Baptism as "teaching," according to Zwingli, means the proclamation that salvation was at hand in Christ who came after John, and of repentance. He appeared to use the concept of baptism as "teaching" to interpret Acts 19, the rebaptism of disciples who had been baptized by John. If baptism means "teaching," in this context for Zwingli, the rebaptism of those disciples who were baptized by John can be explained easily. When John's disciples said they were baptized by John, it could mean that they had received baptism in sense of being taught but not having received water. Accordingly, Paul gave them better instruction and confirmed it with water baptism. The event of baptism in Acts 19, therefore, was to be interpreted as teaching, according to Zwingli.[89] But his attempt to interpret the baptism cited in Acts 19 as having a double meaning (i.e., external water baptism and teaching) is problematic in that it ignores the practice of baptism itself. His arguments about baptism did not address any possible questions as to whether external baptism is needed when one has received teaching as a baptism. Moreover, Zwingli did not show the necessity of infant baptism though he denied the Anabaptists' refusal of infant baptism.[90]

Zwingli's argument was weak in its distinction between baptism in terms of "teaching" and "water baptism." He expanded his treatise on

85. ZL 3:189.
86. Ibid.
87. Ibid., 3:191.
88. Ibid., 3:192.
89. Ibid., 3:194–95.
90. Richards, "Introduction," 23.

baptism in *Von der Taufe, von der Wiedertaufe und von der Kindertaufe*. In spite of expounding his argument at greater length, there are no major changes or developments in Zwingli's view of baptism. Rather, his concern was to identify John's baptism with Christ's in order to demonstrate that there was no need for a second baptism as seen in Acts 19, a passage used by Anabaptists in support of rebaptism.[91] Zwingli moved from his initial interpretations of "water baptism" and baptism as "teaching," to four different interpretations: "water," "Spirit," "external teaching," "faith."[92]

Zwingli asserted that these four different interpretations of baptism can be seen in the New Testament albeit in no particular sequence. Rather, it could be any combination of them.[93] He insisted that any form of baptism could occur independently without any preconditions. For instance, water baptism was exercised without teaching and without the Spirit according to his interpretation of 1 Corinthians or John 4, or the baptism of teaching was often given externally to one who did not believe or accept water baptism according Acts 18.[94] Using these examples of baptism, Zwingli confidently declared that water baptism can be administered before the baptizand has faith, so consequently the administration of infant baptism did not raise any problem. His argument for no particular sequence of baptism seems to be based upon his belief that external elements such as water baptism or external teaching itself cannot save us, but faith can.[95] For Zwingli, external baptism cannot be a sacred thing that cleanses us from sin. Although this primary principle could be used for his argument against Anabaptists, it could also suggest that external elements, in this case water baptism for infants, itself is in fact unnecessary.

Zwingli defined baptism as "a covenant sign which indicates that all those who receive it are willing to amend their lives and to follow Christ."[96] He, however, emphasized that his concept of "sign" for baptism should not be confused with Catholic tradition that justifies the one who is baptized, or it confirms his faith.[97] For Zwingli, the "sign" is just a "sign," but not an efficacious sign of redemption or grace as in the Catholic perspective. Rather, the practice of baptism is simply a covenant sign for the baptizand,

91. Stephens, *Theology of Zwingli*, 198.
92. ZB 132.
93. ZB 133–38.
94. ZB 135.
95. ZB 134.
96. ZB 141.
97. ZB 138.

who pledges themselves to faith and discipleship. In this sense, Zwingli's concept of baptism as pledging faith and discipleship appears to be similar to the Anabaptists' concept of baptism. Although he used the term of "pledge to faith and discipleship" for baptism, he clearly attempted to distinguish his concept from the Anabaptist term of "pledge to faith and discipleship" which was understood to mean a life of absolute perfection.[98] However, this attempt began with a misunderstanding of what the Anabaptists meant by baptism.

Zwingli's other attempt to prove that John and Christ's baptism were the same was to argue that John's baptism had a proper message of Trinitarian character as did the baptism of Christ.[99] For Zwingli, if the baptism of John was administered in Trinitarian mode, there would be no difference between the baptisms of John and of Christ. In other words, the baptism of John could be regarded as the beginning of Christian baptism. Thus, he regarded and interpreted the event of Christ's baptism by John as confirming the Trinitarian character of John's baptism: the Father speaks, the Son is baptized and the Spirit descends like a dove.[100]

From Zwingli's attempt to show the continuity and unity between the baptisms of John and of Christ, we can see that Zwingli's intention to prove both baptisms were the same meant that he was able to attack Catholic tradition which emphasized that the proper form of baptism can convey grace or redeem from sin. Moreover, his theory that the two baptisms were the same could support his argument for the necessity of infant baptism against the Anabaptists' arguments that sharply distinguished between the two baptisms, resulting in an opposition towards infant baptism.

iii. Hubmaier's Understanding of Baptism of John and of Christ

Zwingli's defense and justification of infant baptism by reframing the question to argue that the baptism of John is the same as Christ's, stimulated Hubmaier to respond in, *Von der christlichen Taufe der Gläubigen*. In this treatise, unlike his previous writing, *Eine Summe eines ganzen christlichen Lebens*, which never mentions the issue of John and Christ's baptisms, Hubmaier seems to spend a large part of his writing discussing this issue and rebutting Zwingli's arguments. Even though he aimed to rebut all

---

98. ZB 139.
99. ZB 168–69.
100. ZB 168. Cf. Steinmetz, "Baptism of John," 176.

of Zwingli's arguments,[101] Hubmaier's main concern in this treatise was to demonstrate that Zwingli's identification of John's baptism with Christ's in order to justify infant baptism is an incorrect interpretation of the Bible. In other words, if he could prove that Zwingli had misinterpreted the baptisms of John and of Christ, it would mean that infant baptism could not be justified. However, if Hubmaier only emphasizes the difference between them, it would make it seem that he endorsed the view of medieval Catholicism, which supported infant baptism. He was not willing to do this either. So we must examine how he explained the issue of the baptisms of John and of Christ, and why it was so significant in his theology.

In *Von der christlichen Taufe der Gläubigen*, Hubmaier began with a description of five kinds of baptism in response to Zwingli's four types in *Von der Taufe, von der Wiedertaufe und von der Kindertaufe*. These five types of baptism can be identified as essentially two aspects of baptism, the external act of baptism with water and the internal baptism of Holy Spirit, which brings forth a human response and commitment.[102] After a short introduction to the various types of baptism, Hubmaier focused on the difference between the baptisms of John and of Christ. According to Hubmaier, the office of John the Baptist consists of three parts: "first, he preached; second, he baptized; third, he pointed at or to Christ."[103] In his first office, John preached for repentance of sin, which is based on the curse of the law, with sin, death, the devil, and hell.[104] The purpose of preaching is to lead the hearer to confess that he or she is a miserable sinner and to recognize that he or she cannot help himself or herself nor do anything good as all his or her righteousness is corrupt.[105] The second office is for those who have recognized and confessed their sins. John baptized them, and instructed them that they should do the works which are fitting for a life of repentance.[106] John's third office is to point to Christ who is the "true physician, forgiver of sins, and healer."[107] John the Baptist himself, who was a messenger of Christ, can only point to Christ who would give them a sure forgiveness of sins, and heal their wounds. In short, the

---

101. See the previous section in this chapter, and the introduction of *Von der christlichen Taufe Gläubigen*.

102. The issue will be discussed later. Cf. Pipkin, "Baptismal Theology," 38.

103. HS 123; YP 102.

104. HS 124, 127; YP 103, 106.

105. HS 127; YP 106.

106. HS 124–25; YP 103.

107. HS 126; YP 105.

baptism of John is restricted to baptizands who recognized their sins and could repent of them. For Hubmaier, the baptism of John is only a public testimony which the person receives and is given because he or she confesses and recognizes that he or she is a sinner. It proved that John never baptized infants who cannot recognize and confess in this way. To support his understanding of John's baptism, Hubmaier included in his argument all the passages which deal with the baptism of John. By enumerating the passages about the baptism of John, he reinforced the significance of the order and the nature of the baptizand's response in relation to the administration of baptism itself.[108] He ordered John's baptism thus: (1) Word, (2) hearing, (3) change of life or recognition of sin, (4) baptism, (5) works. Hubmaier therefore insisted that the necessity of preaching and confession before baptism prove that one must be old enough to hear and to respond for baptism to take place.

Hubmaier explained the meaning of Christ's baptism of the apostles in the same way. He argued that the office of the apostles with regards to baptism consists of three parts: first, preaching; second, faith; and third, outward baptism.[109] The preaching of the apostles was to proclaim the works of Christ in order to move the people to recognize their sins.[110] This recognition of sin through preaching can lead people to the faith which believes and trusts in God. Hubmaier's understanding of faith as response to preaching enforces his argument that only those who are mature enough to recognize and repent their sins can be baptized.[111] If a person who recognized and confessed his or her sin by preaching is taught by the Word of God about the forgiveness of his or her sin, and believes it, he or she surrenders himself or herself to God and commits himself or herself internally in his or her heart to live a new life according to the Rule of Christ.[112] As a public testimony of his or her internal faith, he or she accepts water baptism before other believers. In this context, faith must precede baptism with water. After the explanation of the office of the apostles in the baptism of Christ, Hubmaier enumerated the passages on the baptism of Christ as he did for John's baptism. Again, Hubmaier presented five steps for the baptism of Christ: (1) Word, (2) hearing, (3) faith, (4) baptism, (5)

---

108. HS 127–34; YP 106–14.
109. HS 134; YP 115.
110. HS 134–35; YP 115.
111. HS 135; YP 116.
112. HS 136; YP 117.

work. For Hubmaier, this sequence of baptism reinforces the argument that infants should not be baptized.[113]

In spite of the outwardly similar sequence between the two baptisms, Hubmaier asserted that there are significant differences between them. Hubmaier sharpened the split between the two baptisms by restricting the function of John's baptism to the repentance of sins, but not for the forgiveness of sin:

> For that reason water baptism is called a baptism in *remissionem peccatorum*, Acts 2:38, that is, in forgiveness of sins. It is not that only through it or in it sin is forgiven, but by the power of the internal "Yes" in the heart, which the person proclaims publicly in the reception of water baptism, that he believes and is already sure in his heart of the remission of sins through Jesus Christ. Likewise, the baptism of John is also called a baptism of repentance, that is, the one who wants to be baptized confesses and declares himself guilty of sin.[114]

In spite of Hubmaier's description of Christ's baptism as the forgiveness of sin, he strongly denied medieval tradition's arguments for the sacramental efficacy of baptism. He simply asked of the baptizand whether he or she has the will to confess publicly rather than just accept the outward baptismal rite. His placement of John in the Old Testament as a preacher of the curse of the Law shows that the office of John was limited to helping people recognize their sins and lead them to Christ. In this case, we might think that there would be no difference between two baptisms if John the Baptist could help people to recognize their sins and to know Christ. However, Hubmaier's intention was to stress the New Testament which focused on the work of Christ as the saving activity of God; Hubmaier understood John's office to echo that of the prophets' role in the Old Testament.[115] Even though Hubmaier regarded John the Baptist as superior to other prophets of the Old Testament, he insisted that the baptism of John cannot signify the forgiveness of sins in the same way as the baptism of Christ.[116] John led the recipients to recognize their sins, and preached that Christ forgives sin, but never proclaimed forgiveness of the recipients' sins by himself.[117]

---

113. HS 146; YP 129.
114. HS 137; YP 118.
115. HS 123–24; YP 102.
116. HS 124; YP 103.
117. HS 132; YP 113.

Balthasar Hubmaier's Doctrine of Salvation

Hubmaier clearly showed the contrast between the two baptisms and the significance of Christ's baptism for the believers in the New Testament.[118] His distinction between the two baptisms denies Zwingli's assertion that "baptizing" can be understood as "teaching."[119] Hubmaier rejected Zwingli's argument that John administered the same baptism as Christ, but he insisted that the role of John's baptism should be regarded as the forerunner of the baptism instituted by Christ.[120] In this context, Hubmaier's approach to two baptisms can be explained as his developing the medieval argument about the nature of two baptisms. In particular, Windhorst and Steinmetz attempted to show Hubmaier's argument with Zwingli in the context of medieval theology (in particular that of Peter Lombard and Biel), and they have convincingly demonstrated that there are some resemblances between Hubmaier's thought and that of the medieval tradition in considering the two forms of baptism.[121] However, to say that Hubmaier depended on the medieval traditional view of the baptisms of John and of Christ because he accepted that the two baptisms are different is to misunderstand Hubmaier's intention in using it in his argument. For medieval Catholic tradition, as we have seen from Peter Lombard and Biel, the main purpose was to emphasize the differences between the baptisms of John and of Christ in order to explore their view of baptism as a sacrament *ex opere operato*, which concentrates on the correct performance of the external form of the rite. In other words, the stress on the significance of the religious rites for sacraments by using the identity of two baptisms could lead to the conclusion that the correct performance of baptism conveys grace to the recipients, even to infants. Consequently, in the perspective of medieval tradition, the issue of the two baptisms was an important defense for the doctrine *ex opere operato*.

However, for Hubmaier the issue of the nature of two baptisms was used to attack both the view of medieval tradition and that of Zwingli. Hubmaier's interpretation of the baptisms of John and of Christ strongly

---

118. Hubmaier describes two baptisms in *Dialogue with Zwingli's Baptism Book*: "The meaning of the water baptism of John is that it cools, freezes, frightens, kills, and leads into hell. There one sees and recognizes nothing but sin. The water baptism of Christ in this sense means heating, quickening, comforting, making alive, leading again out of hell" (HS 197; YP 209).

119. HS 132; YP 112–13.

120. HS 196; YP 208–9.

121. Windhorst, *Täuferisches Taufverstädnis*, 65-68; Steinmetz, "Baptism of John," 170–73.

depends on his Biblicism rather than on a philosophical assumption.[122] Hubmaier provided evidence to demonstrate the difference between the two baptisms by citing Scriptural passages. His attempt to trace the meaning of the two baptisms using a biblical approach reaches the conclusion that the baptism of John cannot signify the same as the baptism of Christ, what he calls the forgiveness of sins. However, although his conclusion about the two baptisms seems similar to medieval Catholicism, it is difficult to say that his understanding is simply a legacy of that tradition. By his analogizing the sequences between the baptisms of John and of Christ, Hubmaier showed that there are prerequisites for baptism. Baptism, whether it is John's or Christ's, must be based on the preached Word to the recipient. As John in his baptism preached the Word for the repentance of sin, the baptism of Christ involves the Word preached for the forgiveness of sin to the recipients. Even though the context differs, both baptisms require the baptizand to hear the preached Word before his or her baptism. However, the preached Word itself is insufficient for allowing the administration of baptism. For Hubmaier, the actual event of baptism (whether of John or of Christ), depends on the response of the baptizand, namely when he or she heard the preached Word. Unless the recipients respond to the preaching, the baptism itself cannot be accomplished. Consequently, from the sequence of two baptisms, Hubmaier proved that the exercise of baptism can apply only to those who are mature enough to understand the knowledge of God by hearing preaching and by examining themselves. Accordingly, infants should not be baptized in any circumstances.

Hubmaier's general concept of baptism can be summarized in this way: that baptism is a public testimony or confession by the baptizand, and not a sacrament or a sign of covenant:

> From this it follows that the water baptism of John is nothing but a public testimony which the person receives and gives because he confesses and recognizes that he is a miserable sinner, who cannot help himself nor give himself counsel, who does nothing good but that all his righteousness is corrupt and reproachable . . . His awareness and conscience learned from the law, which is knowledge of sin, show this to him.[123] On the other hand, the baptism of Christ is a public and outward confession or oath of faith, that is, that the person inwardly believes the forgiveness of his sins through Christ, for which reason he lets himself be

---

122. Windhorst, *Täuferisches Taufverstädnis*, 66.
123. HS 127; YP 106.

enrolled and outwardly dedicated among Christians, and that he wants to live according to the Rule of Christ.[124]

The biggest difference between the two baptisms from the above description, as we have seen, can be simply summarized thus: the baptism of John as the repentance of sins cannot replace the baptism of Christ which signifies the forgiveness of sins. The meaning of the public testimony is to emphasize that baptism can only be administered by the will of the baptizand, not by any other. In other words, Hubmaier's intention in describing baptism as a public testimony which infants cannot perform appears to be his greatest criticism against paedobaptism.

However, Hubmaier alluded to significant differences between the two baptisms given the common expression of baptism as a public testimony. For Hubmaier, the expression "baptism as a public testimony" with regards to the baptism of John seemed to emphasize the repentance of the recipient. Despite the description of "baptism as a public testimony," Hubmaier never mentioned any relationship between the recipient and the witnesses effected through the baptism. The main purpose of John's baptism, for Hubmaier, is for the recipient to recognize and to confess his or her sin publicly. In other words, the baptism of John as a public testimony means that the recipient would be sealed as a sinner before other people, but there would be no shared responsibility, no relationship between the recipient and the watchers. By the confession of sins the recipient acknowledges himself or herself as a sinner, so that he or she might be isolated from others. Alternatively, the baptism of Christ as a public testimony implies not only the recipient's assurance of the forgiveness of his or her sins through Christ, but also the start of a new relationship between the recipient and the congregation who witness the confession of faith. Here the phrase "public testimony" is applied to the recipient in order to expand his or her relationship from the individual person to the wider community.[125] In the baptism of Christ the confession of the recipient is not only related to himself or herself but also to other believers. From this perspective, the baptism of John, for Hubmaier, cannot properly function as a baptism which creates an interactive relationship between the recipient and other people because the baptism of John remains an individual rather than a corporate event, albeit one that happens publicly. However, the baptism of Christ seems to be regarded as the proper baptism for the baptizand because it means not only the forgiveness of sins through Christ

---

124. HS 196; YP 209.
125. HS 350; YP 389.

but also the starting point of a new relationship with other Christians. It requires the recipient to commit himself or herself to live according to the Rule of Christ with the Christian community.

Hubmaier's distinction between the baptisms of John and of Christ depends on his general concept of baptism which is strongly related to his ecclesiology. This relational perspective for baptism is the foundation stone that explains the necessity of water baptism for entering the church and the importance of the relationship among Christians:

> Where there is no water baptism, there is no church nor minister, neither brother nor sister, no brotherly admonition, excommunication, or reacceptance . . . There must also exist an outward confession or testimony through which visible brothers and sisters can know each other, since faith exists only in the heart.[126]

In distinguishing between the baptisms of John and of Christ by using the concept of baptism as a public testimony, Hubmaier showed that proper baptism is not accomplished through the external form of the baptismal rite, but through the will of the baptizand to confess his faith and to establish a new relationship with other Christians.

iv. Summary

As we have seen above, medieval theologians, Zwingli and Hubmaier have all used the issue of the baptisms of John and of Christ to demonstrate their doctrines of baptism. For the medieval theologians, the baptisms of John and of Christ were interpreted and applied in the perspective of sacramental theology, which concentrates on the significance of the ritual form of baptism. Even though the medieval tradition pointed to the difference between the two baptisms, the main purpose in dealing with this issue was to support the medieval sacramental *ex opere operato* theology rather than to identify its fundamental meaning. Consequently, the medieval perspective of sacraments interpreted the baptisms of John and of Christ as supporting a conviction and justification of infant baptism as the proper form of the baptismal rite.

Zwingli argued against the medieval tradition's sacramental theology by placing the baptism of John and the baptism of Christ on the same level. If he could prove that the baptisms of John and of Christ are the

---

126. HS 145; YP 127.

same, it would substantiate his attack on the root of the sacramental perspective on baptism. Further, it enabled a critique of the Anabaptists, who asserted the baptism of believers, which also acknowledged the distinction between the two baptisms. However, Zwingli's interpretation of the two baptisms seems to depend on his unique assumption that the two baptisms are identical. Zwingli attempted to substitute an interpretation of baptism as "teaching" to replace the baptism of John. However, his redefinition of baptism as teaching seems insufficient for justifying his assumption that the baptisms of John and of Christ are the same to all intents and purposes, especially when interpreting Acts 19. Even though his attempt to place the two baptisms on the same level allowed him to challenge the medieval sacramental perspective on baptism, his definition of baptism as a covenant sign did not deny the role of infant baptism.

For Hubmaier, the proper interpretation of the baptisms of John and of Christ is to be a key point in criticizing both the medieval tradition and Zwingli's justifications of infant baptism. Although Hubmaier acknowledged the difference between two baptisms as stemming from the medieval tradition, he pointed out that medieval Catholicism failed to understand the essential meaning of baptism itself. On the basis of his strong Biblicism to demonstrate the difference between the two baptisms, Hubmaier argued for the importance of personal faith or recognition of sin before any baptism, whether of John or of Christ. This point is vital in showing the obvious difference between the medieval tradition and Hubmaier's interpretation. In this context, Hubmaier argued that infant baptism in either the medieval tradition or in Zwinglian thought cannot be justified for any reason. Hubmaier's intention in using the same phrase "public testimony" for the two baptisms seems to be important not only in attacking both the medieval tradition and Zwingli, but also in developing his theology about the relational impact. From the common denominator of two baptisms as a public testimony, Hubmaier showed their similarity and their difference simultaneously. The similarity is that both baptisms require an outward public testimony or confession which cannot be performed by an infant. In addition, the confession of sin by the baptizand in the baptism of John signifies not only the repentance of sin but also the isolation from the community, but the public testimony of the recipient for the baptism of Christ means a new start by entering into the community of believers with the faith in the forgiveness of sin through Christ. This relational perspective by Hubmaier on the baptisms of John and of Christ is the foundation of his expansion of threefold baptism.

4

Hubmaier's Doctrine of Baptism (II)

1. Threefold Baptism

IN HIS MAJOR WRITINGS concerning baptismal theology, *Von der christlichen Taufe der Gläubigen, Ein Gespräch auf Zwinglis Taufbüchlein,* and *Der uralten und gar neuen Lehrer Urteil (Ausgabe I und II),* Hubmaier argued for believers' baptism instead of infant baptism as advocated by the Catholic theologians and magisterial reformers who relied on varied forms of Biblicism, theology, and the writings of patristic fathers. However, there is no direct description of the threefold baptism, which is one of Hubmaier's most unique ideas, in his most representative writing on baptism, *Von der christlichen Taufe der Gläubigen.* Although the treatise potentially contained the idea of threefold baptism,[1] Hubmaier's argument in this treatise was driven by the need to respond to Zwingli over this issue of the relationship between the baptisms of John and of Christ.

However, in *Ein Gespräch auf Zwinglis Taufbüchlein* there is a notable evolution in Hubmaier's description of baptism. Hubmaier's first enumeration of the five different kinds of baptism in *Von der christlichen Taufe der Gläubigen* against Zwingli's four kinds of baptism[2] is as follows: (1) baptism in water; (2) baptism in water, for or unto change of life; (3) baptism in the Spirit and fire; (4) rebirth out of water and Spirit; and (5) baptism in water in the name of the Father, Son, and Holy Spirit, or in the name

1. See HS 121–22; YP 99–101.
2. ZB 132.

of our Lord Jesus Christ.³ In his *Ein Gespräch auf Zwinglis Taufbüchlein*, Hubmaier revised the five kinds of baptism into three categories: (1) the internal baptism of the Spirit (John 3:5-6); (2) outward water baptism (Matt 28:19); and (3) subsequent suffering (Luke 12:50).⁴ Chatfield suggested that Hubmaier's earlier division, (3) and (4), can be put into the new category, (1) "the internal baptism of the Spirit," and the previous categories, (1), (2) and (5), are grouped into the new category, (2) "outward water baptism."⁵ He further commented that Hubmaier's third category of baptism seems to be an outgrowth of his own experiences and that of other Anabaptists around Zurich.⁶ In spite of Chatfield's suggestion that the concept of suffering in baptism would ensue later from Hubmaier's experience, it is possible to see this concept of suffering in baptism in the fifth category of baptism in water in the name of the Father, Son, and Holy Spirit, as in *Von der christlichen Taufe der Gläubigen*.⁷ Moreover, in the last chapter, *The Order of Christian Justification*, Hubmaier clearly showed the concept of blood baptism where the flesh must be killed daily according to the Rule of Christ.⁸ Even though Hubmaier's concept of threefold baptism is apparently implicit in *Ein Gespräch auf Zwinglis Taufbüchlein*, the direct description of threefold baptism appeared in *Eine kurze Entschuldigung* (A Brief Apologia) and *Eine christliche Lehrtafel* (A Christian Catechism), which were written after his experience of imprisonment (after December 19, 1525), and in *Recantation at Zurich* (January 5, 1526), and *Interrogation and Release* (March 5, 1526). Therefore, it is clear that even though Hubmaier's concept of threefold baptism evolved, it was present from the early stages of his reform efforts.

Importantly, although the expression of threefold baptism was directly mentioned in his major theological treatises on baptism, Hubmaier also clearly specified it in his *Eine christliche Lehrtafel*, which was written for new believers. This must mean that, for Hubmaier, this concept of threefold baptism was not simply an instrument for theological debates, but rather a core tenet of Christian theology, as he wrote:

> Leonhart: After faith what do you desire?
>
> Hans: Water baptism.

3. HS 121; YP 99.
4. HS 182; YP 189.
5. Chatfield, "Clarity of Scripture," 120.
6. Ibid., 120–21.
7. HS 122; YP 101.
8. HS 160–61; YP 145–47.

Leonhart: How many kinds of baptism are there?

Hans: Three kinds.

Leonhart: What are they?

Hans: A baptism of the Spirit, a baptism of water, and a baptism of blood.

Leonhart: What is the baptism of the Spirit?

Hans: It is an inner illumination of our hearts that takes place by the Holy Spirit, through the living Word of God.

Leonhart: What is water baptism?

Hans: It is an outward and public testimony of the inner baptism in the Spirit, which a person gives by receiving water, with which one confesses one's sins before all people. One also testifies thereby that one believes in the forgiveness of his sins through the death and resurrection of our Lord Jesus Christ. Thereupon one also has himself outwardly enrolled, inscribed, and by water baptism incorporated into the fellowship of the church according to the institution of Christ, before which church the person also publicly and orally vows to God and agrees in the strength of God the Father, Son, and Holy Spirit that he will henceforth believe and live according to his divine Word. And if he should trespass herein he will accept brotherly admonition, according to Christ's order, Matt. 18:15ff. This precisely is the true baptismal vow, which we have lost for a thousand years; meanwhile Satan has forced his way in with his monastic vows and priestly vows and established them in the holy place.

Leonhart: What is the baptism of blood?

Hans: It is a daily mortification of the flesh until death.[9]

From this passage in his *Eine christliche Lehrtafel*, Hubmaier gave a short but solid explanation of the meaning of threefold baptism. Mabry argued that an analysis of Hubmaier's presentation of baptism in this passage will help us to see that Hubmaier's general theology must be taken seriously, because, for Hubmaier, baptism refers not only to water baptism, or to the traditional sacramental understanding, but is theologically much richer.[10] However, it is difficult to understand in detail what the baptism of the Spirit and the baptism of blood mean in this short account because it is too condensed. Therefore, this basic concept of threefold baptism expressed

---

9. HS 313–14; YP 349–50.
10. Mabry, *Church*, 126.

in the catechism needs to be expounded in conjunction with Hubmaier's other writings in which there is discussion of the concept of threefold baptism. Furthermore, a comparison with Hans Hut's thought on threefold baptism will be helpful in appreciating the uniqueness of Hubmaier's theology here.

a. Baptism of the Spirit

As we have seen, Hubmaier emphasized that there are three kinds of baptism: the baptism of the Spirit, the baptism of water and the baptism of blood. Hubmaier gave a significant place to each of them in his baptismal theology. Even though three kinds of baptism are all equally important for his theology, Hubmaier regarded the baptism of the Spirit as a prerequisite for the others as shown here:

> Thus, let us go forth to Christ, first of all with a true heart in perfection of faith; second, purified in our heart of an evil conscience, that is, with internal baptism, and third, after that, the body washed with pure water. The outward baptism only comes then, for without the internal baptism it is only hypocrisy.[11]

Hubmaier showed the significance of the sequence of baptism chronologically with the baptism of the Spirit preceding the baptism of water. It means that the outward baptism is meaningless for the baptizand unless he or she has already received the baptism of the Spirit. In emphasizing Spirit baptism, Hubmaier distinguished the procedural order of baptisms: faith, internal baptism, and outward baptism. According to this order, without faith and internal baptism, the baptism of water cannot be administered. This tendency to approach baptism in a chronological order is clearly shown in his *Von der christlichen Taufe der Gläubigen*. Hubmaier insisted on a sequence of five steps in the procedure of baptism: Word, hearing, change of life (or recognition of sin) or faith, baptism, and works.[12] Interestingly, in spite of his assertion that the preached Word and

---

11. HS 239; YP 262.

12. HS 127–28, YP 106; HS 146, YP 129. Hubmaier presented seven passages for the baptism of John, and eleven passages for the baptism of Christ. The passages on the Baptism of John are: Matt 3:1ff., Luke 3:2ff., Luke 7:29f., Mark 1:1ff., John 1:23ff., Acts 19:1ff., Matt 21:25ff. (HS 127–34; YP 106–14). The Scriptures on the baptism of Christ are: Matt 28:18ff., Mark 16:15f., Acts 2: 36ff., Acts 8:4ff., Acts 10:44ff., Acts 16: 13ff., Acts 18:8ff., Acts 19:1ff., 1 Cor 1:13ff., 1 Pet 3:20ff., Heb 10:22f. (HS 146–51; YP 129–36).

personal faith are essential elements for baptism, Hubmaier did not seem to emphasize the significance of the distinction between internal and external baptism in this treatise.[13] From his chronological order of baptism, there are two significant points for understanding Hubmaier's theology of the Spirit baptism. First, there is the possibility in his thinking that the concepts of faith and of the Spirit baptism might be used in a similar sense, or even be interchangeable. In other words, the meaning of the baptism of the Spirit in Hubmaier's theology should be interpreted in tandem with his concept of faith. Second, his premise that the baptism of the Spirit is the essential element for water baptism led to Hubmaier's being labeled a spiritualist.[14] However, Hubmaier's understanding of the baptism of the Spirit is totally different from that of the spiritualists who regard the work of the Holy Spirit as superior to any other element for believers. The question of whether he would be a spiritualist can be answered by examining how Hubmaier understood the baptism of the Spirit.

In *Von der christlichen Taufe der Gläubigen*, Hubmaier stated that: "the baptism of the Spirit is to make alive the confessing sinner with the fire of the divine Word by the Spirit of God."[15] In his *Eine christliche Lehrtafel*, he defined the baptism of the Spirit as: "an inner illumination of our hearts that takes place by the Holy Spirit, through the living Word of God."[16] From these descriptions, we can infer some significant points of his understanding of the baptism of the Spirit. First, for Hubmaier, the baptism of the Spirit is related to two essential elements: the living (or divine) Word of God and the work of the Holy Spirit. By stressing the preached Word as an essential element for the baptism of the Spirit, Hubmaier distinguished his thought from that of Zwingli. Zwingli asserted that the Spirit works independently for salvation "as it will, that is, to whom it will, when it will, where it will."[17] For Zwingli, the work of the Holy Spirit begins with God's

13. Hubmaier pointed out only once about the distinction between the baptism of the Spirit and of water in Heb 10:22f. among eighteen passages of examples. Hubmaier seems to replace the internal baptism with faith.

14. Some Anabaptist theologians have suggested that, although Hubmaier's thought on the baptism of the Spirit seems to be much more moderate than that of Zwingli, he might have been influenced by those spiritualists in Germany such as Thomas Müntzer and the Zwickau Prophets. Johann Loserth, Carl Sachsse, Torsten Bergsten, and Samuel Byung-Doo Nam also take this view. See Loserth, *Balthasar Hubmaier*, 73; Sachsse, *Hubmaier Als Theologe*, 153, 158–60; Bergsten and Estep, *Theologian and Martyr*, 202; Nam, "Baptismal Understanding," 206–7.

15. HS 121; YP 100.

16. HS 313; YP 349.

17. ZL 3:183.

election, and is completely independent of the human will to believe.[18] For Zwingli, the preached words cannot make a person hear and understand the truth; only the Holy Spirit can make them effective. The baptism of the Spirit is accomplished by the work of Holy Spirit without an assumption that it must be preceded by the preached Word; the Word itself does not produce faith, only the Spirit does. Therefore, for Zwingli, the baptism of the Spirit treats the work of the Holy Spirit as the essential element, not the preached Word.

However, Hubmaier rejected the superiority of the Spirit over the role of the preached Word in the baptism of the Spirit. Instead, he seemed to consider that both elements are equally important for Spirit baptism. For him, the outward event of the preached Word initiates internal baptism, but this outward event must be followed by an internal calling of the Spirit:

> The inward drawing is this, that God also illuminates the person's soul inwardly, so that it understands the incontrovertible truth, convinced by the Spirit and the preached Word in such a way that one must in one's own conscience confess that this is the case and it cannot be otherwise.[19]

The preached Word according to Hubmaier, means a pure gift by the grace of God, although he expressed the preached Word as an outward event.[20] Hubmaier's understanding of the work of the Spirit which leads to faith is a pure gift in the same way as is the preached Word,[21] because there is no possibility for the hearer to repent himself or herself without hearing the preached gospel. Hubmaier seemed to regard both elements as the grace of God. Mabry pointed out that the concepts of grace (*gnad*) in Hubmaier's writings are shown in two ways: in the sense of a status of favor before God and in the sense of that which enables one to do what God requires of him or her.[22] The first concept of grace is rarely used,[23] but the second one has appeared to be dominant in his thought. The word *gnad*, in the sense of di-

---

18. Zwingli's understanding of God's work of election should be explained in terms of the freedom of the Spirit. By God's freedom in the Spirit, God elects people even outside the church. For Zwingli, therefore, the election and salvation of the heathen is possible by the freedom of God in the Spirit. Z 9:458.25–459. 10. Cf. Stephens, *Theology of Zwingli*, 131; Nam, "Baptismal Understanding," 144.

19. HS 323–24; YP 362.

20. Snyder, "Anabaptist Spirituality," 43–44.

21. Ibid., 44.

22. Mabry, *Faith*, 76–86.

23. HS 135; YP 116, HS 159; YP 145, HS 421; YP 479.

Hubmaier's Doctrine of Baptism (II)

vine force or power from God, which enables human beings to obey God's commandments, is directly applied to the baptism of the Spirit. Without any Word to believe or recognize, there would be no need for any divine power or force from God in order to believe it. Both the preached Word and the work of the Spirit should be embraced in the category of *gnad*. The preached Word, for Hubmaier, is the element which is indivisible from the work of the Holy Spirit in the baptism of the Spirit. Hubmaier maintained a balance between the significance of both elements for the baptism of the Spirit. His understanding of the baptism of the Spirit develops from the presupposition that the work of the Holy Spirit must be coherent with the preached Word. Even though Hubmaier insisted on the importance of the internal baptism for outward baptism, his thoughts about the necessity of both the preached Word and the work of the Spirit for the baptism of the Spirit showed how he differed from Zwingli and also from spiritualists. Furthermore, for Hubmaier the nature of Spirit baptism means that it can only apply to those who are rational and mature enough to understand the knowledge of God by the preached Word. Therefore, Hubmaier's view of the preached Word as the foundation for Spirit baptism is based on his refusal of not only the spiritualists but also the paedobaptists.

Second, Hubmaier's expression of the baptism of the Spirit as "an inner illumination of our hearts, which occurs from the Holy Spirit through the Word of God,"[24] needs to be interpreted alongside his definitions of free will, which is related to faith. As we saw in the previous chapter, the restoration of free will (in particular, the will of the soul) is effected by the Word of God and the work of the Holy Spirit.[25] In other words, the baptism of the Spirit can be understood in terms of the will of soul which is awakened by the Word of God, and enlightened by the Holy Spirit.[26] For Hubmaier, therefore, "An inner illumination of our heart by the Holy Spirit through the Word of God" means a spiritual rebirth in which the human soul must be reborn through the Spirit of God and the living Word.[27] The inner illumination by the work of the Holy Spirit following the preached Word leads the person to be awakened and to recognize the truth. This concept of the spiritual rebirth is included in Hubmaier's definition of

---

24. HS 313; YP 349.
25. HS 390; YP 439.
26. Ibid.
27. HS 384; YP 431–32.

faith.[28] Without the preaching of the Word of God, faith cannot exist.[29] Only through both hearing the Word of God and the work of the Holy Spirit, can one have faith that is the realization and acknowledgement of God's mercy and His gracious favor, which He has shown to us by offering His Son, Jesus Christ.[30] Hubmaier elaborated thus:

> Baptism signifies not the putting away of the flesh but the certain knowledge of a good conscience toward God through the resurrection of Jesus Christ, who ascended into heaven to the right hand of God. From this, every pious Christian sees and grasps that the one who wants to be baptized with water must beforehand have the certain knowledge of a good conscience toward God through the Word of God.[31]

Hubmaier's definition of baptism is exactly the same as the definition of faith in his *Achtzehn Schlußreden* (Eighteen Theses concerning the Christian Life). The term "baptism" in this passage can be applied to both internal baptism and faith. In this case, faith and the Spirit baptism in Hubmaier's theology appear both to have the same meaning: that of recognizing and knowing God's mercy and grace. Even though Hubmaier's previous explanation of the order of baptism as faith, internal baptism and external baptism seems to regard faith as a premise of internal baptism (or the Spirit baptism), it is difficult to say that Hubmaier actually intended to make a chronological order between faith and the internal baptism. Rather he appears to be insisting that faith and internal baptism should precede external baptism.

What is the difference between faith and the baptism of the Spirit in Hubmaier's theology? In spite of his unclear distinction between them, Hubmaier's definition of faith embraces the concept of the Spirit baptism. Faith is the life that follows from that moment. For Hubmaier, the baptism of the Spirit is used to indicate the moment when the recognition of grace becomes effective. Hubmaier's intention to use both concepts together as a premise for water baptism is what shapes his soteriological understanding of baptism. As we have seen, Hubmaier considered faith, which is linked with human will, as a continuing condition of the relationship between God and human and not as a single accomplished event. Hubmaier's relational perspective on faith means that the baptism of the Spirit is only

28. HS 313; YP 348.
29. HS 135; YP 116.
30. HS 72, 313; YP 32, 348.
31. HS 136; YP 117.

necessary as an expression of the starting point of faith. His concept of faith is not only linked with the baptism of the Spirit but also with water baptism and the baptism of blood. In other words, we can regard the baptism of the Spirit as a part of faith, but it cannot replace faith as a lived expression.

Although the baptism of the Spirit seems to be shown as a basis for the other baptisms, this chronological order of baptism needs to be interpreted according to the relational perspective of Hubmaier's thinking. His intention in emphasizing the Spirit baptism is that it symbolizes the significance of the personal encounter between God and human beings. The realization and acknowledgement of God's mercy by the work of the Holy Spirit through the preached Word of God means the restoration of the broken relationship between God and human beings. It does not, however, mean that the baptism of the Spirit occurs only through God's initiation. In spite of his assertion that both the work of the Holy Spirit and the preached Word are the grace and mercy of God, Hubmaier continued to emphasize the necessity of preaching to create faith in others.[32] The preached Word of God, for Hubmaier, means the expression of God's grace through human words. His purpose in insisting on both elements for Spirit baptism is to show how God's thoughtful consideration towards a human being can start a personal encounter with God. He also pointed out that the baptism of the Spirit is not only an inner illumination of the soul by God's grace, but also the inner commitment to God. The proper meaning of the Spirit baptism for Hubmaier includes an individual's voluntary intention to follow the command of God:

> Accordingly, when he recognizes this grace and kindness, he surrenders himself to God and commits himself internally in his heart to live a new life according to the Rule of Christ.[33]

Thus, the proper meaning of the baptism of the Spirit is accomplished when a person's recognition, by the illumination of the Holy Spirit, through the preached Word, is completed with his own voluntary decision to commit himself to God directly. This shows Hubmaier's understanding that the baptism of the Spirit means the personal encounter with and relationship between God and a person, which make the person alive spiritually. According to Hubmaier, the baptism of the Spirit also means that God invites

---

32. HS 135; YP 116.
33. HS 136; YP 117.

Balthasar Hubmaier's Doctrine of Salvation

human beings to be subject to Him by being acknowledged by Him as children of God.

> For that is the grace and favor of God which he bears to us and with which he embraces us: that power which he offers us through his preached Word, so that we—it lies now in our power—can become children of God, also desire and complete his fatherly will and please him.[34]

In spite of his presupposition that the baptism of the Spirit takes place through the grace of God, Hubmaier's allusion to human response and commitment to God within the concept of the baptism of the Spirit shows that the baptism itself, at least for Hubmaier, is a starting point in the relational perspective beyond the traditional view of baptism as a sacrament or confession of faith. In this concept, baptism of the Spirit can mean not only an inner illumination of the Holy Spirit but also a start of a new relationship with God. Even though Hubmaier seems to bring the concepts of faith, free will and the baptism of the Spirit together in the explanation of external baptism, Spirit baptism—which indicates the relationship between God and human—holds a significant role for his relational perspective on baptism, which is seen in the baptism of water and of blood.

b. Baptism of Water

Hubmaier's understanding of water baptism can be understood in three ways: the confession or testimony of the baptizand's faith with his or her pledge before the congregation of believers, the entrance to the visible church, and the forgiveness of sins by the power of the keys. For Hubmaier, the baptism of the Spirit as the first part of his threefold baptism must then be followed by water baptism; that is, baptism in water with confession of sin and the forgiveness of sin before the congregation of believers. A person who recognizes and realizes God's grace by the illumination of the Holy Spirit through the preached Word of God then requires the baptism of water:

> If now a person who has been brought through the Word of God to recognition of his sin confesses himself to be a sinner, and is further taught by the Word of God that he should call upon God the Father for the forgiveness of his sin for the sake of Christ, and if he does that in faith and does not doubt anything, then

---

34. HS 413; YP 468.

> God has cleansed his heart in this faith and trust and has remitted him all his sin. Accordingly, when he recognizes this grace and kindness, he surrenders himself to God and commits himself internally in his heart to live a new life according to the Rule of Christ. But in order to manifest to other believers in Christ his heart, mind, faith, and intention, he joins their brotherhood and churches, so that from now on he might interact with them and they again with him as with a Christian. Therefore, he accepts and gives a public testimony of his internal faith and lets himself be baptized with water.[35]

Hubmaier clearly showed that the forgiveness of one's sins does not depend on water baptism, but on the internal baptism of the Spirit which brings faith. Even though he emphasized the significance of water baptism as a demonstration of internal faith, it does not mean that the outer baptism remits sins, as in the Catholic tradition. Goertz suggested that the distinction of internal baptism from outer baptism for the remission of sins shows that Hubmaier's concept of internal baptism is linked with Luther's concept of justification.[36] The forgiveness of sins is effected by the baptism of the Spirit and not by any other element, and as such, the baptism of the Spirit is more important than the baptism of water in soteriological perspective. In this sense, Hubmaier's concept of the Spirit baptism is one side of an event which takes place by God's initiative. However, it is vital to note that his understanding of the Spirit baptism is that it contains not only one's conviction of the forgiveness of sins which comes from God's grace, but also one's internal commitment to God to live according to the Rule of Christ as a true believer. For Hubmaier, the baptism of the Spirit is not only something that happens at the initiative of God, but is also an interactive response for the restoration of the relationship between God and human beings. Here, the baptism of the Spirit for Hubmaier cannot be regarded the same as Luther's concept of forensic justification in which only God takes the initiative.

i. Water Baptism as a Public Testimony of One's Faith

If Hubmaier denied the efficacy of outward baptism in the Catholic tradition and believed that our sins are forgiven by faith in Christ, then why did he insist on the practice of water baptism? For Hubmaier, water baptism

---

35. HS 136; YP 117.
36. Goertz, *Anabaptists*, 75.

is an outward confession of faith, which manifests a person's internal faith to other believers. Even though water baptism is meaningless without internal baptism for remitting sins, he held its significance as an outward testimony of one's faith which must follow internal baptism. Although the two baptisms are different and separated events, there is also continuity and unity in that the internal baptism is the premise for outward baptism, but the external baptism only has importance in the context of the experience of internal baptism[37] as he argued:

> The second reason is that water baptism has been instituted and commanded with such powerful and unfathomable words, namely in the name of the Father, the Son, and the Holy Spirit, that nowhere else in the Old or New Testaments can we find such high words put together in such an explicit and clear way. From this we realize once again the seriousness with which Christ wills that those who have been instructed in faith should be baptized. For a serious command demands serious obedience and fulfillment.[38]

Hubmaier insisted that those who believe and have not been baptized have the obligation to allow themselves be baptized according to the command of Christ.[39] In other words, the ceremony of water baptism itself has no efficacy for forgiveness of sins; rather, it is necessary for those who believe in Jesus Christ, in order to keep Christ's commandment:

> We know well that salvation is bound neither to baptism nor to works of mercy. Being unbaptized does not condemn us, nor do evil works, but only unfaith. However, whoever is believing lets himself be baptized and bring forth good fruits, Mark 16:16. Accordingly, if one wants to be a Christian and if he has a baptizer and water at hand, then he lets himself be baptized by virtue of the institution of Christ. If he does not do it, however, then he is not condemned because of his non-baptism, but because of his unfaith, from which his disobedience proceeds, Matt. 7:26.[40]

Hubmaier attempted to avoid the danger of anyone misunderstanding his emphasis on the practice of water baptism being a sacrament in Catholic tradition. Although he held on to the importance of the practice of water baptism, his repeated denial of its sacramental efficacy shows that

---

37. Nam, *Baptismal Understanding*, 209.
38. HS 140; YP 122.
39. HS 140; YP 121.
40. HS 183; YP 191.

Hubmaier's Doctrine of Baptism (II)

his soteriology reflects the reformation slogan that salvation is only by faith. As we have already seen in the previous chapter, Hubmaier's understanding of faith which focused on the active side of human behavior is different from other contemporary reformers' thinking which emphasized the passive side of faith. Despite his denial of the sacramental efficacy of water baptism, he insisted that one who believes in Jesus Christ must commit himself or herself to live according to the Rule of Christ. Accordingly believers must be baptized in water as commanded by Christ. If someone refuses to be baptized with water after his or her internal baptism, it means that his or her faith is inauthentic, because he or she is disobeying Christ's command. For Hubmaier, there is no doubt as to the necessity of the practice of water baptism which is instituted by the command of Christ, although water baptism itself does not affect redeeming sins at all:

> Those who are inwardly baptized will let themselves truly be also outwardly baptized, and they do not despise the command of Christ, where they otherwise are able to have baptizer and water.[41]

ii. Water Baptism as the Entrance into the Visible Church

Then, what does water baptism mean for Hubmaier? In *Eine christliche Lehrtafel*, Hubmaier described water baptism as an outward and public testimony of inner baptism in the Spirit before congregations.[42] For him, the outer and verbal confession of faith proves that internal faith is required for baptism with water. In his contemporary situation, the practice of water baptism of believers was forbidden. Those who are rebaptized from the position of being either a Catholic or mainline reformer are regarded as traitors who should be punished. For the baptizand to receive water baptism it means that he or she must expect to suffer persecution by the government or other religious groups because of their obedience to what they believed to be Christ's command to be baptized. In this context, to be baptized with water with the confession of sins outwardly before congregation proves one's belief in the forgiveness of sins through the

---

41. HS 265; YP 288.

42. HS 313; YP 349. His emphasis on the necessity of outer and verbal confession of faith for water baptism is often shown in his other writings as well. See HS 111; YP 85, HS 122; YP 100, HS 196; YP 209.

Balthasar Hubmaier's Doctrine of Salvation

death and resurrection of Jesus Christ.[43] However, although Hubmaier described water baptism as nothing other than a public confession and testimony of internal faith, the expression "a public testimony of faith" as an essential element in the practice of water baptism does not exhaust the character of this kind of baptism.[44] Rather, Hubmaier added another element, that is, a person's outward commitment and pledge to live according to the Word and command of Christ before the congregation. The emphasis on confession of faith and the voluntary will as key elements in the meaning of water baptism is related to his understanding of the church as visible and congregational:

> Thereupon one also has himself outwardly enrolled, inscribed, and by water baptism incorporated into the fellowship of the church according to the institution of Christ, before which church the person also publicly and orally vows to God and agrees in the strength of God the Father, Son, and Holy Spirit that he will henceforth believe and live according to his divine Word.[45]

For Hubmaier, water baptism is the entrance into the visible church which is constituted by those who confess their faith outwardly and believe in the forgiveness of their sins through Christ. One who is baptized with water through the confession of faith is incorporated into the Christian church, that is, all brothers and sisters who live in faith. In other words, water baptism for the baptizand is the starting point of a new relationship with other believers, by showing his or her will to accept the suffering or trial for faith beyond simple confession of internal faith before congregation. Hubmaier's assertion that the confession of faith should be performed before a Christian church means that the practice of water baptism itself has a significant function in making the connection between the baptizand and other believers. Through water baptism with a public confession of faith, the baptizand can demonstrate the conviction of his or her faith and of the forgiveness of sins. Equally, the congregation can recognize that the baptizand willingly wants to be baptized and to live according to the Rule of Christ within the community of other believers. Thus, for the baptizand, water baptism with the confession of faith functions as one's obedience to Christ's command before a congregation of believers. Then, what does water baptism with the confession of faith mean in Hubmaier's theology? The

---

43. HS 313; YP 349.
44. HS 122; YP 100.
45. HS 313–14; YP 349.

baptizand enters into the community of believers through water baptism. It is also through water baptism that the church acts to accept him or her as a member of the community.

The baptizand's confession of faith and commitment, which is called baptismal pledge or vow, is one of the key elements in understanding Hubmaier's doctrine of water baptism. The baptismal pledge means that the baptizand dedicates himself or herself to live according to the Rule of Christ publicly and orally before the congregation of believers. It also means that he or she willingly accepts the church's admonition when he or she sins against God and neighbors. The pledge of water baptism for Hubmaier is the reciprocal promise between the baptizand and the congregation of believers before God as he argued:

> Where there is no water baptism, there is no church nor minister, neither brother nor sister, no brotherly admonition, excommunication, or reacceptance. I am speaking here of the visible church as Christ did in Matthew 18:15ff. There must also exist an outward confession or testimony through which visible brothers and sisters can know each other, since faith exists only in the heart. But when he receives the baptism of water the one who is baptized testifies publicly that he has pledged himself henceforth to live according to the Rule of Christ. By virtue of this pledge he has submitted himself to sisters, brothers, and to the church so that when he transgresses they now have the authority to admonish, punish, ban, and reaccept him. But this is not the case with those who are still outside.[46]

Through the baptismal pledge, the baptizand enters into a new relationship with other believers who become brothers and sisters in Christ to help and encourage each other to live according to the Rule of Christ. The most important thing for the baptismal vow is the voluntary will of the baptizand which is based on maintaining a visible church. Without the baptizand's entirely voluntary will to submit to the command of Christ, he or she cannot enter into the visible church that has authority over individual believers, and which has the power of fraternal admonition.[47] This is expressly stated in the baptismal liturgy.

> "If now you should sin and your brother knows it, will you let him admonish you once, twice, and the third time before the

---

46. HS 145; YP 127.
47. HS 316; YP 352.

Balthasar Hubmaier's Doctrine of Salvation

church, and willingly and obediently accept fraternal admonition, if so speak":

"I will."[48]

However, the power of fraternal admonition by the community of believers only applies to those who commit themselves to God and other believers without any other enforcement. A visible church, which is the congregation of believers gathered by water baptism, uses the power of fraternal admonition over only those who accepted the authority of church through their baptismal pledge. This is because the power of fraternal admonition is achieved through a reciprocal covenant between the baptizand and believers in the visible church. However, this fraternal admonition applies only to those who make a covenant with the church, so that there is no effect on those who have not come into the church as he wrote:

> Water baptism is given for the forgiveness of sins, Acts 2:38; 1 Pet. 3:21 . . . Therefore, as much as the communion of God the Father, and of the Son, and of the Holy Spirit, yea, also the communion of all the heavenly host and the entire Christian church, and also as much as the forgiveness of sins is important to a person, so much also is water baptism through which he enters and which is embodied in the universal Christian church, outside of which there is no salvation. It is not that forgiveness of sins is a characteristic of the water, but of the power of the keys, which Christ on the authority of his Word commanded in his bodily absence and hung at the side of his bride and immaculate spouse, the Christian church.[49]

iii. Water Baptism as a Forgiveness of Sin by the Power of the Keys

Interestingly, though Hubmaier denied the efficacy of water baptism for the remission of sins in the Catholic tradition, he used the expression that water baptism is given for forgiveness of sins. So, how is Hubmaier's understanding of the phrase, "the forgiveness of sins by water baptism," different from the Catholic view? As we have seen, Hubmaier believed that the forgiveness of sins depends on faith which in turn depends on the baptism of the Spirit. In this sense, he refused the Catholic view of water as sacramental material in the practice of baptism, but he still insisted on

48. HS 350; YP 389.
49. HS 335–36; YP 370–71.

the role of water baptism in the forgiveness of sins. If Hubmaier is being consistent, it is obvious that he must have some understanding of the link between baptism and forgiveness that is not dependent on a traditional sacramental theology. Hubmaier's expression, "the forgiveness of sin by water baptism," does not mean that the baptizand is saved through baptism, but it should be understood as reinforcing his conviction of the significance of the fellowship of the church and of the entering the church through water baptism as much as the importance of forgiveness of sins for a person.

As the above quotation demonstrates, in order to explain the forgiveness of sins, Hubmaier pointed out the importance of the communion of believers alongside the concept of the Trinity which presents a perfect example of fellowship. In other words, although the remitting of sins comes through faith, the fellowship of believers is fundamentally important in understanding the forgiveness of sins. Those who want to be involved in the fellowship of believers should receive water baptism in order to enter the believers' fellowship. However, he also asserted that the meaning of forgiveness of sins is related not only to the practice of water baptism, but also to the function of the power of the keys, which is based on Matt 16:19, "I will give you the keys of the kingdom of heaven; whatever you bind on earth will be bound in heaven, and whatever you loose on earth will be loosed in heaven."

There was significant discussion amongst contemporary theologians about the power of the keys.[50] The traditional understanding was that the "power of the keys" referred to the authority of the priest to declare absolution for those who were forgiven by God, and also gave the power of excommunication and discipline as a remedial practice. In this understanding, the power belonged to the priest alone.[51] Unlike Catholic tradition that stipulates the priests have the authority, Hubmaier asserted that the power of the keys is given to the community of believers and, therefore, it is the community that has the authority to include and exclude persons from this fellowship.[52] In other words, for Hubmaier, the

50. For instance, Luther delivered a sermon at Leipzig on Matt 16:13–19 in conjunction with his disputation with John Eck. Zwingli dealt with the issue of the keys in his *Auslegen und Grüde der Schlußreden* (1523) and in his commentary *De Vera et Falsa Religione* (True and False Religion, 1525). Erasmus also exlained the keys in his *Paraphrase of the Gospel of Matthew* (1522), and *Inquisitio de Fide* (1524). See Leth, "Power of the Keys," 103–17.

51. Leth, "Power of the Keys," 108.

52. Ibid., 115.

power of keys does not belong to an individual office but to the whole community of believers. He insisted that the power of the keys does not mean the power to remit the sins of a person or the power to declare the absolution for forgiveness of sins, rather it means the decision of the whole community as to whether or not they will accept a person into the community, as Hubmaier wrote:

> Namely, to preach the gospel, thereby to create a believing congregation, to baptize the same in water, thus with the first key opening to her the door the portals of the Christian church, admitting her to the forgiveness of sins John 20:22f.[53]

His second explanation of the function of the power of the keys is to exclude people who have already entered into the church and do not demonstrate the will to live in a Christian way, and to close the door to them. This interpretation shows that his understanding of the power of the keys is based on the relational perspective that focuses on the relationship between individual persons and the church.[54] His concept of the forgiveness of sins in explaining water baptism and the power of the keys is that a person who confesses faith and intends to live according to the Rule of Christ with other believers is accepted by and admitted to the Christian church. Accordingly, Hubmaier insisted that there is no salvation outside of the church.[55] Although the power of the keys includes various functions such as admitting, loosing, or excluding, a person from the fellowship of the church, in water baptism the power of the key is to admit a person into the church.[56]

However, these different expressions of water baptism in Hubmaier's writings share a common denominator in that they are all based on the relationship between the baptizand and other believers. Without the encounter between the baptizand and other believers to create a new relationship, for Hubmaier, the practice of water baptism is meaningless. Water baptism is not just a confession of faith or the repentance of sins, nor the forgiveness of sins from a sacramental perspective; rather, it is a new start of a relationship between the baptizand and other believers in order to build up the body of Christ through the encouragement and

---

53. HS 368; YP 412.
54. HS 370; YP 414.
55. HS 172; YP 175.
56. Ibid. The other functions of the keys in Hubmaier's theology are also important for Christian life. This will be further discussed in the next chapter on the Lord's Supper.

admonition of each other. In this context, the meaning of the forgiveness of sins through water baptism is focused upon entering the new relationship with other believers in the commitment to live according to the Rule of Christ. Hubmaier showed the significance of the relational concept between the baptizand and other believers in water baptism as much as the importance of the relationship between a person and God in the concept of the Spirit baptism.

c. Baptism of Blood

For Hubmaier, the meaning of baptism of blood is very rich and multifaceted. It must be understood as a continuing process rather than an event, as are the baptisms of the Spirit and of water. There are two fundamental aspects to the baptism of blood. First, in *Eine christliche Lehrtafel*, Hubmaier described the baptism of blood as "a daily mortification of the flesh until death."[57] From this short sentence, it is quite difficult to know what the baptism of blood means for Hubmaier. Therefore, the concept of "a daily mortification of the flesh until death" needs to be understood in relation of his explanation in *Von der christlichen Taufe der Gläubigen* as elaborated here:

> He expresses his inborn nature and resists the Spirit within the person, that is, he assails the newborn soul so much that the person does not do what he wants according to the Word of God. The flesh must daily be killed since it wants only to live and reign according to its own lusts. Here the Spirit of Christ prevails and gains the victory. Then the person brings forth good fruits which give testimony of a good tree. Day and night he practices all those things which concern the praise of God and brotherly love. By this the old Adam is martyred, killed, and carried to the grave . . . Faith is not idle but is industrious in good Christian works. But only those are good works which God himself has commanded us, and of which he will demand a reckoning from us at the last day, Matt. 25:34ff.[58]

Hubmaier clearly showed that the concept of the mortification of the flesh does not occur from the outside but from the inside. Here, the killing of flesh seems to mean resisting inner wrong desires more than persecution from external factors. In other words, the mortification of flesh can mean

57. HS 314; YP 350.
58. HS 161; YP 147.

the conflict with the sinful nature.[59] According to Windhorst, Hubmaier's concept of flesh in blood baptism points to the old Adam, or the sinful person.[60] In this sense, the baptism of blood is the daily killing of the sinful nature in humans. Hubmaier's baptism of blood could be taken to mean the final destruction of the evil in human beings.[61] Further, for Hubmaier blood baptism could be understood as self-discipline or asceticism and the inner regeneration of individual spirituality.

However, it is difficult to say that Hubmaier's understanding of the baptism of blood indicates only individual self-discipline. Although the word "flesh" in Hubmaier's writings relates to the old Adam or the sinful nature, it actually means the will of flesh in human will, which consist of three different kinds: spirit, soul and flesh. For Hubmaier, the flesh is completely unprofitable and dead to doing good.[62] The will of the flesh can only sin and do nothing good, even after spiritual restoration. The will of the soul after restoration by the Word of God and the work of the Holy Spirit is made healthy and consequently is free to choose to do evil or good. Human behavior concerning sin is totally dependent on the restored will of the soul as to whether it wants to follow the will of God or evil. If the will of the soul decides to follow evil and perform it, then the soul's will becomes an instrument of the flesh, which by its sinful nature is quick to do evil.[63] When the will of the soul restrains the nature of the flesh according to the will of God, it produces good. The most important thing for killing the will of the flesh is the relationship between God and the will of the soul in a human being. In Hubmaier's understanding, the way to maintain a good relationship with God is to follow the will of God in whatever we do, and to give attention to our neighbors. Killing the will of the flesh comes from a right relationship with God and, vitally, is seen in our relationships with other people. Therefore, Hubmaier's concept of blood baptism as "a daily mortification of the flesh" does not insist only on a self-discipline where a person restrains himself or herself from his or her sinful nature, but rather it focuses on the significance of an ongoing relationship with God, which is based on overcoming the wrong desires stemming from our

---

59. Armour, *Anabaptist Baptism*, 54. Armour points out that Hubmaier's concept of blood baptism, which is related to death, might be linked with Luther's view that baptism is a lifelong death to sin and resurrection to new life in Christ.

60. Windhorst, *Täuferisches Taufverstädnis*, 161.

61. Mabry, *Church*, 149.

62. HS 389; YP 438.

63. HS 392; YP 441.

Hubmaier's Doctrine of Baptism (II)

sinful nature. The baptism of blood needs to be understood as self-denial by the believers which is led by the right relationship with God in the relational perspective. In this sense, Hubmaier's concept of blood baptism should be understood to include his understanding of faith, as an active response to God within the personal relationship between them. This is why Hubmaier emphasized the active side of faith—industriousness as exemplified by good Christian works—after the concept of blood baptism. For Hubmaier, believers naturally sanctify their lives through their relationship with God. Therefore, the baptism of blood means that believers restrain their sinful natures, and obey the will of God through their efforts to sustain their personal relationship with God. In this sense, the baptism of blood in Hubmaier's thought can be regarded as a characteristic feature of Anabaptism that holds to moral improvement rather than a one-sided emphasis on either justification or holiness.[64]

Second, Hubmaier insisted that the baptism of blood means not only the inner suffering of believers against sinful nature but also the accompanying external trials and tribulations for faith. In *Eine kurze Entschuldigung*, Hubmaier showed this aspect of blood baptism:

> For I confess three kinds of baptism: that of the Spirit, which takes place inwardly in faith; the second, of water, which takes place outwardly by oral affirmation of faith before the church; and the third, of blood in martyrdom or on the deathbed, of which Christ also speaks, Luke 12:50, for which we are indeed in need of the spiritual wine and oil the Samaritan poured into the wounds of the injured man, Luke 10:34. John calls these three baptisms, with which all Christians must be baptized, the three witnesses on earth, 1 John 5:7.[65]

For Hubmaier, after the baptism of the Spirit and of water, the believer should expect to suffer for his or her faith even unto death. In contrast with the previous concept of blood baptism as self-examination, this suffering comes from external conditions. Those who follow Christ must be willing to enter into suffering for their faith, as Christ suffered. Here, suffering as martyrdom or death should be understood as physical persecution rather than the killing of one's sinful nature. Hubmaier asserted that the fundamental power of believers to endure external persecution or tribulation relies on Christ healing the wounded human being. In *Von der Freiheit des Willens*, Hubmaier interpreted the parable of "the Good Samaritan" as

---

64. Goertz, *Anabaptists*, 59. Cf. Wenger, "Grace and Discipleship," 58.
65. HS 275; YP 301.

Balthasar Hubmaier's Doctrine of Salvation

demonstrating that the fallen human being should be healed in two ways: internally and externally.⁶⁶ The inner wound, which is ignorance of good and evil, is healed through the wine poured by Christ; that is, through the law, in which the human being has his or her conscience restored with regard to what is good and evil before God. The external wound which prevents obedience of the commandments of God in doing and acting is healed by the oil, that is the gospel, so that the human being can obey the will of God. According to Hubmaier, when the wine and oil, that is the law and gospel, are used together by Christ the true Physician, the will of soul becomes righteous and healthy once again able to obey God's commandment.⁶⁷ Hubmaier's concept of blood baptism contains both inner and external transformation, as the parable "the Good Samaritan" indicates. The healing by the Samaritan Christ is necessary for the generative power to overcome the suffering whether internally or externally. The inner healing that is the restoration of human recognition and judgment about good and evil is connected with discipline by killing the sinful nature in the concept of blood baptism. Without recognizing good or evil, one cannot discipline himself or herself in a right way. This inner healing must be linked with the external healing of the wound. True faith is not only internal in human beings but must be shown through external actions. One whose external wound is healed by the gospel can follow God's commandments. Healing by the Samaritan represents the relationship between God and the wounded one. On this foundation, the believers must be ready to suffer for faith in the world. The parable of "the Good Samaritan" denotes that the baptism of blood contains both meanings: the daily killing of the flesh and the suffering or persecution that the believers must endure. Moreover, it shows that through a right relationship with God, the believers can endure suffering in the world.

As we have seen, Hubmaier's theology delineates a threefold baptism. If the baptism of the Spirit occurs between the believer and God, and the baptism of water is accomplished in the relation between the believer and the congregation of believers, then, how does the baptism of blood as suffering take place? It is clear that the encounter reflected in the baptism of blood exists between the believer and the world. In other words, if the world did not exist, blood baptism would be unnecessary. When the believer encounters persecution and tribulation in the world because of the gospel, it is a testimony to his or her faith because the world hates light and

---

66. HS 395–96; YP 445–46.
67. HS 396; YP 446.

Hubmaier's Doctrine of Baptism (II)

life.[68] The baptism of blood is begun with the relationship with the world. For Hubmaier, the baptism of blood is to prove his or her faith which keeps the gospel in the world despite suffering, as he elaborated:

> For whoever wants to cry with Christ to God: "Abba, pater, dear Father," must do so in faith, and must also be cobaptized in water with Christ and suffer jointly with him in blood. Then he will be a son and heir of God, fellow heir with Christ, and will be jointly glorified with Christ, Rom. 8:17. Therefore no one should be terrified of persecution or suffering, for Christ had to suffer and thus enter into his glory, Luke 24:26. And also Paul writes: "All who desire to live so devoutly in Christ Jesus will be persecuted," 2 Tim. 3:12. This is indeed precisely the third baptism or last baptism in which people should indeed be anointed with the oil of the holy and comforting gospel (in order that we may be meek and ready to suffer).[69]

The baptism of blood, which is based on persecution and suffering in the world, shows the relationship between God and His children. For Hubmaier, if we are children of God, it is right for us to follow the way of Christ which leads to suffering for the will of God. Believers are encouraged to accept suffering realizing that to do so is a sign that one is a child of God. One cannot escape persecution or suffering for Christian faith, rather it must be encountered. Mabry rightly pointed out that, for Hubmaier, believers should be willing to suffer, and even do so joyfully, as Christ bore his suffering.[70] In other words, believers should show their faith in order to live in the world, not to escape from the world. Hubmaier's purpose in insisting that the baptism of blood take place in the world is to test whether the believer lives in faith according to the will of God. Therefore, suffering or persecution has meaning for the believers when the world is against the will of God. Whether the world is evil or not, the most important thing for believers is to keep and live in their faith under any circumstances.

Hubmaier's inclusion of believers' voluntary will to suffer in the world is a significant key in understanding his view on the role of government and separatists, which differed from many other Anabaptists. Hubmaier expected the community of believers to be involved and interested in all social and governmental functions,[71] so he showed a posi-

---

68. HS 112; YP 86.
69. HS 275; YP 301.
70. Mabry, *Church*, 148.
71. Snyder, *History and Theology*, 58–59.

Balthasar Hubmaier's Doctrine of Salvation

tive attitude toward government in his treatise *Von dem Schwert* (On the Sword). Snyder rightly pointed out that *Von dem Schwert* presents three reasons to support the function of government against *Schleitheim's Confession* that insisted on the strict ethic of "doing what Jesus did."[72] First, Hubmaier emphasized that even as we remain human, our kingdom is still of this world.[73] Second, even though Christ was sent on a mission of salvation, He could not possibly play all social roles. Therefore, everyone should continue in their proper office and calling, be it in government or in obedience.[74] Third, Hubmaier asserted that God did not ordain two opposed kingdoms, but rather intended a harmony to exist between church and government.[75] Hubmaier insisted that the role of a governor or judge or any other secular worker in the world is not so very different from the works of Christians when it serves the common good according to the will of God. He wrote thus:

> For God thus wants to do many things through his creatures as his instruments which he could well do alone and without them. But he wants to use us so that we serve one another and are not idle, but that everyone fulfill his office to which he has been called by God. One should preach, the other protect, the third cultivate his field, the fourth do his work in another way so that we all eat our bread in the sweat of our brow. Truly, truly whoever rules rightly and in a Christian way has enough to sweat.[76]

Hubmaier's insistence that believers act their office in their calling can be related to the baptism of blood which takes place in the world. Hubmaier never encouraged believers to separate or escape from the rule of secular government, rather he urged them to live and to keep their faith there. Windhorst rightly pointed out that Hubmaier argued that believers and non-believers should live together peacefully in society until the day of the Lord's judgment.[77] The relational perspective on baptism in his theology influences his view of the world which is also a subject for the relation

---

72. Snyder, *History and Theology*, 192–93.

73. HS 436; YP 497: "We are stuck in it [this world] right up to our ears, and we will not be able to be free from it here on earth."

74. HS 439; YP 500: "Just as Christ wanted to do justice to his office on earth, likewise we should fulfill our office and calling, be it in government or in obedience."

75. Snyder, *History and Theology*, 192.

76. HS 448; YP 511.

77. Windhorst, *Täuferisches Taufverstädnis*, 145; Estep, *Anabaptist Story*, 85; MacGregor, *Radical and Magisterial Reform*, 149.

with believers. Believers should keep and live in faith not out of the world, but in the world. In this sense, for Hubmaier, the concept of separatism cannot be accepted, because Christians should live their calling according to the will of God. The baptism of blood in Hubmaier's theology is understood to mean the relationship not only between God and believers, but also between believers and the world in the present context. One's attitude toward his or her sinful nature depends entirely on what relationship one has with God. One cannot overcome the temptation of the sinful nature, and endure suffering or persecution in the world, unless he or she has a proper and strong relationship with God.

d. Hans Hut's Threefold Baptism

As we have seen above, Hubmaier's distinguishing three kinds of baptism reflects his unique approach towards baptism. It is worth noting he was not the only one to use this language. The distinction of baptism into three parts is echoed later by Hans Hut, who was one of the south German Anabaptist's leaders along with Hans Denck. Hut's view on baptism was particularly influenced by Thomas Müntzer's thought that inner baptism of the Spirit was a *Bund*, but also by Denck's emphasis that the outer expression of inner baptism in the action of water baptism was a covenant which pledged one's faithfulness to God.[78] Moreover, Müntzer's thought around the necessity of suffering for Christian life had a significant influence on Hut's idea of the "Gospel of All Creatures" where: "God had revealed in all creation the fundamental gospel that human being must be subject to, and suffer, at the hand of God."[79] From his recognition of the necessity of suffering for Christians, Hut regarded the main theme of gospel of all creatures as the understanding of the suffering of Christ. Accordingly, Hut considered the relation between the gospel of all creatures and the suffering of Christ as the starting point for the process of baptism.[80] From the concept of covenant and the necessity of suffering for baptism, Hut expanded his understanding of baptism in order to follow the concept of Hubmaier's threefold baptism[81] as shown in this passage:

---

78. Armour, *Anabaptist Baptism*, 76.
79. Snyder, *History and Theology*, 71.
80. Baylor, *Radical Reformation*, 156–57.
81. Klaassen, *Anabaptism in Outline*, 346.

> Baptism has three parts, that is Spirit, water, and blood. These three are one and witness upon the earth. Firstly, the Spirit is the assurance in and surrender to the divine Word that a man will live according to what the Word proclaims. This is the covenant of God which God makes with them through his Spirit in their hearts. Secondly, beyond that God has given them the water as a sign of the covenant. In this one indicates and confesses that he wishes to live in true obedience towards God and Christians and to live a blameless life. And whoever transgresses and does not live right and acts against God and love, he is to be chastised by the others with words. That is the ban about which God speaks. It is to be a witness before the church. The third is blood which is the true baptism which Christ shows his disciples when he says that they are to be baptized with the baptism which witnesses to the whole world when a disciple's blood is spilt. This is what he holds concerning baptism since he has understood it.[82]

In this text, Hut's distinction of baptism in three parts echoes Hubmaier's concept of threefold baptism which is distinguished by the object of baptism: the baptism of the Spirit as the covenant between God and person, the baptism of water as the covenant between God and the baptizand or the baptizand and believers, the baptism of blood as the relation between the baptizand and the world. Although Hut's shape of threefold baptism is similar to Hubmaier's one, it does not mean that Hut's threefold baptism followed Hubmaier's chronological order for threefold baptism. Rather, Hut's understanding of water baptism that prepared for inner baptism seems to invert the order between the baptism of the Spirit and of water as argued by Hubmaier.[83] For Hut, the function of water baptism is to let the baptizand agree to submit to inner baptism: "the waters which press on the soul are temptation, trouble, anxiety, trembling and worry—so then baptism is suffering."[84] Thus, his concept of baptism is expanded in the concept of suffering, which is the real essence and power of baptism.[85]

However, his understanding of baptism in a covenantal aspect seems to develop according to Müntzer's mysticism that true baptism depends on a process of suffering, and is fulfilled through the work of the Spirit. Furthermore, his baptismal thought is also influenced by Müntzer's

---

82. Ibid., 169–70. Cf. Schornbaum, *Markgraftum Brandenburg*, 43.
83. Goertz, *Anabaptists*, 78.
84. Rupp, *Patterns of Reformation*, 395.
85. Ibid., 390.

apocalyptic emphasis on baptism as the sealing of the elect on the Last Days.[86] From this point of view, Seebaß rightly pointed out that Hut's understanding of believers' baptism is an outward expression of the apocalyptic sign for the elect on the Last Days.[87]

From this account of Hut's understanding of baptism, we can see that the concept of threefold baptism in his theology is not the same as Hubmaier's, which focused on the significance of its chronological order for his relational perspective of soteriology. Hut's threefold baptism showed how it can support the significance of suffering in Christian life according to his apocalyptic and mystic perspective.

2. Relationship between Original Sin and Infant Baptism

Hubmaier's unique understanding of baptism is found not only in his concept of threefold baptism, but also in his discussion of the relationship between original sin and infant baptism. There are two main responses to Augustine's establishment of the definition of baptism for everyone, including infants, as the sacrament for the remission of previous sins and original sin.[88] The first response, following an Augustinian, approach, argues that baptism should be given to infants for the remission of original sin, otherwise infants cannot be saved. The second response rejects the Augustinian presupposition of original sin and argues that, since a human being is not damned through original sin, infant baptism is unnecessary.

There is also a much less common view, that original sin is a reality, but infant baptism does not remit it. In other words, on the whole, the acknowledgement of original sin seems to emphasize the necessity for infant baptism in order to remit original sin. This view of baptism continued in the Reformation era. Catholic and most mainline reformers tended to adhere to the Augustinian view of original sin and infant baptism, but most Anabaptists and radical reformers denied the validity of remitting sins by infant baptism and the existence of original sin. However, there are some exceptional cases on each side: in the former group that accepts infant baptism there is Zwingli, and in the latter group that deny infant baptism there is Hubmaier.

86. Snyder, *History and Theology*, 72.

87. Seebaß, "Hans Hut," 138–64.

88. Augustine, *de natura et gratia* 3.3–4.4. Cf. McGrath, *Christian Theology*, 427–30; idem, *Reader*, 219.

Zwingli's view of the relationship between original sin and infant baptism does not appear to follow the traditional view of baptism, particularly the Augustinian view. For Zwingli, original sin which is inborn in us: "is a disease, not a sin, because sin implies guilt, and guilt comes from a transgression or trespass on the part of one who designedly perpetrates a deed."[89] In this sense, Zwingli would not necessarily have accepted the reason for the practice of infant baptism for remission of original sin for two reasons: first, he said, original sin does not damn the infant and therefore does not need to be remitted;[90] second, baptism does not remit sins anyway but only the blood of Christ does.[91] If original sin does not affect an infant's salvation, why did Zwingli assert the necessity of infant baptism? If infant baptism is not needed to remit any sin, including original sin, would he do better to argue that infant baptism is unnecessary as do Anabaptists or radical reformers?

Zwingli's defense of infant baptism can be explained through an examination of the historical context of his own struggle against Anabaptism. Since being influenced by Erasmus in his notion of original sin, Zwingli had difficulties in relation to infant baptism when he was faced with the question of justifying whether its practice is biblical. However, the so-called "First Zurich Disputation" of January 29, 1523 for determining whether Zwingli's sixty-seven *Schlussreden* were in accordance with Scripture, was a significant event. The city council decided that Zwingli's *Schlussreden* was the right interpretation of the Bible. In other words, this disputation meant not only a triumph for Zwingli, but also that the city council was authorized to interpret and make this judgment.[92] The city council declared that it had the right to interpret the Bible for the citizens of Zurich, and gave notice that it intended to exercise that right.[93] Zwingli deemed that if the functions of city and church were equivalent in Zurich, then a Christian city could not be anything other than a Christian church.[94] His understanding of the relationship between state and church was the starting point for his political hermeneutic which related his covenant theology for the doctrine of sacraments.

---

89. ZL 2:5.
90. ZL 2:23.
91. ZL 2:27.
92. Oberman, *Masters of the Reformation*, 187–209.
93. McGrath, *Reformation Thought*, 164.
94. Z 14:424. Cf. George, "Zwingli's Baptismal Theology," 82.

Zwingli earlier understood sacrament in the sense of "oath" or "pledge," considering the sacraments of baptism and the Lord's Supper as the signs of God's faithfulness to his people and those of his promise of forgiveness.[95] In *An Exposition of Articles* (1523), he used the word "sacrament" to refer to those things that "God has instituted, commanded, and ordained with his Word, which is as firm and sure as if he had sworn an oath thereto."[96] However, Zwingli's misgivings about continuing the practice of infant baptism in the early 1520s had disappeared by 1524, when he started to develop a theory of baptism which supported its necessity while denying the existence of original sin in infants.[97] Even though he continued to use the word for sacrament as "oath" or "pledge" in *Von der Taufe, von der Wiedertaufe, und von der Kindertaufe* (1525), Zwingli had changed its reference to our pledge of obedience and loyalty to a new life before God and to one another, rather than God's pledge of faithfulness to us.[98] From his experience as a chaplain in the army of the Swiss Confederacy, he could apply the concept of "oath" or "pledge" for sacrament to baptism and the Lord's Supper. For Zwingli, the believer pledges loyalty to the church community through baptism, and he or she demonstrates his or her loyalty publicly in the Lord's Supper.[99] In this sense, Zwingli could develop the idea as covenant theology to defend and justify infant baptism. He asserted that as circumcision was not a sign to confirm faith, but a sign of pledging one's children to God, so baptism has the same purpose.[100] Moreover, he pointed out that, although Abraham received circumcision after his faith, circumcision was given to infants before they had faith, and therefore argued that baptism can also be given to infants who would have faith later.[101] This justification for infant baptism which was practiced without any confession of faith, was an attempt to answer the question of the relationship between infant baptism and original sin. For Zwingli, just as the children of Israel were not damned by original sin because of the covenant, shown by circumcision in the Old Testament, Christian children were also not damned by original sin because they

---

95. McGrath, *Reformation Thought*, 180.
96. Stephens, *Theology of Zwingli*, 180.
97. George, "Zwingli's Baptismal Theology," 79–82.
98. ZB 131, 150. Cf. Stephens, *Theology of Zwingli*, 181.
99. McGrath, *Reformation Thought*, 180.
100. ZB 138.
101. ZB 138.

were also included in the community of covenantal promise.[102] His understanding of circumcision as a sign of the covenant between God and the Israelites in the Old Testament could apply to the practice of baptism as a sign of the covenant between God and believers. In other words, just as the children of Israel belonged to the community of God by circumcision, infant baptism was equally a sign of belonging to a community of God.

With this covenantal concept of baptism at least, Zwingli could argue against anti-paedobaptists despite continuing his views on original sin. In his understanding of the Christian city as a Christian church, sacrament meant not only loyalty to the church, but also loyalty to the state. If anyone refused to allow their children to be baptized, it was an act of disloyalty to the Zurich city community. In this context, those who refused to allow infants to be baptized had to be expelled because they represented revolt, faction or heresy. This means that Zwingli's interpretation was particularly associated with the political hermeneutic from the first Zurich disputation.[103] With Zwingli's understanding of baptism in both its religious and political aspects, the reformation of Zurich would accelerate and enforce conformity.[104] However, his method of interpreting the Bible on the issues of baptism and original sin utilizing a political perspective means that, as far as Hubmaier is concerned, Zwingli's argument on the doctrine of sacrament is far removed from actual and correct biblical interpretation.

In this context, Hubmaier criticized the weakness of Zwingli's interpretation of sacrament in a covenantal perspective. Unlike Zwingli, he acknowledged the traditional concept of original sin—that we are conceived and born in sin so that there is no good in us.[105] He clearly denied Zwingli's understanding of original sin as a weakness or lack, but regarded original sin as the matrix and root of all sins, by and through which those who are not in Christ, and who follow the flesh, will be damned.[106] He even asserted that Zwingli's defense for infant baptism will lead people to misunderstand the concept of original sin in human beings.[107] If one depends on an argument regarding the issue that is not biblically grounded, he maintained, it could encourage further misinterpretations of the Bible. In other words, for Hubmaier, Zwingli's views on infant baptism and

---

102. ZL 2:21.
103. McGrath, *Reformation Thought*, 163.
104. Walton, "Reformation at Zurich," 497–515.
105. HS 158; YP 144.
106. HS 473; YP 540.
107. HS 263–64; YP 284–85.

original sin are both unbiblical and incorrect.[108] In this sense, Hubmaier found himself at total odds with Zwingli, in that he accepted original sin in humans, but denied the necessity and effectiveness of infant baptism.

However, Hubmaier's premise that infant baptism is not biblical, but original sin is biblical might be problematic for his efforts to explain the relation between the two concepts. Traditionally, the relationship between original sin and infant baptism has been understood through the transactional perspective of the efficacy of the sacraments to mediate redemption from sin. Any question about the justification of infant baptism must consider the issue of original sin. Using a transactional objective approach one (original sin) is a cause, and then the other (the necessity for infant baptism) is a result. Those who support infant baptism accept the existence of original sin, because infant baptism can remit original sin in infants. On the other hand, those who ignore infant baptism do not acknowledge original sin, because the infant does not have any sin which needs to be remitted. In other words, the traditional view of the relation between original sin and infant baptism is understood in the transactional and objective perspective on soteriology. This premise that one element is subordinate to the other means that either could be manipulated to defend a given perspective. In any case, this position lends itself to a primarily philosophical interpretation, rather than a biblical one.

Hubmaier's denial of the traditional approach towards interpreting the relationship between original sin and infant baptism is based on his principle of Biblicism—what is not commanded in Scripture is already forbidden in those matters; as such, infant baptism is not biblical.[109] Moreover, given his conviction that whatever the Scripture says is right, original sin which is obviously indicated in Scripture should be accepted.[110] It could be easier for him to show evidence for justifying each issue if he dealt with them separately. However, if he understood the relation between original sin and infant baptism in the traditional way, with a transactional perspective of soteriology, it would be difficult for him to defend himself against criticisms from either the Augustinian side or the Pelagian side. Hubmaier's theology needs to demonstrate an understanding of the relation between original sin and infant baptism as an explanation of how the place of baptism in the salvation of infants is understood.

---

108. HS 263; YP 285.
109. HS 261; YP 250.
110. HS 473; YP 540.

Balthasar Hubmaier's Doctrine of Salvation

For Hubmaier, it is clear that the salvation of infants cannot be affected by the practice of infant baptism. As we have seen, for him, baptism itself does not contain any efficacy of forgiveness of sin. Rather it has meaning when the one who repents sins and confesses faith is baptized as he wrote here:

> For that reason water baptism is called a baptism in *remissionem peccatorum*, Acts 2:38, that is, in forgiveness of sins. It is not that only through it or in it sin is forgiven, but by the power of the internal "Yes" in the heart, which the person proclaims publicly in the reception of water baptism, that he believes and is already sure in his heart of the remission of sins through Jesus Christ.[111]

From this passage, MacGregor argued that Hubmaier held on to his position in the Catholic tradition because he described infant baptism as an initial sign in the forgiveness of sin.[112] However, MacGregor, who wanted to show a strong relation between Catholic tradition and Hubmaier's theology, has misrepresented Hubmaier's argument by replacing "water baptism" with "infant baptism" from Hubmaier's original text.[113] Hubmaier clearly distinguished his understanding of baptism from the Catholic view of sacraments, *ex opere operato*, that the transactional transformation of man is effected through the external rites of the church.[114] Even though he emphasized the significance of baptism for those who believe in Jesus Christ as their Lord and Savior, it was on the basis of the command of Christ which indicated the institution of baptism for believers.[115] Hubmaier's refusal to follow the traditional Catholic view of baptism (or other sacraments) led him to deny the assumption that infant baptism is related to infant salvation. In this sense, for Hubmaier, there is no reason to practice infant baptism for remitting original sin.

As previously indicated, Hubmaier's definition of baptism is based on the premise of individual faith before the candidate is baptized. He

---

111. HS 137; YP 118.

112. MacGregor, *Radical and Magisterial Reform*, 95.

113. HS 137; YP 118: "Auß dem grundt würdt der *wasser tauff* genent ein tauff in remissionem peccatorum, Actorum am ij. cap. [V. 38], das ist in verzeyhung der sünden. Nit, das durch jn oder inn jm die sünde erst verzigen werden, sonder inn krafft des innwendigen Ja im hertzen, das der mensch offenlich bezeügt mit empfahung des wasser taufß, das er glaube vnd gwiß sey schon im hertzen der nachlassung seiner sünden durch Jhesum Christum, ..." (Hubmaier, *Von der christlichen Taufe*).

114. Steinmetz, "Scholasticism," 128.

115. HS 174; YP 178, HS 196; YP 208, HS 318; YP 355, HS 350; YP 389.

asserted that baptism is not remitting sin, but a public testimony of internal faith commitment.[116] In other words, the ceremony of baptism itself is meaningless unless one is ready to confess faith and to commit to living according to the Rule of Christ. According to Hubmaier, those who are unable to confess their own faith with knowledge of God through hearing the Word of God are unqualified for baptism, because Christ commanded that only those who have been instructed in faith should be baptized.[117] In this sense, infant baptism is only a human device and is against the will of God. His accent on faith as the essential element for baptism is an argument not only against the Catholic stance on baptism, but also against those who baptize infants in the supposition of a future faith. Like Zwingli, those who refuse an *ex opere operato* theology, but want to defend the practice of infant baptism, tend to replace a future faith with faith for infant baptism. However, Hubmaier showed a strong objection against this assumption in *Von der christlichen Taufe* as shown in this passage:

> But that one alleges to baptize infants on the grounds of a future faith is really a mocking casuistry, for under no circumstances was that the institution of Christ. He says, "Teach all nations, and then baptize them in the name of the Father, and the Son, and the Holy Spirit." One does not know whether at a later time it will be the will of the child or not. It is the same thing to baptize infants for a future faith as to hang up a barrel hoop at Easter in hope of future wine which is not to be casked until fall, and of which one does not know whether it will be ruined beforehand by hail, hoar frost, or other kinds.[118]

As we have seen in the discussion on the definition of faith in the previous chapter, the characteristic feature of faith for Hubmaier is that it is relational and subjective. He understood the concept of faith in the context of the present tense and as an expression of relationship. Baptism is not a sign of guaranteed faith or salvation. It is based on the conviction that faith is only meaningful in the present. As we have seen in the discussion on free will, Hubmaier's emphasis is always on the ongoing present moment as the place where relationship is expressed. He refused to be drawn into discussions about the status of past or future. This is also true in his discussions of baptism and faith.

---

116. HS 122; YP 100.
117. HS 140–41; YP 122.
118. HS 137; YP 118.

Balthasar Hubmaier's Doctrine of Salvation

Even though Hubmaier pointed out that nobody can be assured of an infant's future faith in Jesus Christ, the point is not simply that Hubmaier rejected the dependence on something as uncertain as the infant's future faith. Rather the point is his emphasis on the significance of faith which should be applied to baptism in the present time, "here" and "now." So Hubmaier said:

> Immelen: We have it that God loves children and that they have the promise. Why then should one not baptize them?
>
> Balthasar: Well then, let God love the children, still you have not proved that one should baptize them. For baptismal Scriptures do not apply to them but to those who *now* believe and confess their faith orally.[119]

For Hubmaier, baptism itself can be meaningful only when one repents sin and confesses faith before other believers. If the one who wants to be baptized does not have faith, baptism cannot be administered despite what a person did in the past or will do in the future in terms of faith. In his understanding of faith which focuses on the present time, a theology of infant baptism that is based on the supposed ground of future faith cannot be accepted. Consequently, Hubmaier showed the invalidity of infant baptism both by denying the efficacy of the sacrament for the remitting of original sin and by defining faith as something which has reality only as a present relationship.

Hubmaier's assertion about the necessity of faith for baptism and the rejection of the efficacy of sacrament for remitting sin seems to be similar to the views of other Anabaptists, although his understanding of faith is different. However, this different view of original sin requires another look at the issue of the relationship between original sin and an infant's salvation. Hubmaier insisted that original sin, which is indicated in the Bible, is the cause of human damnation and as such infants would be condemned.[120] Even so, he also presented an opposite opinion that God: "can save the infants very well by grace since they know neither good nor evil."[121] Pipkin asserted that the two totally opposed concepts of infant salvation are based on Hubmaier's pastoral concerns.[122] In other words, although Hubmaier believed on the basis of Scripture that infants would be damned

119. HS 264; YP 286.
120. HS 154–55; YP 139–40.
121. HS 155; YP 140.
122. Pipkin, "Baptismal Theology," 41.

as a result of original sin, he was open to a possibility of infant salvation as a result of God's grace because of his pastoral concern for believers who have children. If Pipkin's assumption that Hubmaier's conclusion about infants' salvation was led by his pastoral concern rather than his biblical conviction is correct, why then did he not accept infant baptism? For Hubmaier, it is impossible to admit both the practice of infant baptism and the denial of original sin in his biblical understanding, because giving up one to choose the other is wrong. His concern about the salvation of infants is not based on the transactional perspective. Salvation depends neither on baptism nor on works of mercy. "Being unbaptized does not condemn us, nor do evil works, but only unfaith."[123] For Hubmaier, we do not know whether an infant has faith or not, only God knows. That is the reason for Hubmaier arguing that the issue of infant salvation belongs to the sovereignty of God, despite his conclusion that infants are damned by original sin.[124] Therefore, Hubmaier's conclusion about this issue of the relationship between original sin and infant baptism is, I suggest, not led by his pastoral concern, but it is based on his refusing the transactional approach on this issue. The matter of infant salvation cannot be understood as our concern, but is better left to the providence of God. As an answer to the question about infant salvation within the issue of infant baptism and original sin, Hubmaier wrote:

> Third, I confess here publicly my ignorance. I am not ashamed not to know what God did not want to reveal to us with a clear and plain word. He said to me as he said to Peter, "What business is it of yours, as to what I will to do with infants? Follow me, look to my Word and will," John 21:22. But yet I will humbly and earnestly beseech him that he be a merciful Father to them. I commit this into his hands. His will be done. With this I will leave it. For if he does not want it to be done, then even if on a thousand times, it would still not help because water does not save.[125]

Hubmaier insisted that whether infants are saved or condemned is not related to the issue of baptism. Rather, he encouraged people to examine for themselves whether they are ready to follow the command of Christ now. The meaning of baptism is important to us when we recognize the

---

123. HS 183; YP 191.
124. HS 154–55; YP 139–40.
125. HS 155; YP 140–41.

Word and will of God, but it is meaningless when it applies to future faith for infants.

3. Hubmaier's Understanding of Baptism in Dynamic and Relational Perspective

As we have seen in the previous chapter, the most useful method for understanding Hubmaier's doctrine of faith is to see his definition of faith as relational and subjective. Traditionally, the issue of human salvation has been interpreted by an objective and transactional perspective which leads to the danger of a fatalistic belief in achieving salvation by divine will. However, Hubmaier's understanding of faith as the relationship between God and human beings in relational perspective is helpful to escape from the danger of a fatalistic belief. Hubmaier's understanding of baptism, which stands on the concept of faith, needs to be understood relationally in the same way as the meaning of faith. Although he sometimes borrowed phrases or concepts from the Catholic tradition or the Protestant reformers to defend his theology on baptism, he never accepted their theories on baptism for his doctrine of baptism. Instead, he used them in different ways to develop his own understanding of baptism. Therefore, it is difficult to say that Hubmaier's doctrine of baptism was influenced primarily by the Catholic tradition or by Anabaptism or other Protestant traditions. Rather, we can see that all three different views on baptism co-exist together in his writings. Thus we need to understand Hubmaier's concept of baptism from his own texts as they stand, rather than trying to fit them into other people's positions. Hubmaier's understanding of baptism does not belong to any one traditional view of baptism and needs to be understood on its own terms.

As we have seen in the previous section, the characteristic feature of his baptismal theology is shown in his argument about the meaning of the baptisms of John and of Christ against Zwingli's defense for justifying infant baptism. Although his external structure in arguing for two baptisms is similar to a Catholic approach, his main concern in this argument is to show that the difference between the baptisms of John and of Christ is not dependent on the exercising of outward forms of baptism, but on what kind of relationship exists between the baptizand and the witnesses through baptism. His emphasis on the significance of the relationship between baptizand and the witnesses in Christ's baptism shows that the meaning of baptism needs to be understood in relational perspective. This relational perspective on baptism from the issue of the baptisms of John and of Christ seems to be solid and expanded in his doctrine of threefold baptism. Hubmaier's phrase "the forgiveness of sins" with respect to the baptism of Christ does not clearly show how it is different from the Catholic tradition. His intention to use the phrase "the forgiveness of sins" for the baptism of Christ can be understood clearly when it is linked with his concept of threefold baptism.

For Hubmaier, the baptism of the Spirit, which is the premise of the other two baptisms, is explained through his emphasis on the active side of faith by human beings and on the importance for the concept of faith of the relationship between God and human beings. The baptism of the Spirit means not only a one-sided event on the initiative of God, but also the voluntary will of humans to obey God. For him, the baptism of the Spirit is the starting point of faith and is also a new relationship between God and human beings. However, he distinguished his concept of the Spirit baptism from Luther's concept of justification by faith which he believed led to a compromised immorality. The baptism of the Spirit is the starting point of new life, but not the completion of salvific process. In this respect, for Hubmaier, there is a new relationship between the baptizand and other believers through water baptism for following together the Rule of Christ. Hubmaier's relational perspective of water baptism is clearly shown in his baptismal liturgy *Eine Form zu taufen*.

> After the church has completed his prayer, the bishop lays his hands on the head of the new member and says:
>
> "I testify to you and give you authority that henceforth you shall be counted among the Christian community, as a member participating in the use of her keys, breaking bread and praying with other Christian sisters and brothers. God be with you and your spirit. Amen."[126]

Hubmaier asserted that the baptizand is counted as a member of church, and started a new relationship with other Christians in the church after water baptism. Using this relational perspective, we can understand why Hubmaier distinguished the baptism of Christ, which is the forgiveness of sins, from the baptism of John, which is the repentance of sins. The meaning of the baptism of blood for Hubmaier is also understood relationally between believers and the world. God never commands His people to leave the world in order to keep their faith, rather He asks them to live

---

126. HS 350; YP 389.

in the world as true Christians who follow Christ by obeying the Rule of Christ. Christian life in the world involves trials and suffering, but God's Will will be done through them.

Through the difference between the baptisms of John and of Christ and his understanding of baptism as threefold, Hubmaier showed that baptism is not regarded as a sacrament in the way of traditional theology, but as a means to make a new relationship between God and human beings, between the believer and other believers, and between the community of believers and the world. The meaning of baptism that requires personal faith cannot be separated from the meaning of salvation which emphasizes the relation perspective. Therefore, for Hubmaier, baptism is an essential element in explaining the meaning of salvation in terms of relational perspective.

4. Conclusion

Hubmaier's doctrine of baptism must be understood in terms of his understanding of faith which is his premise for baptism. His basic view of salvation, similar to that of other contemporary reformers, is that we are saved only by faith. Therefore, the concept of faith is the most important element to explain the doctrine of salvation. But his theology of the concept of faith refers not to the passive understanding where faith is given or infused by God nor does it refer to the assumption that a human being can have faith by himself or herself, but rather it means the formation of the personal relationship between God and the human being. Although Hubmaier avoided the transactional question as to who initiates the process of salvation between God and human beings, he stressed the current conditions of a believer's relationship with God. From this point of view, as we saw in the previous chapter, Hubmaier's concept of faith needs to be understood in a subjective and relational perspective and is directly related to his doctrine of salvation in order to sustain the contemporary motto for the Reformation, "justification by faith." In other words, unless there is a paradigm shift from a transactional and objective perspective to the relational and subjective perspective in understanding Hubmaier's concept of faith, there will be misunderstanding of his doctrine of salvation.

Hubmaier's premise that faith is a prerequisite for baptism also means that his doctrine of salvation must be linked with his concept of a baptism which requires faith before its administration. In this sense, the doctrine of baptism must be regarded as the essential element for understanding

Hubmaier's soteriology. If Hubmaier has a unique explanation of faith for salvation, he will apply his understanding of the concept of faith to his doctrine of baptism. In other words, if we need a new perspective to see Hubmaier's concept of faith for the understanding of his soteriology, his doctrine of baptism can also be understood using the same methodology. A new perspective on the Hubmaier methodology pertaining to his concept of faith via a dynamic and relational perspective helps us to understand how he refuses the concept of contemporary views of baptism as an instrument for sacramental efficacy by Catholicism and as a sign of covenant between God and the baptizand by Zwingli.

Hubmaier's relational perspective on baptism is shown in his distinction of two baptisms, the baptism of John and the baptism of Christ. For Hubmaier, the difference between two baptisms is not only based on the functional existence of the forgiveness of sins, but the existence of a new relationship with others. Furthermore, the concept of baptism is explained as a relationship between God and a baptizand or between believers and a baptizand or between the world and a baptizand in the relational perspective. His understanding of baptism in a relational perspective can also be explained in three categories: the baptism of the Spirit as the relationship with God, the baptism of water as the relationship with other believers, the baptism of blood as the relationship with the world.

Moreover, the threefold baptism that is developed with the concept of faith is linked with the procedure of salvation which suggests that the baptism of the Spirit is the starting point of salvation but the baptisms of water and of blood are ongoing processes of salvation through the life of faith. His emphasis on the significance of the ongoing process of salvation in his concept of water baptism and of blood baptism is related to his relational perspective which focuses on the present context of the believer's life for his soteriology. His emphasis on the baptizand's confession for water baptism in the present context could solve the difficulty in reconciling the fact that he refused the practice of infant baptism though he acknowledged original sin. Consequently, his concept of baptism has been shown in the relational perspective as his way of explaining the meaning of faith for salvation. Hubmaier's doctrine of salvation cannot be explained without understanding his doctrine of baptism as requiring faith as the essential element for his soteriology. But his accentuation on the ongoing process of salvation in the concept of baptism is developed more with his doctrine of the Lord's Supper, which is called a pledge of love. Therefore, in the next chapter I shall examine the significance of the Lord's Supper for his soteriology.

5

Hubmaier's Doctrine of the Lord's Supper

Introduction

As WE HAVE SEEN in the previous chapter, Hubmaier was most concerned with the issue of baptism—both the understanding of the sacrament and its practice. His emphasis on baptism as an important element for Christian life did not depend on the assumptions of medieval sacramentalism, but on his theology of the significance of faith, which he regarded as a prerequisite for baptism. For Hubmaier, the practice of water baptism, which is based on the believer's public confession of faith, is directly related to his understanding of the human will. From this point of view, his doctrine of baptism and the freedom of the human will are central to his concept of salvation. However, his refusal of the medieval sacramental perspective on baptism also means that his understanding of the Lord's Supper is different from that of the Catholic tradition. Hubmaier's program for church reform—as seen in Waldshut and Nikolsburg—always involved both the question of the practice of believers' baptism and of the Lord's Supper after believers' baptism.

If Hubmaier rejected the sacramental perspective of Catholic tradition for interpreting the Lord's Supper, what *does* the Lord's Supper mean for him, and why is it so significant for his doctrine of salvation? To answer these questions, I shall first survey Hubmaier's writings on the Lord's Supper in order to chart how his view of the Supper evolves. Secondly, I shall look at his methodology, and at what assumptions he makes for

Hubmaier's Doctrine of the Lord's Supper

developing his view of the Eucharist. To help in understanding his methodology, I shall also survey the background of the controversy over the Lord's Supper in his days. Thirdly, I shall present Hubmaier's unique understanding of the Lord's Supper in order to interpret his primary texts. In this way, I shall be in a position to suggest why Hubmaier had to insist on the necessity of fraternal admonition and Christian excommunication as being at the heart of his understanding of the meaning of the Lord's Supper in soteriological perspective.

1. Appearance of the Lord's Supper in Hubmaier's Writings

Hubmaier's concern with the issue of the Lord's Supper deepened after he became involved in the discussions at the second Zurich disputation (October 26–28, 1523) regarding the doctrine of the Mass and whether or not it should be understood as a sacrifice. His interest in the issue of the Lord's Supper appears in various writings, such as letters, theological treatises, the Catechism, and even apologia. For Hubmaier, the issue of the Lord's Supper is one of the most significant tasks for the reforming church with regard to the practice of believers' baptism. In his first published work, *Achtzehn Schlußreden* (1524), Hubmaier clearly rejected the stance of medieval Catholicism, affirming that the Mass is not a sacrifice and cannot be offered up for the living or for the dead, although he did not include any particular feature of Anabaptist theological thought about the doctrine of baptism.[1] At that time, his understanding of the Supper tended to follow the Zwinglian interpretation of it as a "memorial."[2] In his first writing as an Anabaptist, *Eine Summe eines ganzen christlichen Leben* (July 1525), a treatise attacking Catholic tradition, the Lord's Supper along with baptism was the main issue. He continued to reject the Catholic tradition's concept of the Supper as a re-presentation of Christ's sacrifice, but maintained its meaning as a memorial of Christ's suffering.[3] The significance of the Lord's Supper for Hubmaier is also seen in his *Eine christliche Lehrtafel*, which, as we have seen earlier, contains what he considered the basic and

---

1. HS 73; YP 32.

2. Bergsten, *Balthasar Hubmaier*, 211–12. Cf. Bergsten and Estep, *Theologian and Martyr*, 156. Hubmaier's early concept of the Lord's Supper was influenced not only by Zwingli but also by Karlstadt. Their influence is clearly shown in Hubmaier's *Etliche Schlußreden vom Unterricht der Messe*.

3. HS 114; YP 88.

most important doctrines of Christianity for believers. In his catechism, Hubmaier dealt with the issue of the Lord's Supper as the beginning of the second part of the dialogue after the issue of baptism. In contrast to previous accounts of the Lord's Supper, he focused on its meaning as a public sign of the obligation to brotherly love, rather than criticizing the Catholic theology of the Mass as offering Christ's sacrifice.[4]

a. Etliche Schlußreden vom Unterricht der Messe

Although most of his writings on the Lord's Supper include the issue of baptism, there are three specific treatises which Hubmaier devoted to a study of the Lord's Supper: *Etliche Schlußreden vom Unterricht der Messe, Ein einfältiger Unterricht,* and *Eine Form des Nachtmahls Christi.* Hubmaier's early understanding of the Lord's Supper is shown in his first treatise on the Eucharist, *Etliche Schlußreden vom Unterricht der Messe* (January 1525), after the Second Zurich Disputation. Here Hubmaier, as a supporter of Zwingli, spoke publicly in favor of raising the question of the mass, disputing Catholic doctrine.[5] In this early treatise, Hubmaier showed his rejection of the mass and preferred the concept of the Lord's Supper as a "remembrance" (*Wiedergedächtnisor*) or "memorial" which was suggested by Karlstadt who also influenced by Zwingli.[6] Moreover, his interpretation of the word "body" in the phrase "this is my body given for you," as meaning the *physical* body of Christ at the Last Supper, not the bread on the table, is influenced by Karlstadt.[7] Hubmaier's intention in this treatise was to insist that the Lord's Supper is a commemoration of, rather than the actual presence of, the suffering of Christ and also the proclamation of his death until he comes.[8] Although he rejected the Catholic tradition of the sacrificial presence, Hubmaier emphasized the significance of believers gathering for the Supper.[9] However, this treatise did not contain a detailed explanation of the Lord's Supper by expositing the meaning of Christ's words in the institution of the Eucharist.[10]

4. HS 317–18; YP 354–55.
5. Sachsse, *Hubmaier Als Theologe*, 13. Cf. YP 73.
6. Bergsten, *Balthasar Hubmaier*, 259.
7. Ibid. Cf. HS 102; YP 75.
8. Windhorst, "Abendmahls Bei Balthasar Hubmaier," 122.
9. HS 103; YP 75.
10. YP 74.

b. Ein einfältiger Unterricht

Hubmaier's second major writing on the Lord's Supper is *Ein einfältiger Unterricht*, which was written in late 1526 while he was reforming churches in Moravia. In this treatise, Hubmaier continued to deny the Catholic doctrine of transubstantiation, and further developed his doctrine of the Lord's Supper beyond *Etliche Schlußreden vom Unterricht der Messe*. He attempted to interpret the meaning of the Lord's Supper as memorial within his Christology and this position afforded the counter argument to the Catholic concept of Mass. Hubmaier believed that Jesus Christ was physically absent after his ascension from the earth until he comes again. As such, the bread of the Lord's Supper cannot be the real body of Christ since that is in heaven with His Father God.[11] In this Christology, he also differed from the Lutheran view of the Supper as the real presence of Christ.[12] For his argument against the rite of Mass in the Catholic tradition, Hubmaier presented many expositions of biblical texts including Matt 26:26ff., Mark 14:22ff., and 1 Cor 11:23ff., which he used to criticize it.[13] For instance, in his exposition of the biblical text "take" in Matt 26:26, as he explained:

> "Take": He gives to the disciples and not they to him. Therefore we have wrongly and without any basis made out of taking a giving and sacrificing. Here you see that the mass is not a sacrifice, for Christ did not say "sacrifice," but receive it from me.[14]

Even though he pointed out the weakness in the view of the Eucharist by Catholics, Lutherans and even Karlstadt in this treatise, there was no further explanation of the Lord's Supper as the pledge of love[15] in any practical way. This omission may be because Hubmaier was focused more on the theological issues concerning the Lord's Supper against transubstantiation or real presence of Christ, which was still an ongoing debate in Moravia at that time.

---

11. HS 293; YP 324.
12. HS 294–95; YP 325–26, YP 314.
13. Bergsten, *Balthasar Hubmaier*, 432. HS 297–301; YP 329–34.
14. HS 297–98; YP 330.
15. The phrase "pledge of love" is a part of Hubmaier's published liturgy and will be discussed later.

c. Eine Form des Nachtmahls Christi

Hubmaier completed his final writing about the Lord' Supper, *Eine Form des Nachtmahls Christi*, sometime during 1526–1527 in Nikolsburg. While Hubmaier had reformed the churches in Nikolsburg, he felt that there was still a need to restructure congregational life and practice in the church community. This liturgy was an extension of Hubmaier's catechetic instruction with his *Eine Form zu taufen* after his catechism, *Eine christliche Lehrtafel*, for church members. Hubmaier also wrote two other booklets, *Von der brüderlichen Strafe* and *Von dem christlichen Bann*, in which he asserted the necessity of fraternal admonition and of excommunication for the correction of errant church members. For Hubmaier, the true meaning of both water baptism and the Lord's Supper imply the believer's obligation to live according to the Rule of Christ. In this context, his purpose was very different from his previous writing *Ein einfältiger Unterricht*, which focused on pointing out the falseness of other views of the Supper. Thus, although this liturgy did not deal much with the theological debates about the Supper, Hubmaier explained the meaning of the Lord's Supper and the significance of its practice by an easily accessible biblical account.

2. Hubmaier's Methodology in the Doctrine of the Lord's Supper

Hubmaier continued to depend explicitly upon the Bible text itself to support his doctrine of the Lord's Supper, as he did for believers' baptism. As far as he was concerned, the most important issues for the church reform program in Waldshut and Nikolsburg were to redefine the meaning of baptism and the Eucharist, not only against Catholic tradition, but also against the magisterial reformers. Hubmaier defended his convictions concerning infant baptism by utilizing direct evidence from biblical texts and raising the question of whether infant baptism is based on the Bible. However, although Hubmaier's writings on the Supper were also supported by the biblical texts, his main counterargument against other views depended more on the hermeneutical assumptions related to his Christology. In order to reform the ceremony of the Lord's Supper, in contrast to the practice of the Catholic Mass, Hubmaier had to argue against two essentials of the traditional thinking: whether the interpretation of Mass as an offering of Christ's sacrifice was biblical; and, how to interpret the phrase of Jesus' words at the Last Supper, "This is my body." Hubmaier insisted that those who partake in the Lord's Supper are qualified only after their public confession of faith through water baptism. In this prerequisite for the Supper, Hubmaier showed how his view of the Supper is distinct from that of the Catholics and Luther and Zwingli, who allowed people to take part in the Lord's Supper without reverence and hearts desiring the grace of a believers' baptism.[16] Therefore, his Christology and the prerequisite of water baptism before the Lord's Supper are significant elements for understanding his doctrine of the Lord's Supper. To survey the background of the contemporary controversy on the issue of the Lord's Supper, it will be helpful to understand Hubmaier's methodology for his Eucharistic thoughts.

a. Background of Controversy on the Lord's Supper in Hubmaier's Day

Controversy in the early Reformation era was not only concerning the doctrine of baptism but also the Lord's Supper, which was much contested even among the Reformers who agreed on much else. In particular, there was conflict between two representative reformers, Luther and Zwingli, who both supported infant baptism and rejected believers' baptism. Although the distinction between mainline reformers and radical reformers tended to depend on the issue of how to understand and exercise baptism, the issue of the Lord's Supper split the mainline reformers. In particular, there was disagreement over how to interpret the phrase, "This is my body," in the Scripture for the rite of the Eucharist. Tracing the different interpretations for the Lord's Supper in Hubmaier's day will help us to understand more fully Hubmaier's notion of the Lord's Supper.

i. Catholic Tradition of the Eucharist

During the Reformation, the traditional theology and practice of Eucharist was attacked by the protestant reformers. In particular, the reformers opposed the doctrine that the priest participates in the sacrifice of the body and blood of Christ, and the doctrine of transubstantiation. The medieval theologians understood that sacrifice literally means "to consecrate" or "to make holy" and taught that consecration in the Eucharist transformed the bread and wine as the gifts of the church into the body and blood of

---

16. HS 364; YP 407. Cf. MacGregor, *Radical and Magisterial Reform*, 181.

Balthasar Hubmaier's Doctrine of Salvation

Christ, which convey to the partakers the grace of Christ's atoning sacrifice on the cross.[17] The significance of the Mass as a sacrifice of Christ was affirmed by Peter Lombard in his *Sentences* that: "From the these passages we gather that what is done at the altar both is called and is a sacrifice, and that Christ was offered once and is offered daily, but in a different manner then and now."[18] Moreover, Thomas Aquinas asserted that the Mass is "the reactualization of the sacrifice of Christ."[19] In this sense, the same benefits gained in the atoning sacrifice are actually conveyed to the recipients through the sacrament, and the elements are the means of this conveying.[20]

This theology of the Mass as a sacrifice of Christ could not be understood apart from the notion of the nature of the bread and wine for the Eucharist in Catholic tradition. Although there had been controversy among the theologians with regard to the definition of the character of the bread and wine in the rite of the Eucharist, the doctrine of transubstantiation was formally affirmed by the Fourth Lateran council in 1215, as stated:

> There is one universal church of the faithful, outside of which no one is saved. In this church Jesus Christ Himself is priest and sacrifice, whose body and blood are truly contained in the Sacrament of the Altar under the species of bread and wine, the bread having been transubstantiated into the body, and the wine into the blood by divine power.[21]

Here, the concept of transubstantiation was founded upon Aristotle's distinction between "substance" and "accident" though the term "accident" was not used at all.[22] The "substance" of something is its essential nature as true reality, whereas its "accidents" are its perceptible characteristics such as its color, smell and so forth.[23] This use of the Aristotelian notions of "substance" and "accidents" to explain the nature of bread and wine for the Lord's Supper was made clear by Thomas Aquinas. According to Thomas Aquinas, although the accidents of the bread and wine (their outward

---

17. Senn, *Christian Liturgy*, 253.

18. Peter Lombard, *IV Sent.* d. 12 c. 5. Cited in Senn, *Christian Liturgy*, 254.

19. Thomas Aquinas, *ST* III. q. 83. a. 1. "Celebratio autem huius sacrament I . . . est imago quaedam est repraesentative passionis Christi quae est vera ejus immolation." Cf. Senn, *Christian Liturgy*, 254.

20. Senn, *Christian Liturgy*, 255.

21. Denzinger and Schönmetzer, eds., *Enchiridion Symbolorum*, 430. Cited in Senn, *Christian Liturgy*, 251.

22. Senn, *Christian Liturgy*, 250.

23. McGrath, *Christian Theology*, 512.

characteristics, taste, smell and shape) remain unchanged at the moment of consecration, the substance of the bread and wine is changed into that of the body and blood of Christ.[24] While we are sharing the bread and wine in the rite of the Eucharist, Christ is truly present so that we partake of the body and blood of Christ by means of this bread and wine without the change of physical accidents of the bread and wine.[25] From this point of view, the bread and wine for the Supper are the real body and blood of Christ through the consecration in the rite of Eucharist.

However, this doctrine of transubstantiation brought some results which the Reformers deplored. If the bread and wine for the Eucharist were in substance transformed into the body and blood of Christ at the consecration, it is natural that the elements which convey the grace of God should be adored and worshipped. While attendance at Mass could be seen as a virtuous practice for a good Christian in Catholic tradition, the Reformers feared that it would lead to gross superstition and idolatry.

ii. Luther's Concept of the Lord's Supper

Luther attacked Catholic tradition concerning the Mass in order to deny that the Mass is a good work and a sacrifice.[26] This meant that Luther rejected not only that the Mass is offered to God as a good work which merits God's favor, but also that the Mass is offered to God as a sacrifice.[27] If the Mass is understood as a good work of human acting for God's favor, it was not acceptable in terms of his doctrine of salvation as justification by faith alone. For Luther, when the Mass is used as a form of work-righteousness it becomes a way of ignoring the work of Christ.[28] Moreover, Luther's objection to the Mass being called a sacrifice was based on his understanding of sacrament that "the sacrament itself is not an offering, but is a gift of God."[29] Accordingly, for Luther, "the consecrated elements cannot be offered to God because they are the gift of God to the people."[30] In this sense, for Luther, the doctrine of transubstantiation for the Supper seemed to be an absurdity. As Luther wrote:

24. Thomas Aquinas, *ST* III qq. 75–77. McGrath, *Christian Theology*, 512.
25. Colwell, *Promise and Presence*, 164.
26. LW 36:35.
27. Senn, *Christian Liturgy*, 271.
28. WA 15:776.24–25.
29. WA 30/2:614.23.
30. Senn, *Christian Liturgy*, 272.

> Therefore it is an absurd and unheard-of juggling with words to understand "bread" to mean "the form or accidents of bread," and "wine" to mean "the form or accidents of wine." Why do they not also understand all other things to mean their "forms or accident"? And even if this might be done with all other things, it would still not be right to enfeeble the words of God in this way, and by depriving them of their meaning to cause so much them.[31]

Here Luther clearly rejected the Thomistic idea of a change in the substance of the elements while accidents remain, which had been the basis of the doctrine of the Supper for the last three hundreds years in Catholic tradition. But it does not mean that he denied the real presence of Christ in the rite of the Eucharist. Rather he accepted the phrase "This is my body" and "This is my blood" literally. Concerning this issue of the Real Presence, he was convinced that the words of Scripture in themselves compelled him to take this position. He argued that what was true of Christ's nature was also true of the sacramental nature of the elements.[32]

> What is true concerning Christ is also true concerning the sacrament. In order for the divinity to dwell in a human body, it is not necessary for the human nature to be transubstantiated and the divinity contained under the accidents of human nature. Both natures are simply there in their entirety, and it is true to say: "This man is God; this God is man." Even though philosophy is not capable of grasping this, faith is. And the authority of God's Word is greater than the capacity of our intellect to grasp it. In the same way, it is not necessary in the sacrament that the bread and wine be transubstantiated and that Christ be contained under their accidents in order that the real body and real blood may be present. But both remain there at the same time, and it is truly said: "This bread is my body; this wine is my blood," and vice versa.[33]

His understanding of the real presence of the Lord's Supper should be distinguished from the doctrine of transubstantiation. For Luther, to believe the fact itself that Christ is bodily present in the Lord's Supper and that his body is received by all who partake of the bread and wine is more important than any particular theory or explanation, even though we do not see the real presence of Christ in the Eucharist. In this sense, the elements of

31. LW 36:31.
32. Althasus, *Theology of Luther*, 383.
33. WA 30/2:509.22–512.4.

bread and wine themselves cannot be become materials of superstition or idolatry. Although Luther rejected transubstantiation, he was unwilling to abandon the conviction of Christ's objective presence. In order to make the difference between the traditional theology and his new understanding clear, he needed a different way to explain this presence. He did this through the theology of the Real Presence—Christ's presence in, with and under the consecrated elements.

However, there was another obstacle to his defense of the doctrine of the Real Presence through the doctrine of consubstantiation. If Christ is really present in the rite of the Eucharist, then how can the nature of Christ be understood after His ascension? In addressing this question, Luther stated that:

> We teach not that the body and blood of Christ are visibly present in external things, but that they are hidden in the sacrament. Nor do we say that he is and must be in particular places and is not free to be in all. Rather we claim that he and the bread and wine are and must be free in regard to all localities, places, times, and persons.[34]

Here Luther's notion of the Real Presence of Christ in the Supper seems to accept the ubiquity of Christ even after His ascension in terms of the Word-Flesh Christology, which focused on the explicit Johannine portrayal of Christ's deity and implicit portrayal of His humanity, where the "Word became the flesh." This had become understood according to "the Platonic concept of man as a body animated by a soul or spirit, which was essentially alien from it."[35] Moreover, this view of the incarnation as the union of the Word with human flesh could mean that there was "no allowance for a human soul in Christ."[36] Although the Word was incarnated as a human by taking flesh, He does not become different, but remains the same in that He continued to exercise sovereignty over the universe.[37] This view postulated the doctrine of the *communicatio idiomatum* (communication of attributes) that "the human nature of Christ partakes of the divine attributes without either losing its own '*idiomata*' or conferring human, finite '*idiomata*' upon the divine nature."[38] In other words, as MacGregor pointed out, "every necessary attribute of the divine Word before

34. LW 40:221.
35. Kelly, *Early Christian Doctrines*, 281.
36. Ibid.
37. Ibid., 284.
38. Muller, *Latin and Greek*, 73.

the incarnation, such as omniscience, omnipotence, and omnipresence or ubiquity, are transferred to human nature of Jesus."[39] Accordingly, the human Jesus can be present everywhere without time and space barriers.[40] In this sense, Luther could assert the doctrine of the Real Presence of Christ in the Lord's Supper.

iii. Zwingli's Concept of the Lord's Supper

Zwingli was one of the main opponents of Luther's view on the Supper and criticized the doctrine of the Real Presence. His understanding of the nature of the Lord's Supper was based on the memorial of the suffering and death of Christ but refused the concept of offering a sacrifice in the Catholic tradition. This memorialist theology of the Supper by Zwingli was developed in his different interpretation of the phrase "This is my body," which was accepted literally by Luther and Catholic theologians. Zwingli believed that if we understand the word "is" literally in the Scripture, this would create many problems of misinterpretation.[41] For instance, if we interpret the words of Christ "I am the vine" literally, then Christ must be a real vine. This speech of Christ should be understood figuratively rather than literally. For Zwingli this figurative and symbolic understanding of the speech of Christ ought to be applied to the phrase "This is my body." "This" [the bread] should be regarded as a symbol or figure of Christ's body for the memory of Christ's suffering and death for us. So Zwingli asserted that:

> Therefore the word "is" cannot be taken literally, for the bread is not the body and cannot be, as we have seen already. Necessarily, then, it must be taken figuratively or metaphorically; "This is my body," means, "The bread signifies my body," or "is a figure of my body." For immediately afterwards in Luke 22 Christ adds: "This do in remembrance of me," from which it follows that the bread is only a figure of his body to remind us in the Supper that the body was crucified for us.[42]

In this way of interpreting the phrase "This is my body," Zwingli criticized not only transubstantiation but also Luther's doctrine of consubstantiation

---

39. MacGregor, *Radical and Magisterial Reform*, 185.
40. Frank, *Work of Christ*, 291.
41. ZB 189–90.
42. ZB 225.

Hubmaier's Doctrine of the Lord's Supper

teaching that somehow Christ is corporeally in, under, and with the element.[43]

However, Zwingli's notion of memorialism is based on his understanding that the divine and human nature of Christ should be considered separately in thinking about the Lord's Supper. For Zwingli Christ's divine nature is omnipresent and ubiquitous but it did not mean that Christ's human nature is also.[44] In contrast with Luther, Zwingli's understanding of Christ's nature seems to follow Word-Man Christology, which is focused on the humanity of Jesus where "the Word united Himself with a complete human being, including not only a visible body but also a particular soul." This approach to Christology draws on "the Aristotelian theory of man as a psycho-physical unity."[45] Accordingly, the nature of Jesus is first considered as a human person, and then His divinity is explained through it. Here, Jesus as fully human must be limited in knowledge, power, and presence although He is also the divine One.[46] Word-Man Christology refused any attribution of Christ's divinity to His human nature.[47] Thus, the issue of the real, or corporeal, presence of Christ in the Lord's Supper must be understood differently from Word-Flesh Christology which was used by Luther. After Jesus' ascension, His physical presence was not possible on earth, because He was seated at the right hand of the Father God until He comes again. In this sense, Zwingli could assert that:

> The flesh may fume, but the words of Christ stand firm: he sits at the right hand of the Father, he has left the world, he is no longer present with us. And if these words are true, it is impossible to maintain that his flesh and blood are present in the sacrament.[48]
> ... The fact that he is wherever he wills does not mean that he is everywhere at once. For in the body he does not will to be anywhere except at the right hand of the Father.[49]

Therefore, through this understanding of the human nature of Christ in a Word-Man Christological perspective, Zwingli could attack both the Catholic and Luther's assertion of the doctrine of the real presence of Christ for the Lord's Supper.

43. Osterhaven, "Lord's Supper," 655.
44. ZB 212.
45. Kelly, *Early Christian Doctrines*, 281.
46. MacGregor, *Radical and Magisterial Reform*, 185.
47. Pelikan, *Reformation of Church*, 157–59.
48. ZB 214–15.
49. ZB 218.

b. Hubmaier's Christology and the Lord's Supper

As already mentioned, one of the most significant concepts for the understanding of the doctrine of the Lord's Supper is how to understand the issue of the real presence of Christ within the rite of the Eucharist. The Catholic doctrine of transubstantiation and the Lutheran doctrine of the Real Presence, demonstrate the Christology underlying each. Hubmaier's distinctive response to the doctrine of the real presence of Christ in the Lord's Supper and his Christology are essential elements for understanding his doctrines.

Hubmaier's doctrine of the Supper seems to depend more on the Word-Man Christology than the Word-Flesh Christology. It is shown in his *Eine Form des Nachtmahls Christi* that:

> Although the majority of people who stand by the gospel recognize that bread is bread and wine is wine in the Lord's Supper, and not Christ, Acts 1:9; Mark 16:19; Heb. 1:3; 12:2; Matt. 22:44; Ps. 110. For the same ascended into heaven and is sitting at the right hand of God his Father, whence he will come again to judge the living and the dead. Precisely that is our foundation, according to which we must deduce and exposit all of the Scriptures having to do with eating and drinking. Thus Christ cannot be eaten or drunk by us otherwise than spiritually and in faith. So then he cannot be bodily the bread either but rather in the memorial which is held, as he himself and Paul explained these Scriptures, Luke 22; 1 Cor. 11.[50]

In this text, Hubmaier clearly rejected the possibility of a real, or corporeal, presence of Christ in the ceremony of the Lord's Supper, adhering to the Word-Man Christological perspective on the nature of Christ. For Hubmaier, eating the bread and drinking the wine in the Lord's Supper does not mean that the partakers actually eat or drink the body and blood of Christ, because His physical body is still with the Father God in heaven after His ascension. Hubmaier's strict denial of the physical omnipresence or ubiquity of Jesus since His ascension is more clearly shown in *Von dem christlichen Bann*:

> For he is with who himself by his grace until the end of the world, Matt. 28:20, although bodily he has ascended into heaven where he sits at the right hand of his heavenly Father there in heaven, Mark 16:19; Acts 1:9. Yea, it was in heaven that Stephen

---

50. HS 364; YP 407.

saw him; there he sits bodily according to his humanity. He has a particular place "in heaven, in heaven" and not everywhere, as deity is omnipresent. Yea, neither in the bread nor in the wine nor in other creatures.[51]

This text suggests that Hubmaier's understanding of Christology is much closer to those reformers who adhere to Word-Man Christology such as Zwingli.[52]

Another characteristic feature of Hubmaier's doctrine of the Lord's Supper is that his Christology is related to the doctrine of the church. Although Hubmaier denied the real presence of Christ in the Supper, he insisted on the significance that Jesus Christ is still with His church until the end of the world, as exemplified through the communion with the body of Christ spiritually and in faith through the Supper.[53] Here, the communion with the body of Christ does not point to Jesus Christ who is the second person of Trinity, but rather points to those who believe in Jesus Christ as their Savior and commit themselves to Him:

> . . . although we present ourselves to be members of the church in the reception of this symbol, also to do the same for all those who with us are members of the body of Christ, which his church.[54]

For Hubmaier, it is clear that the body and blood of Christ in the Supper represent and are represented by the believers who are parts of the church as the body of Christ. Although the partaker in the Lord's Supper does not eat and drink Christ, he or she can nevertheless experience communion with Christ through other believers who are a part of Christ's body on earth. In this sense, Hubmaier could say that Christ is present with His church, although His physical body has been absent from earth since His ascension. This point seems to show that Hubmaier also acknowledges the nature of Jesus which is omnipresent, ubiquitous or universal through

---

51. HS 370; YP 414–15.

52. However, in spite of his observation of the trend in which the sixteenth-century contemporary theologians defend their eucharistic theology, MacGregor nevertheless classifies Hubmaier's position of the Supper into Word-Flesh Christology along with Catholics and Lutherans. This might be caused by his desire to reinforce the premise that Hubmaier's theology should be linked with Lutherans or Catholics who pursue sacramental significance. See MacGregor, *Radical and Magisterial Reform*, 184–85.

53. HS 103; YP 75.

54. HS 102; YP 74–75.

partakers in the Lord's Supper. Thus, there is a way in which Hubmaier can be seen as arguing for a theology of presence.

In sum, whether one classifies Christology as Word-Flesh or Word-Man is based on a transactional perspective, which stems from whether one accepts the real presence of Christ in the Supper (Word-Flesh Christology) or not (Word-Man Christology). However, Hubmaier's doctrine of Christology expressed in the Supper is not entirely either Word-Flesh or Word-Man Christology. Rather, it seems to contain both interpretations of Christology. Therefore, we need to find the reason why Hubmaier distinguished his doctrine of the Supper from Zwingli's view, where the bread and wine in the Lord's Supper is only symbolic or signifying. Hubmaier asserted that the bread and wine should not be accepted as a sign or symbol of the body and blood of Christ, but instead they must be the body and blood of Christ in remembrance.[55] Hubmaier thought that if the bread and wine in the Supper simply signified the body and blood of Christ, this might reduce the importance of the Lord's Supper, which was instituted by Christ for Christian life. Therefore, Hubmaier's compounded Christology in his doctrine of the Supper needs to be understood in subjective and relational perspective rather than in objective and transactional perspective and this will be discussed in the later part of this chapter.

c. Hubmaier's Prerequisite for the Lord's Supper

As we saw in the previous chapters, Hubmaier insisted that the precondition for baptism is that the one who wants to be baptized must confess before the congregation of believers his or her own faith, which comes from hearing the Word of God. As this prerequisite for baptism depends on his concept of faith, the prerequisite for the Lord's Supper can also be found within his concept of baptism. In *Eine christliche Lehrtafel*, Hubmaier defined the meaning of the Supper as follows:

> It is a public sign and testimonial of the love in which one brother obligates himself to another before the congregation that just as they now break and eat the bread with each other and share and drink the cup, likewise they wish now to sacrifice and shed their body and blood for one another; this they will do in the strength of our Lord Jesus Christ, whose suffering they are now commemorating in the Supper with the breaking of bread and the sharing of the wine, and proclaiming his death until he

55. HS 291–93; YP 321–24.

> comes. Precisely this is the pledge of love in Christ's Supper that one Christian performs toward the other, in order that every brother may know what good deed to expect from the other.[56]

From this passage, Hubmaier's understanding of the Supper can be summarized in two main ways: first, as a public sign of Christian love, and second, as a commemoration of the suffering of Jesus Christ and a proclamation of His death. However, we can see that this ceremony of the Supper, which includes this pledge of love and commemoration of the death of Jesus Christ, is required only of those who are members of the church. In other words, one who wants to join the Lord's Supper must become firstly a member of the community of believers through being baptized, with an attendant confession of faith. Through this baptism, which includes one's confession of faith and commitment to live according to the Rule of Christ, one enters into the church and is incorporated into the fellowship of the church. For Hubmaier, the meaning of baptism is to proclaim publicly and thus create the relationship between the baptized person and God, and also between the baptized person and other believers. For Hubmaier therefore, there is no meaning for the practice of the Lord's Supper unless the partaker has been baptized:

> For just as water baptism is a public testimony of the Christian faith, so is the Supper a public testimony of Christian love. Now he who does not want to be baptized or to observe the Supper, he does not desire to believe in Christ nor to practice Christian love and does not desire to be a Christian.[57]

From this passage, Mabry asserted that for Hubmaier, the meaning of the Supper is a public confirmation of a covenant, which is enacted first between God and the church member and second between the member and other members of the church.[58] However, Hubmaier seems to show a different emphasis in each ceremony although he regarded both ceremonies as a public testimony for Christian life. Hubmaier's expression of "a public testimony of Christian faith" for water baptism focuses on a vertical relationship between God and the believers, but his expression of the Lord's Supper as "a public testimony of Christian love" is focused more on the horizontal relationship between believers. However, this horizontal relationship cannot exist unless the vertical relationship between God and

56. HS 317; YP 354.
57. HS 358–59; YP 399.
58. Mabry, *Church*, 168.

a believer also exists. For that reason, these two ceremonies which were instituted by Christ must be held together for Christian life. The community of believers as the body of Christ can only consist of those who have committed themselves to live according to the Rule of Christ. The obligation to love one another by the pledge of love in the Supper cannot be given to those who have not yet committed themselves through water baptism to the congregation of the church. One who has been baptized must abide by the order of Christ that we love each other, confirming one's commitment to God. As such, the practice of believers' baptism is a prerequisite for the Lord's Supper.

The relationship between believers' baptism and the Lord's Supper shows how we should interpret Hubmaier's doctrine of the Supper. As we have seen in the previous chapters, Hubmaier's doctrine of believers' baptism, which requires the baptizand's personal faith, is best understood in the relational perspective because his concept of faith had been developed in the relational perspective. Therefore, to understand Hubmaier's doctrine of the Lord's Supper, we also need to interpret it through the relational perspective found in his baptismal theology.

3. Hubmaier's Understanding of the Lord's Supper in Dynamic and Relational Perspective

Hubmaier's understanding of the Lord's Supper can be summarized in two ways: the Lord's Supper as the memorial of Christ's death and His work on the earth, and the Lord's Supper as the pledge of love. The former theme is demonstrated in his earlier writing, *Achtzehn Schlußreden* (1524), which was written after he became interested in the issue of the Eucharist. In it we see that for Hubmaier, the memorialist theology of the Lord's Supper is a significant element in the development of his general understanding of the Lord's Supper. Most of his writings concerning the mass or the Eucharist assert that the Lord's Supper is a memorial or remembrance. The meaning of memorial or remembrance for the Lord's Supper is not just mere remembrance of the past event mentally or spiritually, but includes a connection with outward action. In this sense, Hubmaier presented the second concept of the Supper as the pledge of love. However, this concept does not mean that we accept and forgive any sins or errors of any kind, but it does mean that we need to help one who is errant to return to the right path. Hubmaier introduced two important treatises, *Von der Brüderlichen Strafe*, *Von dem christlichen Bann*, to help explain his perspective on the Supper as a pledge of love. Therefore, I shall examine the meaning of memorial and of the pledge of love for the Lord's Supper. Moreover, I shall present his unique understanding of the Lord's Supper through the significance of Christian ban and fraternal admonition for the Supper in his writings.

a. The Lord's Supper as Memorial in the Context of Present Perspective

Hubmaier's analysis of the Eucharist issue in *Achtzehn Schlußreden* begins with his conviction that the Catholic understanding of the Mass as a sacrifice of Christ is incorrect. Interestingly, his concern over the Eucharist in this treatise seems not to relate to his understanding of baptism, a connection that would develop later. His earlier focus was on correcting the meaning of the Mass in terms of Catholic tradition as he wrote here:

> 5. The mass is not a sacrifice, but a memorial of the death of Christ, for which reason it cannot be offered either for the dead or for the living. Hereby requiem masses and memorial masses of the seventh day, the thirtieth day, and of the anniversary collapse.

> 6. As often as such commemoration is held, the death of the Lord shall be proclaimed in the tongue of every land. Here all dumb masses fall on one heap.[59]

From these theses, Hubmaier showed his early understanding of the Eucharist which is based on his denial of the doctrine of Catholic Mass. Here, we see that Hubmaier's early understanding of the Eucharist as a memorial of the death of Christ is similar to Zwingli's idea about the Lord's Supper for reforming the church. In his sixty-seven theses (1523), Zwingli insisted that:

> Since Christ once sacrificed himself, being eternally a pardoning valid sacrifice for the sins of all believers, it follows that the mass is not a sacrifice, but a commemoration of the sacrifice and an assurance of the redemption which Christ proved to us.[60]

From the above explanations of the Eucharist, there is a common pattern in which both Hubmaier and Zwingli clearly denied the Catholic doctrine

---

59. HS 73; YP 32–33.
60. Z 1:460 and Z 2:111. Cf. YP 32.

of transubstantiation and Luther's doctrine of the Real Presence by arguing for the Eucharist as the memorial of the death of Christ. However, Zwingli's understanding of the Eucharist is not just a ceremony commemorating the death of Christ, but also salvific assurance for the recipients. For Zwingli, believers remember the work of Christ and His death for the forgiveness of sins through attendance at the Supper, so that it brings them the confidence of salvation. However, Hubmaier had not yet developed the concept of the Supper as a memorial within a soteriological perspective in *Achtzehn Schlußreden,* which focused more on a critique of the Catholic tradition of sacramental ceremony. His accentuation of the meaning of the Supper focuses more on the proclamation of the death of Christ and His work for those who still need to know the gospel for salvation, than on the recipients' salvation. From this early writing on the Supper, we see that Hubmaier's understanding of the Lord's Supper was related to the concept of memorial, as advocated by Zwingli.

What does "memorial" mean for Hubmaier in his understanding of the Lord's Supper? In his first treatise on the Lord's Supper, *Etliche Schlußreden vom Unterricht der Messe* (1525), Hubmaier expanded his explanation of the meaning of the Lord's Supper as memorial, which is basically supposed in the concept of proclamation of Christ's death for us as he wrote in *Achtzehn Schlußreden*.[61] However, in this second treatise, he expanded the meaning of the Supper further from remembering the death of Christ and His work to regarding it as an outward sign or symbol instituted by Christ.[62] However, this remembrance of Christ's death in the Lord's Supper is not focused on ourselves but on others. For Hubmaier, the practice of the Lord's Supper is no longer regarded as a memorial for improving one's own faith or assurance of salvation, but rather for reminding us of our responsibility to live for our neighbor as Christ gave Himself for us. Hubmaier elaborated here:

> From all these words follows the final conclusion that the bread offered, broken, taken, and eaten is the body of Christ in remembrance. Thus also the cup taken, distributed, and drunk is the blood of Christ in remembrance. Now the general true thesis or maxim is known: *Talia sunt subiecta qualia permittuntur ab eorum predicates,* that is: The preceding words should be understood according to the following words. In the power of this saying everyone must confess and say that this baked bread is

61. HS 102; YP 74.
62. Ibid.

the body of Christ who was crucified for us. Now, however, this bread in itself is not the body, for this bread was not crucified and did not die for us, so the bread must be the body of Christ in remembrance, so that all the words of Christ can remain in their plain and simple sense, for he always spoke in the most simple fashion, so that it would be understood clearly as his parting word by his disciples.[63]

Here, Hubmaier's key point concerning the Lord's Supper is that the bread and wine are meaningless unless we recognize the work of Christ and His death for us. When we eat and drink the bread and wine in remembrance of Christ, they become the body and blood of Christ. In other words, that which the past action of Christ had done for us becomes the present event for ourselves through believing His works in remembrance. The death and work of Christ is no longer a past event, but is the present reality for us as we recognize them through the Lord's Supper. However, Hubmaier clearly distinguished the meaning of the body and blood of Christ present in remembrance, from the Catholic doctrine of transubstantiation.

As we have seen in the previous section, participants are required to confess their faith by believers' baptism before they attend the Lord's Supper as a remembrance of the death of Christ. The requirement of faith before attendance at the Supper is related to the meaning of the Supper as memorial, which needs to be understood in the relational perspective. We have seen the meaning of faith as the significance of the relationship between God and a human being in the relational perspective with the active side of free will. Moreover, using this relational approach means that faith, in Hubmaier's theology, is understood as the realization of God's grace together with the human's response to it.[64] His prerequisite that the participants should have declared their faith before the Lord's Supper means that the significance of the Supper is based on recognizing the grace of God and sustaining a right relationship with Him. For Hubmaier, therefore, the rite of the Supper itself, where we break the bread and share the drink, is meaningless unless we recognize the grace of God through our relationship with Him in faith. In his *Eine Form des Nachtmahls Christi*, Hubmaier showed the importance of this relationship with God for partaking in the Supper:

It is not a fellowship for the reason that bread is broken, but rather the bread is broken because the fellowship has already

63. HS 293; YP 324.
64. HS 72; YP 32.

> taken place and has been concluded inward in the spirit, since Christ has come into flesh, John 4:27. For not all who break bread are participants in the body and blood of Christ, which I can prove by the traitor Judas, Matt. 26:25. But those who are partakers inwardly and of the spirit, the same may also worthily partake outwardly of this bread and wine.[65]

Hubmaier insisted that Jesus Christ presented the best example through Judas that one's attending the ceremony of the Supper itself is not important, but rather whether he or she is ready for it spiritually by trusting in God. The value of the Lord's Supper depends on the partakers' examination of each other as to whether they have kept a right relationship with God through obeying the Rule of Christ, not on the attendance itself. In this respect, he argued the emphasis on the significance of attending the Eucharist according to Catholic tradition is human invention and not scripturally based.

Hubmaier's understanding of the Lord's Supper as memorial, linked with his view that Christ's physical absence on earth after His ascension is also his key point for arguing against both the Lutheran doctrine of the Real Presence of Christ according to "communication of attributes" (*communicatio idiomatum*),[66] and the Catholic doctrine of transubstantiation.[67] For Hubmaier, Luther's doctrine of the Real Presence of Christ was an erroneous development stemming from his Christological view that Jesus Christ's humanity after His ascension is omniscient, omnipotent or ubiquitous, even being present in the Supper.[68] He also argued that the Catholic doctrine of transubstantiation was based on a misunderstanding of the nature of Christ.

Accordingly, Hubmaier clearly rejected the Catholic and Lutheran perspectives on the Eucharist as his Christology is in accordance with Zwingli based on the conviction that Christ's physical body, after His ascension, is in heaven at the right hand of God the Father.[69] Thus Hubmaier approached the theology of the Lord's Supper from a subjective rather than objective position. Hubmaier elaborated here:

> For these words, "in my memory," testify in the entire previous saying that the breaking, distribution, and eating of the bread is

65. HS 358; YP 398.
66. Muller, *Latin and Greek*, 72-74; HS 290; YP 320.
67. HS 290; YP 319; Rempel, *Lord's Supper*, 72.
68. HS 370; YP 414-15.
69. Gäbler, *Zwingli*, 134; Mabry, *Church*, 171.

Hubmaier's Doctrine of the Lord's Supper

> not a breaking, distribution, and eating of the body of Christ, who is sitting at the right hand of God the Father in the heavens, but all that is a remembrance of his being broken and distributed in suffering. It is also an eating in faith, that he was thus taken, broken, and divided for us, that is, captured, martyred, and died for us, so that we remember this and be aware of his death.[70]

His emphasis on faith as the prerequisite for the Supper means that spiritually the Supper is nothing unless the partakers have the right relationship with God, and recognize His grace.[71] When the partakers participate in the Supper in their faith, the bread and wine become the body and blood of Christ, not materially, but spiritually.

The Lord's Supper is not a remembrance of the past event of Christ's death by crucifixion but is rather a present event for the partakers in their recognition. With regards to the meaning of the Supper, Hubmaier's emphasis on the importance of transferring the past event of Christ's death into the present recognition of it by the partakers echoes his understanding of faith, where faith is a human recognition and response to God's grace in the present tense experientially. By his experiential understanding of the Supper, the significance of the Lord's Supper does not depend on the sacramental rite of the Eucharist itself or on the partakers' attendance at it, but it does depend on their recognition of the love of Christ through His death. For Hubmaier, the Supper as memorial of Christ's death and work means an invitation to partakers to realize the present reality of Christ's love by living it in action. So he emphasized on the significance of the action to love neighbor in the liturgy *Eine Form des Nachtmahls Christi*.

> "I [Christ] was hungry and you fed me. I was thirsty and you gave me drink. I was naked, in prison, and homeless, and you clothed me, visited me, and housed me," Matt. 25. He says I, I, I, me, me, me. From this it is certain and sure that all the good that we do to the very least of his, that we do to Christ himself. Yea, he will not let a single drink of cool water go unrewarded, Matt. 10:42. If one is thus inclined toward his neighbor, he is now in the true fellowship of Christ, a member of his body, and a fellow member with all godly persons, Col. 1:4.[72]

In this sense, Hubmaier's expression of "memorial" for the Lord's Supper also means partakers participating in Christ's suffering and death through

70. HS 293–94; YP 324.
71. HS 364; YP 407.
72. HS 357–58; YP 397.

Balthasar Hubmaier's Doctrine of Salvation

their actions beyond just mental and spiritual recognition of Christ's death and work. Both intellect and willed action are implied in this recognition. Thus, the partakers' recognition of Christ's love through His death in the Lord's Supper is part of their resolve to live according to the example of Jesus Christ's life. Hubmaier continued to insist that in this liturgy:

> Fourth: So that the church might also be fully aware of a person's attitude and will, one holds fellowship with her in the breaking of bread, thereby saying, testifying, and publicly assuring her, yea, making to her a sacrament or a sworn pledge and giving one's hand on the commitment that one is willing henceforth to offer one's body and to shed one's blood thus for one's fellow believers. This one does not out of human daring, like Peter, Matt. 26:33, but in the grace and power of the suffering and the blood shed by our Lord Jesus Christ, his (i.e., meaning Peter's) only Savior, of whose suffering and death the human being is now celebrating a living commemoration in the breaking of bread and the sharing of the chalice.[73]

Hubmaier's stress on the significance of believers acting in the meaning of the Supper is shown in his explanation of the Supper as a word "living" with commemoration. This expression of "living memorial" for the Supper means that the partakers will offer their lives for each other now as Christ did for all of them. For this reason, Hubmaier emphasized the pledge of the love in his liturgy in which partakers repeated the pledge and so were reminded of it.

> If you will love your neighbor and serve him with deeds of brotherly love, Matt. 25; Eph. 6; Col. 3; Rom. 13:1; 1 Pet. 2:13f., lay down and shed for him your life and blood, be obedient to father, mother, and all authorities according to the will of God, and this in the power of our Lord Jesus Christ, who laid down and shed his flesh and blood for us, then let each say individually:
>
> I will.[74]

Hubmaier's understanding of the Supper is not just the partaker's remembrance of the past event of Christ's death, but the examination of their lives and their commitment to imitate the life of Christ for others. In this context, Rempel asserted that Hubmaier's concept of the Lord's Supper shows the equal significance from two originally different acts of remembering

---

73. HS 358; YP 397–98.
74. HS 362; YP 403.

in faith and acting in love.⁷⁵ Although Rempel rightly pointed out that the Supper in Hubmaier's theology equally emphasizes remembering and acting, he did not connect these two different acts—"remembering" and "acting"—to Hubmaier's understanding of faith. Thus, the Lord's Supper for Hubmaier is not the partaker's simple remembrance of the death of Christ but proof of their faith through their imitation of the life of Christ, who gave Himself for all. For partakers, attendance at the ceremony of the Supper is the living experience of Christ's love through their realization and practice of it in the present. So in the liturgy, Hubmaier let the congregation call out:

> Stay with us, O Christ! It is toward evening and the day is now far spent. Abide with us, O Jesus, abide with us. For where thou art not, there everything is darkness, night, and shadow, but thou art the true Sun, light and shining brightness, John 8:12. He to whom thou dost light the way, cannot go astray.⁷⁶

For Hubmaier, the Lord's Supper is the transformation of the past work of Christ's love through His death into a present event for believers in an experiential perspective. Therefore, the Lord's Supper requires the partakers to love and live willingly for their neighbors now as their present obligation. In this sense, Hubmaier's concept of memorial for the Lord's Supper cannot be separated from his concept of the Lord's Supper as a pledge of love in relational perspective.

b. The Lord's Supper as the Pledge of Love in Relational Perspective

With his concept of memorial for the Lord's Supper in the experiential perspective, Hubmaier ruled out not only the Catholic belief that each practice of the Mass is an effective re-enacting of the sacrifice of Christ, but also the more modest claims of the Supper as a sacrament in the Lutheran sense.⁷⁷ It is clear that Hubmaier had a negative view of traditional notions of sacrament in function, although he wanted to sustain the significance of the Supper as an ordinance of Christ in Christian life. In this

---

75. Rempel, *Lord's Supper*, 82.

76. HS 356; YP 395.

77. Cf. HS 73; YP 32–33, HS 102; YP 74, HS 113–14; YP 87, HS 161–62; YP 147, HS 290–91; YP 319–20, HS 358; YP 398. Rempel rightly points out that a Calvinist view on the Supper would be ruled out by Hubmaier's understanding of the Supper as memorial. See Rempel, *Lord's Supper*, 63.

Balthasar Hubmaier's Doctrine of Salvation

context, he had to present a new concept of sacrament which challenged the traditional custom that the materials—water, bread and wine—are regarded as sacramental:

> That we have called the water of baptism, like the bread and the wine of the altar, a "sacrament"; and held it to be such, although not the water, bread, or wine, but in the fact that the baptismal commitment or the pledge of love is really and truly sacrament in the Latin; i.e., a commitment by oath and a pledge given by the hand which the one baptized makes to Christ, our invincible Prince and Head, that he is willing to fight bravely unto the death in Christian faith under his flag and banner.[78]

Hubmaier's attempt to argue against the traditional view of a sacramental function that has the power to take away sin and to make holy, is developed by using Zwingli's expression of sacrament as a commitment or pledge.[79] Although they shared a common expression for the definition of sacrament, Hubmaier did not fully depend on Zwingli's notion of sacrament as a sign. In *Ein einfältiger Unterricht*, Hubmaier clearly distinguished himself from Zwingli's interpretation of "is" as "signifies" in the phrase, "This is my body," although he used the same expression "memorial" for the Supper as Zwingli did.[80] Hubmaier's concept of sacrament is focused more on the event of commitment or pledge of love by believers, because this event, commitment or pledge of love, forms the relationship between God and believers. For those who take part in a sacrament, creating a relationship through that sacrament is a present event, not a past or future one. From this point of view, Hubmaier's concept of the Lord's Supper as the pledge of love needs to be understood according to his relational perspective as shown:

> We conclude that the bread and wine of the Christ meal are outward word symbols of an inward Christian nature here on earth, in which a Christian obligates himself to another in Christian love with regard to body and blood. Thus as the body and blood of Christ became my body and blood on the cross, so likewise shall my body and blood become the body and blood of my neighbor, and in time of need theirs become my body and

---

78. HS 352; YP 391.
79. See ZB 131.
80. Z 4:476–77. Cf. HS 291; YP 321.

blood, or we cannot boast at all to be Christians. That is the will of Christ in the Supper.[81]

In this passage, Hubmaier showed that the concept of the pledge of love in the Supper comes from his concept of memorial. The past event of Christ's death is transferred to the present event for us. The transference from the past event to the present one in the Supper means that the past event of Christ's suffering and death as a remembered account becomes the present event with subjective force for partakers in their recognition. In this sense, Hubmaier could apply the sacrifice of Christ for all to the obligation of partakers to love each other. This obligation is not a side responsibility for them, but a reciprocal action between believers in terms of Hubmaier's personalizing concept for relationship. For Hubmaier, the true practice of the Lord's Supper with the pledge of love is begun with the partakers' recognition of their relationship not only with God, but also with other believers. However, for true breaking of the bread and sharing of the wine for the Supper, the partaker should begin with inner communion which is a right relationship with Christ and other believers through the remembrance of Christ's love, before he or she shares the Supper with other believers. It is the same pattern as in Hubmaier's doctrine of baptism—that the inner baptism (the baptism of the Spirit) should precede outward baptism (water baptism). For Hubmaier, the outward practice of the baptism and the Supper is meaningless unless the internal baptism or communion has occurred:

> A parable: We do not believe because we have been baptized in water, but we are baptized in water because we first believe. So David says: "I have believed, therefore I have spoken," Ps. 116:10; Matt. 16:16; Acts 8:30. So every Christian speaks equally: "I have believed, therefore I have publicly confessed that Jesus is Christ, Son of the living God, and have thereafter had myself baptized according to the order of Christ, the high priest who lives in eternity." Or: "I have fellowship with Christ and all his members, 1 Cor. 10:16, therefore I break bread with all believers in Christ according to the institution of Christ." Without this inner communion in the spirit and in truth, the outward breaking of bread is nothing but an Iscariotic and damnable hypocrisy. It is precisely to this fellowship and commitment of love that the Supper of Christ points, as a living memorial of his suffering and death for us, spiritually signified and pointed to by the breaking

---

81. HS 104; YP 76.

> of bread, the pouring out of the wine, that each one should also sacrifice and pour out his flesh and blood for the other.[82]

Hubmaier insisted on the significance of inner communion, which is the right fellowship with God and our neighbor, as the foundation for the accomplishment of the obligation of the Lord's Supper that requires us to sacrifice ourselves for each other as Christ did for us. To eat the bread and to drink the wine in the ceremony of the Supper cannot be truly eating and drinking the body and blood of Christ unless we have faith, that is described as fellowship with God. But the requirement to partake in the Supper is to sustain good relationship with one's neighbor, in the same manner as a right relationship with God. When the partaker has a good relationship with his or her neighbor, he or she will sacrifice for his or her neighbor, but he or she can also give himself or herself up for the partaker. This reciprocal response between believers is Hubmaier's characteristic feature of the relational perspective. For Hubmaier, if the partaker does not have a right relationship with both God and other believers, he or she cannot be qualified for participation in the Supper. The heart of the meaning of the Lord's Supper understood as the pledge of love, is to share Christ's love in the fellowship with other believers. But this obligation of the pledge of love for others is required only for those who now recognize the love of Christ through the Supper. The present recognition of God's grace and Christ's love through the Lord's Supper is the present motivation of the partaker to love others. For Hubmaier, the Supper is the present obligation of the partaker to love their neighbors in action, as Christ sacrificed Himself for us. According to this point of view, the meaning of the Supper is not the memorial of a past event but a present reality for the partaker[83] as shown here:

> Likewise, in love, in which he obligates himself now, and with this breaking of the bread and drinking of the cup publicly before the church commits himself and promises that for the sake of his neighbor he is also willing to let his flesh and blood be broken and sacrificed, with which he has now become one bread and one drink.[84]

However, Hubmaier's concept of the partaker's will to love others through the pledge of love in the Supper needs to be understood along with the

---

82. HS 358; YP 398.
83. Rempel, *Lord's Supper*, 63.
84. HS 301; YP 333–34.

doctrine of the freedom of human will. As we saw in the previous chapter, Hubmaier's understanding of human will is directly linked with the condition of the relationship between God and a human being. Although Hubmaier emphasized the necessity of human action for doing good works as proof of being a Christian, he denied that human capability of the will is able to do good by itself, as he wrote in his liturgy, *Eine Form des Nachtmahls Christi*:

> Answer: Certainly for the Adamic human nature. But all things are possible to the Christian, Mark 9:23, not as persons, but as believers, who are one with God and all creatures, and are (except for the flesh) free and independent of themselves. For God works such willing and doing in his believers, Phil. 2:14, through the inward anointing of his Holy Spirit, so that one stands in complete freedom to will and to do good or evil. The good one can do is through the anointing of God. The evil comes from one's own innate nature and impulse, which evil will one can, however, master and tame through the grace given by God, Deut. 30:1ff.; Gen. 4:17; Rom. 10; Matt. 19; John 1:12.[85]

For Hubmaier, the obligation of the believer cannot be fulfilled by our human will or power, but only by the grace of God. He assumed that the possibility of fulfilling the obligation of Christ in the Supper to love one another is restricted to believers only. The definition of a believer as the person who is in relationship with God is a crucial point for understanding Hubmaier's relational perspective on the Supper, because that can only be accomplished by the partaker's relationship with God. This relation between God and the believer is not formed by our human will, but by the inward change caused by the work of the Holy Spirit. His emphasis on the work of the Holy Spirit for molding the relationship between God and man as we have seen means that he avoids the danger of being regarded as a Pelagian, insisting on the role of human works and playing down the idea of divine grace for salvation. Hubmaier's relational concept between God and the believer does not mean a permanent static relation but one that can be changed. So Hubmaier asserted the necessity of continually sustaining the relationship with God, which in turn is the source of power to imitate the love of Christ. Therefore, the mission of the pledge of love for the Supper is accomplished by one's inner communion with God.

Consequently, Hubmaier's concept of the Lord's Supper as a pledge of love means that the believer who sustains a relationship with God in his or

---

85. HS 360; YP 400.

her recognition lives and loves for others according to the order of Christ. For believers, to recognize the grace of God and to obey the command of Christ through the Supper means that there is a present responsibility for them to love and sacrifice now for others as Christ did for us. But the proper enacting of the love for others in the community of believers is only possible when the believer has fellowship with other believers which ensues from a shared relationship with God. Hubmaier's understanding of the commitment of love for others in the Lord's Supper is developed in his relational perspective that emphasizes the relationship between God and believers and between a believer and other believers as the source of loving one another. This relational view of the Supper in his theology shows why Hubmaier insisted on the necessity of fraternal admonition and Christian ban for the practice of the Lord's Supper.

c. Fraternal Admonition and Christian Ban in Hubmaier's Doctrine of the Lord's Supper

So, his understanding of the Lord's Supper can be explained as defining the meaning of the practice of love. His most explicit requirement for love is a sacrifice which is shown in the example of Christ who gave Himself and died for us. Anybody who wants to follow the life of Christ has to give up his or her life not only for Christ, but also for neighbors. For Hubmaier, this concept of the practice of love in the Lord's Supper is begun as we have seen with the relational presupposition that we (the believer and other believers) are all brothers and sisters in Christ:

> Since our brotherly love requires that one member of the body be also concerned for the other, therefore we have the earnest behest of Christ, Matt. 18:14ff., that whenever henceforth a brother sees another erring or sinning, that he once and again should fraternally admonish him in brotherly love. Should he not be willing to reform nor to desist from his sin, he shall be reported to the church. The church shall then exhort him a third time. When this also does no good, she shall exclude him from her fellowship.[86]

The concept of love in the Lord's Supper, which is based on the relationship between the partaker and other believers, can have a wider meaning beyond that of sacrifice for others. As we have seen in Hubmaier's concept

---

86. HS 363; YP 406.

of relationship in his doctrine of free will, he focused on the personalism that is accomplished by the recognition of and concern with each other. He emphasized the concept of faith as the personalizing encounter between God and a person, and as such the meaning of relationship cannot exist without reciprocal efforts. In this respect, Hubmaier's purpose in insisting on love in the Supper does not mean that each person always forgives and accepts the one who sins and errs. The brotherly love shown in the Supper is meant to help each other to improve his or her life by imitating the example of Christ with encouragement and discipline. If one ignores the sins and errors of others, it does not demonstrate love. Rather, it means that there is not a proper relationship of love which leads to concern for the other.

The public confession of faith that one will live according to the Rule of Christ through water baptism and the pledge of love to live for others through the Supper means that one has promised to follow the way of Christ beyond simply living with a good heart and doing good. Those who follow the way of Christ, must examine themselves to overcome sins or errors. This is accomplished by helping and encouraging each other within a right relationship. With this relational perspective, we may see the reason why Hubmaier stressed the importance of fraternal admonition and Christian ban for the Lord's Supper as he wrote here:

> Christ, rather, gives to his church a second key, namely the authority to exclude again persons who had been received and admitted into the Christian congregation if they should not will to behave in a right and Christian way, and to close her doors before them, as he says, "Whose sins you retain, to them they shall stand retained," Matt. 18:18 [John 20:23].[87]

For Hubmaier, the keys which were given to the community of believers by Christ are distinguished in two ways: first, there is the authority to admit those who desire to enter the community of believers to follow the way of Christ by public confession of faith through water baptism; and, second, the authority to exclude those who refuse to live according to the Rule of Christ from the community. The concept of keys—entrance and exclusion—shows how important the concept of relationship is in Hubmaier's theology. In particular, his relational understanding of the Christian ban is clearly shown in his *Von dem christlichen Bann* in this passage:

---

87. HS 370; YP 414.

> It is to be noted that the ban is a public separation and exclusion of a person from the fellowship of the Christian church because of an offensive sin, from which this person will not refrain, recognized according to the earnest and express command of Christ, decided by a Christian congregation, and publicly proclaimed, so that the Word of God and the whole Christian church might not be shamed, calumnied, and despised, and so that the novices and the weak might not be caused to stumble by his evil example or to be corrupted, but rather that because of this punishment they might be startled, afraid, and might know henceforth better how to protect themselves from sins and vices.[88]

Hubmaier's intention in highlighting the practice of Christian ban, as the public separation or exclusion from the community of believers of the one who has confessed faith but who refuses to turn from his or her sin, is not to condemn individuals but to express a desire for the individual to leave sin and to return the community again. To examine myself means to have a motivation to inspect myself as to whether I trust in God in a good relationship. The reason for separation from the community of believers is that one has not lived according to the Rule of Christ, even though one undertook to do so before congregation of the church. If a person was attempting to sustain a right relationship with God when they fell into sin, they will be willing to listen to the advice of other believers so that they could leave behind their sinful life. For Hubmaier, therefore, the Christian ban which is imposed on those who do not want to leave sin shows not only that the excommunicated person is now excluded from the community of believers but also that he or she has already broken their relationship with God. If a person had sustained a good relation with God and then other believers gave advice for him or her to depart from sin, then, he or she would recognize sin and turn from it. The main purpose of Christian ban in Hubmaier's theology is not to condemn or judge the excommunicated person, but to give him or her the opportunity to recognize his or her fault, repent of sin and return to God and his or her community. In this respect, if there is no exercise of the fraternal admonition and ban for the Christian community, water baptism and the Lord's Supper are nothing better than infant baptism and baby feeding in the traditional way of sacraments.[89] Consequently, the exercise of the fraternal admonition and Christian ban is not an expression of hatred or harm to the excommunicated person,

---

88. HS 367–68; YP 410–11.
89. HS 346; YP 384.

but an expression of love among believers in order that the sinful person has a chance to examine him or herself.[90] Therefore, when one who was excommunicated from the church is renewed and returned from their sin, the community of believers must admit him or her with true heart of love for attempting to follow the life of Christ.[91] Christian ban and fraternal admonition through water baptism and the Supper is a rule to enable believers to live according to the commandment of Christ, and an opportunity for the excommunicated person to examine their relationship with God and turn from sin by exclusion from the community. According to Hubmaier's relational perspective on the doctrine of the Supper, the fraternal admonition and Christian ban are essential elements for Christian life that imitates Christ.

4. Conclusion

As we have seen in this chapter, Hubmaier asserted that the meaning of the Lord's Supper must be an essential element for Christian life beyond just a simple rite in the tradition of church. For Hubmaier, however, partakers in the Supper are only qualified if they have confessed their faith and entered into the community of believers. In this context, the meaning of the Lord's Supper must be understood within the context of a personal confession of faith through water baptism before a congregation of believers, which is related to his or her understanding of salvation. In other words, just as Hubmaier understood the concept of faith in dynamic and relational perspective, so he developed his understanding of the Lord's Supper also in those perspectives.

First, his characteristic feature of the Lord's Supper is his critique of the real or corporeal presence of Christ in the rite of the Supper, as exemplified in the Catholic doctrine of transubstantiation or Lutheran doctrine of consubstantiation. For Hubmaier, like Zwingli or other Anabaptists, according to the Bible, the body of Christ cannot descend after His ascension, because He is sitting at the right hand of God the Father until He comes again on the earth. Accordingly, the Catholic and Lutheran understandings of the real presence of Christ in the Supper are unacceptable. Hubmaier instead asserted that the Lord's Supper should be understood as the memorial of the suffering and death of Christ for us. As he rejected the real or corporeal presence of Christ in the Supper, he also insisted that the

90. HS 375; YP 421.
91. HS 343; YP 380.

presence of Christ on earth is present in the community of believers as the body of Christ. It is difficult to understand what assumption his Christology is based on, either Word-Flesh or Word-Man, if one looks at it in the light of a transactional perspective. Rather, his Christology in the Supper is better understood through an experiential perspective.

Second, using this relational and subjective perspective for understanding his Christology helps us to see why Hubmaier emphasizes the significance of the Lord's Supper for Christian life. For Hubmaier, there are two central concepts of the Lord's Supper in his theology: first, the Supper as the memorial of Christ's suffering and death; second, the Supper as the pledge of love. The former concept of the Supper is entirely different from the meaning of remitting sins in Catholic tradition or the concept of the real or corporeal presence of Christ in the Supper. Hubmaier also did not accept that the bread and wine just signify the body and blood of Christ. The meaning of the Lord's Supper is that the past event of Christ's suffering and death for us, which happened two thousand years ago, becomes a present event for the partakers who are able to attend it *now* in their recognition.

Hubmaier's second concept of the Supper as the pledge of love shows that we need to understand the meaning of the Lord's Supper in a relational perspective. The concept of the Supper as a recognition of Christ's suffering and death for us in the subjective and relational perspective implies the relationship between God and the partaker, but the concept of the Supper as the pledge of love emphasizes the significance of relationship between the partaker and the others in relational perspective. The practice of the Lord's Supper means that the partakers must live for others in love as Jesus Christ showed His love for us even unto His death. The Lord's Supper, which is based on the pledge of love, is meaningless without a relationship with other believers in Christ. For Hubmaier, the Lord's Supper implies the significance of relationship not only with God, but also with other believers. Hubmaier's relational perspective on the Lord's Supper shows why he insisted on the importance of fraternal admonition and excommunication in the community of believers. If one has been excommunicated from the community of church, he or she has to be concerned with his or her relation with God and other believers. This excommunication by the community is not a punishment for or judgment on the sinner, but an opportunity for him or her to restore the right relationship with God and other believers.

Consequently, for Hubmaier the Lord's Supper must be regarded as important for Christian life and faith beyond being simply a church rite or tradition. His understanding of the Lord's Supper in the experiential perspective leads us to recognize the grace of God by the work of Christ in the present time. This recognition of the love of God through Christ's death lets us hold on to the good relationship not only with God, but also with other believers. Through the Supper, believers can imitate Christ day by day according to his instructions for loving God and others. For Hubmaier, the Lord's Supper must be regarded as the essential element for believers to improve their lives by imitating Christ.

6

Conclusion: A Fresh Perspective on Hubmaier's Doctrine of Salvation

THIS THESIS HAS AIMED to identify and explore a better way of understanding Hubmaier's doctrine of salvation and it has done so by exploring the primary texts of his writings for church reform. As we come to a conclusion, I suggest that the new reading we have explored means that Hubmaier's writings are important not only for what they tell us of the breadth of sixteenth-century Anabaptism, but also for reflection on the nature of the church today. In this concluding chapter, I shall draw together the threads of the discussion so far and also sketch some possible ways in which Hubmaier's theology can enrich our current thinking.

1. A Fresh Perspective on the Studies on Hubmaier's Theology

We have seen that the most common method of analysis of Hubmaier's writings, tracing the influential sources, is not a satisfactory way of understanding Hubmaier's intentions in writing. Previous researchers' accounting of Hubmaier's theology, in terms of background influences, is what we have been calling a transactional perspective, that is, one where the emphasis is on the cause that brings the result. But this approach does not give a full explanation of Hubmaier's theology, because his individual approach to certain theological issues does not fit easily into such straightforward categorizing. As I argued in chapter 3, Hubmaier's rejection of

Conclusion: A Fresh Perspective on Hubmaier's Doctrine of Salvation

the practice of infant baptism despite his acknowledgement of original sin in human beings, is not easily explained by such a transactional perspective. Although previous researchers provide considerable evidence that Hubmaier's theology was similar to some specific theological schools of thought—such as medieval Catholicism, or the teachings of Erasmus, Zwingli, and other contemporary theologians—they have tended either to avoid or to ignore any attempt to account for these issues in their arguments. This is why I suggest that previous research methodologies evaluating Hubmaier's thought on the basis of its influences are not sufficient to explain the characteristic aspects of his theology. We need to read Hubmaier's theology in terms of his own writings, not merely in terms of influences.

If we use this methodology to study Hubmaier's theology, we will see that the main purpose of Hubmaier's writings was the reform of the church. Hubmaier's concern for church reform began with correcting the way in which the phrase "justification by faith," the motto of the Reformation was used. Since he dedicated himself to reform, he saw that many people who lived in ways that were compromised by sin believed that they would be saved because of their faith regardless of how they acted. In this context, he believed that this phenomenon of people's continuing to live sinful lives arose from a misunderstanding of the meaning of salvation by faith because of what he was convinced was the mistaken Lutheran perspective on faith. As we saw in his thesis *Von der Freiheit des Willens*, although he like Luther, used the term "justification by faith," he understood the concept of faith differently. Consequently, the purpose of Hubmaier's theses is to present the proper understanding of the meaning of "salvation by faith." Therefore, the issues he raised in his theses are linked to his soteriological perspective. So, we can see that Hubmaier's doctrine of salvation was demonstrated not only in one specific area of his thinking, but in all of his arguments for church reform.

In order to sustain "justification by faith" as the motto of the Reformation, at least for Hubmaier, the understanding of faith must be directly related to his understanding of salvation. His understanding of faith is shown in three main categories of his writings: the freedom of the will, baptism and the Lord's Supper. All three topics in his theses show how each is related to the definition of faith which is the key to soteriology. For Hubmaier, the concept of the freedom of the will is the starting point for developing his doctrine of salvation in dynamic subjective and relational terms. Those who enter the community of believers freely through baptism are required to confirm their life of faith and love through partaking in the Lord's Supper which helps them to live according to the Rule of Christ. In this sense, none of these three can be excluded for purposes of understanding Hubmaier's soteriology. As we have looked at Hubmaier's theses in the light of the new methodology, there are two specific features of Hubmaier's understanding of faith that have emerged as part of his soteriology.

2. Martin Buber's Dialogical Personalism and Hubmaier's Soteriology

The approach which Hubmaier takes to soteriology and in particular of the relationship between the doctrines of free will, baptism, and the Lord's Supper, is to understand each issue in a relational and subjective way rather than in a transactional and objective way. In this context, Martin Buber's philosophy of personal relation, which is a dynamic rather than a static approach to identity helps us to understand more fully how Hubmaier maintained the concept of free will in his soteriology.

Martin Buber presented a personalist philosophy, which is normally called "dialogical personalism," as seen in his writing *I and Thou*.[1] He asserted that human beings experience things in two different ways: *experience* and *encounter*. Buber explained that there are two kinds of relation: an "I-It" relation, which is designated as *experience*; and, an "I-Thou," one which is designated as *encounter*.[2] The "I-It" relation means that some*one* as an active subject faces some*thing* as a passive object. Here, an active subject, that is, the "*I*," has the initiative to make and develop a relation to a passive object, "*It*." That is, the initiative for this relation between *I* and *It* belongs to the subject, "*I*," all the time, and not to the object, "*It*." It is a one-sided and dependent relationship because the object itself is experienced, but it does not do anything to build a relationship with the subject.[3] The concept of the "*I-It*" relation clearly shows the initiator who starts and builds the relationship. Accordingly, it is a transactional approach, depending on the difference between object and subject.

In contrast, the concept of the "*I-Thou*" relation as *encounter* is dynamic and mutual.[4] The "*I-Thou*" relation rejects one-sided choosing or

1. McGrath, *Justification by Faith*, 98.
2. Buber, *I and Thou*, 4.
3. McGrath, *Justification by Faith*, 99.
4. Buber, *I and Thou*, 8.

Conclusion: A Fresh Perspective on Hubmaier's Doctrine of Salvation

initiative to develop the relationship. Relation is reciprocity, according to Buber:

> The *Thou* meets me. But I step into direct relation with it. Hence the relation means being chosen and choosing, suffering and action in one.[5]

In the concept of an "*I-Thou*" relation, *I* and *Thou* both should be subjects and neither is an object. If one of them becomes an object for the other, the "*I-Thou*" relation does not exist anymore but becomes an "*I-It*" relation. When the relation to the *Thou* is direct, it is related in direction to me. I only become the subject, *I*, when I have a direct relation to the *Thou*. Buber continued:

> In face of the directness of the relation everything indirect becomes irrelevant. It is also irrelevant if my *Thou* is already the *It* for other *I*'s ("an object of general experience"), or can become so through the very accomplishment of this act of my being.[6]

His dialogical personalism emphasizes the personal character and mutuality of relationship. It means that whatever is not relative to me as a subject is meaningless. Despite the other subject having its own significance, if it is not directly related to me, then it will not be a subject to me anymore. Rather it will be transformed into an object for me. The direct relation can only exist in the present time:

> . . . but the real, filled present, exists only in so far as actual presentness, meeting, and relation exist. The present arises only in virtue of the fact that the *Thou* becomes present.[7]

Buber's dialogical personalism stresses the significance of the *present relationship* with God in order to obtain a new perspective in understanding soteriology. It is a move from a static and transactional to a dynamic and relational approach. McGrath argued that Buber's concept of personalism in speaking of God as a person is extremely important in demonstrating the nature of God as personal in a number of biblical texts.[8] In the theory of dialogical personalism, therefore, to regard God as personal will mean that *I*, human, also exist as *a person*, a subject, when I meet God. This is because a personal relationship can only exist when both

5. Ibid., 11.
6. Ibid., 12.
7. Ibid.
8. McGrath, *Justification by Faith*, 102.

sides are subjects. Here, "person" means an "individual who is involved in relationship."[9] The encounter between God and a human being is meant to make a personal relationship, not one forced by either party.

Another important aspect of dialogical personalism is that it is valid or applicable in the present moment. For instance, the encounter between God and a human being in relationship needs to be focused on the moment of its occurrence. For such a relationship, the question of most concern is what kind of relationship a subject, *I*, has with the other subject, *Thou* in the *present*.

Therefore, Buber's concept of dialogical personalism can be summarized in three main points: first, personal relationship is mutual, dynamic and changeable; second, this relationship is valid in the present, otherwise it would not be a personal relationship anymore; third, a "subject" or "person," means an individual who participates in relationships. To be a subject as a person also means that the relationship cannot be forced by the other subject. These points are, however, co-related with each other. This personal relation demonstrates what I am calling a subjective and relational perspective, which focuses on a person and a relationship in the present time. The perspective of the dialogical dimension is useful in grasping Hubmaier's intentions in discussing free will.

3. Hubmaier's Doctrine of Salvation in Dynamic and Relational Perspective

a. Concerning the Freedom of the Will

Hubmaier's understanding of faith for salvation occurs in the context of a personal relationship. This personal relationship is the relation not only between God and human beings, but also among believers and between believers and the world. In chapter 2, I argued that Hubmaier's understanding of faith in his doctrine of free will showed that the meaning of faith must be understood as an instrument to create a *personal relationship* between God and human being. Martin Buber's dialogical personalism is an effective way of understanding the concept of personal relationship as *encounter*. To sustain the mutual and dynamic relation in the personalist view means that there is no initiative to make a relation between them unlike a one-sided and dependent *I-It* relationship. As we have seen all through this discussion, part of Hubmaier's originality is the way in which,

9. Ibid.

Conclusion: A Fresh Perspective on Hubmaier's Doctrine of Salvation

by using such an approach, he escapes from questions that dominate other thinkers—for example, Erasmus and Luther's discussion on free will. If one forces the other to build a relationship, the other one becomes an object rather than a subject. In other words, there is no personal relationship since the initiator led the other into a relationship. From this point of view, emphasizing the significance of the human will in salvation in Hubmaier's theology does not mean that our salvation depends on the freedom of human will or that such a position weakens the initiative of God in effecting human salvation. Rather the emphasis on the human will in salvation by Hubmaier shows how much God regards human beings as most precious. Although God always wants all human beings to be saved, He has never forced anyone to be saved. This is because, in His care He wants to encounter each human being as a subject in a personal relationship, not as an object. For Hubmaier, the significance of the personal relationship between God and a human being in terms of salvation is not best understood through an objective and transactional perspective because this loses the characteristic feature of God as a personal being. However, an understanding of human will through a relational perspective reinforces the understanding of the personal character of God.

His understanding of faith in subjective and relational perspective allows him, as we have seen, to escape from fatalism and from what turned out to be sterile questions around initiative, particularly in terms of salvation. As shown in chapter 2, Hubmaier's concept of trichotomism when worked out through the freedom of the will argues that the meaning of free will for faith needs to be understood in a dynamic and relational perspective. His emphasis on the significance of free will for salvation did not answer the question as to who takes initiative for human salvation: God or human beings. For Hubmaier, an answer to this transactional question of free will in terms of salvation would lead to one of two extreme conclusions: the non-necessity of human will for salvation, that is fatalism, or the necessity of human initiative for salvation. His attempt to avoid these extreme views of soteriology created by the transactional perspective is shown in his understanding of faith in terms of the concept of human will. For him, in terms of his dynamic understanding of salvation, the meaning of human will for faith is best understood as the instrument for expressing the relationship between God and a human being.

b. Concerning Baptism

Hubmaier's relational perspective of faith in his soteriology is more clearly shown in his doctrine of baptism. chapter 3 shows Hubmaier's characteristic features of baptismal theology in relational perspective in two ways. First, his argument about the difference between the baptisms of John and of Christ was developed according to this relational perspective. In the traditional view of Catholicism, the baptisms of John and of Christ were used to illustrate the significance and necessity of a proper sacramental rite. For Catholics, the baptism of John, which was not practiced in the name of God the Father, Son and Holy Spirit, could not be regarded as a proper baptism in terms of sacramental theology *"ex opere operato"* where the correct and churchly performance of the rite conveys grace to the recipient. This interpretation of two baptisms in traditional thinking enforced the significance of a proper form for sacraments. The emphasis therefore fell not on an immediate and personal encounter, but on a transaction, with its *I-It* shape.

Zwingli's interpretation of the two baptisms in which he identified the baptism of John with the baptism of Christ criticized not only Catholic sacramentalism, which seemed to focus on the external form of the rite for sacraments, but also the Anabaptists who insisted on the necessity of believers' baptism by distinguishing the differences between the two baptisms. Even though his attempt to show the meaning of John's baptism as the same as the baptism of Christ through interchanging the term "baptism" in sense of "teaching" or "water baptism" was an attempt to argue against the Anabaptists' refusal of infant baptism, Zwingli instead failed to justify and reinforce the necessity of infant baptism in biblical perspective.

In his relational perspective, however, Hubmaier understood that the confession of sin by the baptizand in the baptism of John meant not only the repentance of sin but also the isolation of the baptizand from the community, whereas the baptism of Christ for the forgiveness of sin meant a new start of relationship by entering into the community of believers.

c. Threefold Baptism

Secondly, this relational aspect was expanded through the concept of threefold baptism as one of the most characteristic features in his theology. In his threefold baptism, Hubmaier emphasized that the meaning of baptism should be understood through the perspective of salvation

Conclusion: A Fresh Perspective on Hubmaier's Doctrine of Salvation

understood beyond the concept of ritual sacraments. According to his chronological order of a threefold baptism, the baptism of the Spirit precedes the baptism of water and the baptism of blood. The baptism of the Spirit as the precondition for water baptism occurs through the preached Word and the work of the Holy Spirit. In this sense, the meaning of the baptism of the Spirit is understood in the same way as his understanding of faith that is on the basis of the relationship between God and a human being.

Hubmaier's application of this relational aspect of the baptism of the Spirit to the baptism of water leads us to recognize the significance of the relationship between believers as part of salvation. For Hubmaier, through the baptism of water, the baptizand enters into the community of believers as a visible church, and starts a new life with other believers by showing his or her will to accept all responsibility for being a believer according to the command of Christ. Again, this emphasis on the theological necessity of the relationship between the believers draws us toward what Buber is talking about in *I-Thou* relationships. Moreover, the forgiveness of sins in the baptism of water involves the decision of the whole community to accept or reject a person into their community—a multiple *I-Thou* experience.

Hubmaier's understanding of the baptism of blood is best explained in relational perspective using two concepts: first, blood baptism as the mortification of flesh is to do with the significance of an ongoing relationship with God, based on overcoming the wrong desires stemming from our sinful nature; and second, blood baptism as even unto martyrdom or death for their faith is the external suffering such as the physical persecution by others for keeping faith in the world. Hubmaier's insistence on the baptism of blood is not to be understood as the necessity of the separation of believers' community from the world, but to do with living within the context of the world.

Consequently, Hubmaier's emphasis on the threefold baptism in his theology further develops his concept of faith. His relational perspective on baptism shows why his baptismal theology is so important for his soteriology. Therefore, his theology of baptism as threefold can be well explained by this relational perspective identifying the relationships between God and a person with the baptism of the Spirit, between believers with water baptism and between believers and their world with blood baptism. Accordingly, Hubmaier's relational approaches of baptism to his soteriology have much wider comprehensive concepts of relationship than Buber's terms which only focus on the relationship between God and a human being.

d. Concerning the Relation between Original Sin and Infant Baptism

The characteristic feature of Hubmaier's theology of baptism which focused on the present moment is shown in his understanding of the relationship between original sin and infant baptism. As shown in chapter 4, there have been two contrasting responses to this issue of the relation between original sin and the validity of infant baptism. First, there is the argument that baptism should be given to infants for the remission of original sin so that they can be saved. This opinion builds on Catholic sacramentalism where a proper rite of sacrament conveys the grace of God.

Second, there is the argument that there is no need for infant baptism because human beings are not condemned because of original sin. During the Reformation, with regards to this, Catholic and magisterial reformers tended to hold to the former view, but Anabaptists and radical reformers tended to support the latter view. In other words, this tendency to correlate the validity of infant baptism with the understanding of original sin is explained in an objective perspective with regard to future salvation. However, Hubmaier's understanding of the relationship between infant baptism and original sin cannot be categorized in this way since it is clear that he rejects the validity of infant baptism although he acknowledges original sin. In all of his theology, Hubmaier argued for the primacy of Scripture over tradition. In his understanding, the concept of original sin is found in the Bible, but the practice of infant baptism is not. Hubmaier's understanding of the relation between infant baptism and original sin needs to be understood in his definition of faith through a subjective and relational perspective. In this perspective, his characteristic understanding of faith is that faith is only meaningful in the present tense, but not in the past or future tense. In this context, the relation between original sin and infant baptism for the salvation of infants is unimportant. This example shows that Hubmaier's doctrine of baptism, which requires faith as prerequisite, needs to be understood in a subjective and relational perspective rather than in an objective and transactional perspective.

e. Concerning the Lord's Supper

In chapter 5, Hubmaier's understanding of the Lord's Supper as a living memorial of Christ's death understood, experientially showed that the Supper includes the commitment and pledge of love for others by the

Conclusion: A Fresh Perspective on Hubmaier's Doctrine of Salvation

partaker. The partaker's present realization of Christ's death through the Lord's Supper leads to the partaker's commitment to love and sacrifice for other neighbors mirroring the way that Jesus Christ showed His love to us through His sacrifice even unto the death. To realize and live in the relationship between God and the partaker through the Lord's Supper helps to let the partaker to look at the relationship between the partaker and other believers. Here, the Lord's Supper as the pledge of love is understood in terms of a relational perspective such that it is depended on the relationship between God and a partaker and between the partaker and other believers.

However, this obligation which is formed by the partaker's pledge of love is not a one-sided responsibility which is given to an individual partaker of the Supper, but rather a reciprocal duty among all those who participate in the Supper with their commitment to live according to the commandments of Christ. The choice to live according to the Rule of Christ through the pledge of love is not accomplished by singular effort only but through the efforts of others to help and encourage each other to follow the way of Christ. In this sense, for Hubmaier, the fraternal admonition and Christian ban are essential elements for sustaining the community of believers in terms of his relational emphasis for the Lord's Supper.

We also saw Hubmaier's experiential perspective on the doctrine of salvation in his Christology for the Lord's Supper. The contemporary Christology of Hubmaier's day can be distinguished in two different ways: Word-Flesh Christology and Word-Man Christology. As shown in the previous chapter, Catholics and Luther held what can be understood as a Word-Flesh Christological perspective which was expressed in the doctrine of the Real Presence of Christ in the Lord's Supper. Alternatively, the Word-Man Christology, which asserted that the physical Christ cannot be present on the earth after His ascension, was held by such as Zwingli and the Anabaptists, who rejected the traditional understanding of the real presence of Christ in the Lord's Supper. However, the Christology that characterizes Hubmaier's theology of the Lord's Supper cannot be explained solely by either Word-Flesh or Word-Man Christological approaches. Although Hubmaier seemed to depend more on the Word-Man perspective for rejecting the real presence of Christ in the Supper, he also grafted the Word-Flesh Christology into his doctrine of church. Hubmaier's intention in using this compounded Christology for the Supper showed that a transactional perspective of Christology for the Supper in traditional view is not sufficient to describe the Christology he adopts.

Hubmaier's focus on the present tense in relational perspective towards the Lord's Supper is shown in his definition of the Supper as memorial, which is based on his Christology. Although his theology of the Supper as the remembrance of the death of Christ appeared similar to Zwingli's, there were some differences between them. For Zwingli, the meaning of the Supper as memorial is to give an assurance of salvation to the partakers through remembering the past event of Christ's death for us. For Hubmaier, this understanding means the transferring of the past event of Christ's death into the present event for the partakers through their recognition from the point of view of experience. However, understanding the Supper as a memorial does not only mean mental or spiritual recognition of Christ's love through His death, but also the partakers' participating in Christ's suffering and death through their lives to love and live willingly for others as their present obligation now. In this sense, the meaning of the Supper must be linked with the concept of pledge of love.

Hubmaier's dynamic understanding of salvation can be seen in the central aspects of his theology, the freedom of human will, baptism, and the Lord's Supper. His dynamic and relational understanding of salvation argues that the meaning of faith for salvation is not only the inward change in a human being, but also the outward change of human life willingly. Hubmaier explained the significance of baptism and the Lord's Supper in dynamic and relational terms for salvation and showed that for believers the continual recognition of God's grace in the present time is essential for their salvific lives to sustain their relationship with God and to live according to the Rule of Christ.

4. The Implication of Hubmaier's Doctrine of Salvation for Today's Christian Life

As I have suggested, Hubmaier's writings are not only relevant for the study of the past, but for reflection on our current situation. In this section I will indicate three broad areas where I argue he can help us: the nature of salvation, the nature of the church as community and the significance of the sacraments.

a. The Nature of Salvation

Hubmaier's doctrine of salvation with its subjective and relational perspective is distinguished from other contemporary soteriology which was

Conclusion: A Fresh Perspective on Hubmaier's Doctrine of Salvation

marked by a transactional perspective. As we have already seen, his motive for arguing for church reform came from seeing the phenomenon of people compromised after their baptism and the consequent misuse of the phrase "justification by faith." In this context, Hubmaier felt that the motto of the Reformation "justification by faith" was being misunderstood as it ignored the significance of Christian life as lived in everyday contexts. Through his understanding of faith in dynamic and relational perspective, Hubmaier showed that the meaning of faith for salvation does not ignore, but in fact reinforces, the importance of Christian life. In his doctrine of salvation, Hubmaier did not focus on the meaning of faith as either a human emotional experience of the Holy Spirit or a simple acceptance of historical knowledge of Christ's death and resurrection. Although he accepted that we are saved only by faith as other contemporary reformers did, he wanted to show how Christian life is important for salvation through redefining the concept of faith.

The failure to see Hubmaier's redefinition of the concept of faith, as we have already seen in previous research methodologies that focus on the transactional perspective, leads to the weakening of the significance of his doctrine of salvation for Christian life. Hubmaier's understanding of faith in dynamic and relational aspect suggests a new perspective on the doctrine of salvation, which can overcome the weaknesses of the transactional perspective for soteriology. For Hubmaier the meaning of faith as the relationship with God is understood not in the view of the past or future tense but in the view of "here" and "now" of the *present* context. The meaning of salvation in Hubmaier's theology does not mean simply the assurance of the ticket to heaven after death nor the transferring the status of a believer to being a child of God. For him the meaning of salvation is based on a believer's recognition that he or she lives in the grace of God. His intention in emphasizing salvation is for believers to examine their lives according to the question of whether they live as proper Christians in seeking the right relationship with God day by day.

For Hubmaier salvation by faith is a relationship with God which means that a believer sustains the relationship with God by pleasing Him through living according to the Rule of Christ. If our relationship with God needs to be a continual reality, evidenced by the sanctifying of our lives then should we fear that it may not be sufficient to ensure our permanent salvation? "Relationship with God" requires us to be holy like Him.[10] However, it does not mean we have to live in fear all the time wor-

---

10. Cf. Lev 11:44–45, 19:2; Exod 31:13; 1 Cor 1:2; Col 1:22; 1 Thess 4:7.

rying about what God requires of us. We are instead meant to enjoy our relationship with God. If we always have a relationship with God in fear and trembling, it would not be a truly personal relationship. The "personal relationship with God" is to become a motive power of our lives provoking a dynamic and active choice to follow His will. The relational view of salvation places appropriate emphasis on the "here" and "now" which is turn enables a more practical understanding of problems in the Christian life.

Hubmaier's understanding of salvation by faith in dynamic and relational perspective can be applied to our contemporary Christianity which also faces the same issue in the Christian life as in the Reformation era. In our contemporary Christian society, there is still a tendency for the meaning of salvation to be understood in either an extreme view of predestination in fatalism or over-emphasis on the assurance of faith which could reduce the significance of Christian moral life. In contrast, there are also those who are living in fear of God all the time because of a legalistic understanding of salvation. Hubmaier's understanding of faith in a dynamic and relational perspective reduces the possibility of these extreme tendencies in Christian life, because his concept of faith for salvation cannot be understood without the life of the believer. However, his emphasis on the significance of Christian life is not based on legalism but it is understood as a changed life in the relationship with God, which is dynamic but not static. Thus, Hubmaier's concept of faith offers us the reason to know what we should do as a Christian in order to sustain the relationship with God. In this sense, it would become natural that our lives in Christ do not ignore the necessity of an improving moral life according to the Rule of Christ. For believers to imitate the life of Christ is their pleasure for God in this personal relationship between them. Here Hubmaier's emphasis to sustaining the right relationship with God is not to focus on an ascetic practice such as a monastic life in the medieval period. If his concept of faith as the relationship with God would mean only a self-denial expressed in asceticism, this life would not be different from a monastic life.

b. The Nature of Church as Community

Hubmaier, however, insisted that the change of Christian life through living according to the Rule of Christ is accomplished within the relationship with other believers. From this point of view, he regarded the practice of believers' baptism as the essential element for Christian life. In his relational understanding of faith for salvation, Hubmaier also insisted on the

Conclusion: A Fresh Perspective on Hubmaier's Doctrine of Salvation

significance of the role of believers' community as the body of Christ. For Hubmaier, entrance into this community of believers by means of baptism was accompanied by the baptizand's commitment to accepting and following the Rule of Christ. The newly baptized person also accepted the responsibility to live by this Rule. The role of this community of believers is to help and encourage each other to live according to the Rule of Christ. The believer's life which is progressing in following the way of Christ is to be enforced in order to live together with other believers. In this sense, all members of the same community of believers should know and look after each other regarding each other as brothers and sisters in the love of Christ. From this point of view, the community of believers requires relationship between believers to sustain the community.

Unless we have concern for each other to encourage, correct and rebuke with great patience and with careful instruction in love, we will find it difficult to live as Christians according to the Rule of Christ. From this point of view, Hubmaier's understanding of the role of the community for believers draws our attention to rethink the role of church as the community of believers in our day. There is a tendency for some church communities to hold on to a vision of the church as constantly seeking growth for its own sake.[11] To create a bigger size of community, churches tend to accept people without examining their sincere commitment to Christ as expressed through the community. This situation can result in there being no strong relationship between church members. The chase for a larger community can lead to the loss of the essential function of a church in looking after each other to help each other live according to the will of God. In this context, the significance of the relationship between believers at church is weakened, so it tends to ignore the situation that many people just attend a service on Sunday as nominal Christians without it affecting their lives. But the proper function of the church is to lead a member to live for Christ through concern for each other. Therefore, we need to be more concerned about the fundamental role of church in helping believers to live and grow as children of God than on how we can expand our community.

---

11. In particular, this tendency is strongly present in American and South Korean churches. For instance, Saddleback Church (Pastor Rick Warren), Willow Creek Community Church (Pastor Bill Hybels), Lakewood Church (Pastor Joel Osteen), Yoido Full Gospel Church (Emeritus Pastor Yong-Gi Cho), Onnuri Community Church (Pastor Jae-Hoon Lee), and Sarang Community Church (Pastor Jung-Hyun Oh) are regarded as models of very successful churches.

Balthasar Hubmaier's Doctrine of Salvation

c. The Significance of the Sacraments

Hubmaier's concept of baptism and the Lord's Supper draws us to reevaluate the significance of the sacramental rites for Christian life. Hubmaier's stress on the exercise of water baptism which is a confession of the baptizand's faith with his or her commitment to live according to the Rule of Christ implies that both the baptizand and the church should remember how costly it is to be a Christian. Unless the baptizand is ready to follow the commandment of Christ, he or she should not be baptized. This will remove the danger of abusing the practice of baptism as the entry of the baptizand into the community of believers.

Hubmaier believed that too much emphasis on the toleration of sinners in the church without any concern about it disturbs people in their pursuit of the way of Christ. For him, this problem regarding Christian life could be resolved by placing the emphasis on the meaning of the Lord's Supper involving the exercise of fraternal admonition and Christian ban. The fraternal admonition and Christian ban in the Lord's Supper may only be exercised properly when believers in the community sustain strong relationships with each other. The proper exercise of fraternal admonition and Christian ban in the context of the Lord's Supper can help church members recognize his or her sin, and repent of it. The reason for these practices is not to condemn or judge those who have sinned, but to enable the restoration of the relationship between God and the believers, and the reconciliation between believers through them. Through attending the Lord's Supper, the partakers recognize the necessity of forgiving the one in the community who sinned as we are forgiven by the grace of God. As the Lord's Supper shows the forgiveness and love of God for our sins, we also need to confess our sins to be forgiven and to be reconciled with other members of the community. Hubmaier's understanding of the Lord's Supper involving fraternal admonition and Christian ban will help us to examine whether we are following the way of Christ, and to rethink the importance of the community as the body of Christ. This reinforces the ongoing relationship with God, and with other believers in the life of salvation.

In looking at the characteristics of Hubmaier's doctrine of salvation, this thesis offers a fresh perspective within which to understand the meaning of salvation. It is clear that his doctrine of salvation, understood through a dynamic and relational approach, showed the necessity of asserting the significance of Christian life for salvation even though he maintained the motto of the Reformation, "justification by faith." From

Conclusion: A Fresh Perspective on Hubmaier's Doctrine of Salvation

this point of view, I suggest that studies on the doctrine of salvation need further consideration and development using a dynamic and relational perspective, which can complement objective and transactional perspective for soteriology. This thesis does not claim that Hubmaier was the only one who was concerned with the issue of the immorality of people who called themselves Christians. Both in Hubmaier's days and since, there are others who have also been concerned with this issue and might construct an argument around the question of salvation in Hubmaier's particular way. For them, the methodology of this thesis for the study of Hubmaier's theology would, I suggest, be valuable in re-examining their theology and in understanding it from a different perspective.

Bibliography

Primary Sources

Aquinas, Thomas. *Summa Theologica*. 5 vols. Westminster, MD: Christian Classics, 1981.
Augustine of Hippo. *de correptione et gratia*. In *PL* 44:915-46.
———. *de diversibus quaestionibus ad Simplicianum*. In *CC*, edited by A. Mutzenbecher, 44:620-27. Turnholt: Brepols, 1970.
———. *de gratia Christi*. In *CSEL* 42:128.1-29.
———. *de natura et gratia*. In *CSEL* 60:235.8—236.6.
———. *de peccato originale*. In *CSEL* 42:175.22-7.
———. *de spiritu et littera*. In *CSEL* 60:157.10-24.
Baylor, M. G., editor. *The Radical Reformation*. Cambridge: Cambridge University Press, 1991.
Bergsten, Torsten, and Gunnar Westin, editors. *Balthasar Hubmaier: Schriften*. QGT IX. Gütersloher: Mohn, 1962.
Biel, Gabriel. *Collectorium Circa Quattuor Libros Sententiarum*. 4 vols. Tübingen: Mohr/Siebeck, 1975.
Denzinger, H., and A. Schönmetzer, editors. *Enchiridion Symbolorum Definitionem et Declarationem*. 33rd ed. Rome: Herder, 1965.
Erasmus von Rotterdam. *De libero diatribe sive collatio*. Edited by Winfried Lesowsky. Ausgewählte Schriften 4. Darmstadt: Wissenschaftliche Buchgesellschaft, 1969.
Harder, Leland, editor. *The Sources of Swiss Anabaptism. The Grebel Letters and Related Documents*. Classics of the Radical Reformation 4. Scottdale, PA: Herald, 1985.
Hugh of St. Victor. "De sacramentis fidei christianae." In *PL* 176:174-618. Paris, 1880.
Klaassen, Walter, editor. *Anabaptism in Outline: Selected Primary Sources*. Classics of the Radical Reformation. Scottdale, PA: Herald, 1981.
Luther, Martin. *D. Martin Luthers Werke: Kritische Gesamtausgabe*. 73 vols. Weimar: Böhlau, 1883–.
———. *Luther's Works*. American Edition. 55 vols. Edited by Jaroslav Pelikan and Helmut T. Lehmann. Philadelphia: Muhlenberg, 1955-75.
Pelagius, "Letter to Demetrias." In *PL* 33:1110A-B.
Peter Lombard. *Sententiae in IV Libris Distinctae*. Vol. 2. Edited by I. C. Brady. 3rd ed. Grottaferrata: Collegii S. Bonaventurae ad Claras Aquas, 1971-81.
Pipkin, H. Wayne, and John H. Yoder, editors. *Balthasar Hubmaier. Theologian of Anabaptism*. Classics of the Radical Reformation 5. Scottdale, PA: Herald, 1989.

Bibliography

Rupp, E. G., and P. S. Watson, editors. *Luther and Erasmus: Free Will and Salvation.* LCC 17. London: SCM, 1969.

Schornbaum, Karl, editor. *Markgraftum Brandenburg.* QGT II. Leipzig: Nachfolger, 1934.

Williams, G. H., and A. M. Mergal, editors. *Spiritual and Anabaptist Writers. Documents Illustrative of the Radical Reformation.* Philadelphia: Westminster, 1977.

Zwingli, Huldreich. "Declaration of Huldreich Zwingli Regarding Original Sin." In *The Latin Works of Huldreich Zwingli*, vol. 2, edited by W. J. Hinke. Philadelphia: Heidelberg, 1922.

———. *The Latin Works of Huldreich Zwingli.* Vol. 3. Reprinted as *Commentary on True and False Religion*, edited by S. M. Jackson and C. N. Heller. Durham, NC: Labyrinth, 1981.

———. *Zwingli and Bullinger*, edited by G. W. Bromiley. LCC 24. London: SCM, 1963.

Secondary Sources

Althaus, Paul. *The Theology of Martin Luther.* Philadelphia: Fortress, 1966.

Armour, Rollin S. *Anabaptist Baptism: A Representative Study.* SAMH. No. 11. Scottdale, PA: Herald, 1966.

Barr, James. "The Pelagian Controversy." *The Evangelical Quarterly* 21 (1949) 253–64.

Beachy, Alvin J. *The Concept of Grace in the Radical Reformation.* Bibliotheca Humanistica & Reformatorica 17. Nieuwkoop: De Graaf, 1977.

Bender, Harold Stauffer. "Anabaptist Vision." In *The Recovery of the Anabaptist Vision*, edited by G. F. Hershberger, 29–54. Scottdale, PA: Herald, 1957. cf. Presidential address, the American Society of Church History, December 1943. Reprinted from *Church History* 13 (1944) 3–24 and *MQR* 18 (1944) 67–88.

Bergsten, Torsten. *Balthasar Hubmaier: Seine Stellung Zu Reformation Und Täufertum, 1521–1528.* Kassel: Oncken, 1961.

Bergsten, Torsten, and William. R. Estep. *Balthasar Hubmaier: Anabaptist Theologian and Martyr.* Valley Forge, PA: Judson, 1978.

Bonner, Gerald. *Augustine and Modern Research on Pelagianism.* Villanova: Villanova University Press, 1972.

Brecht, Martin. *Martin Luther Shaping and Defining the Reformation 1521–1532.* Minneapolis: Fortress, 1994.

Brewer, Brian C. *A Pledge of Love: The Anabaptist Sacramental Theology of Balthasar Hubmaier.* Milton Keynes: Paternoster, 2012.

Brown, Peter. "Pelagius and His Supporters." *Journal of Theological Studies* 19 (1968) 93–114.

Buber, Martin. *I and Thou.* Edinburgh: T. & T. Clark, 1958.

Chatfield, G. R. "Balthasar Hubmaier and the Clarity of Scripture: A Study in the Development of Reformation Hermeneutics." PhD diss., University of Bristol, 1993.

Clark, S. J. F. *Eucharistic Sacrifice and the Reformation.* 2nd ed. Oxford: Blackwell, 1967.

Clasen, Claus-Peter. *Anabaptism: A Social History, 1525–1618.* Ithaca, NY: Cornell University Press, 1972.

Colish, M. L. *Peter Lombard*, vol. 2, edited by A. J. Vanderjagt. 2vols. Brill's Studies in Intellectual History. Leiden: Brill, 1994.

Bibliography

Colwell, John E. *Promise and Presence: An Exploration of Sacramental Theology.* Milton Keynes: Paternoster, 2005.

Davis, Kenneth R. "Erasmus as a Progenitor of Anabaptist Theology and Piety." *MQR* 47 (1973) 163–78.

———. *Anabaptism and Asceticism.* Scottdale, PA: Herald, 1974.

Enninger, W. "The Second Zurich Disputation in 1523: A Discourse-Analytical Approach." *MQR* 65 (1991) 407–26.

Erickson, Millard J. *Christian Theology.* Grand Rapids: Baker, 1995.

Estep, William R. *The Anabaptist Story: An Introduction to Sixteenth-Century Anabaptism.* 3rd ed. Grand Rapids: Eerdmans, 1996.

Ferguson, John. *Pelagius: A Historical and Theological Study.* Cambridge: Heffer, 1956.

Frank, Robert S. *A History of the Doctrine of the Work of Christ.* Eugene, OR: Wipf & Stock, 2001.

Friedmann, Robert. "The Doctrine of Original Sin as Held by the Anabaptists of the Sixteenth Century." *MQR* 32 (1959) 206–14.

———. "Peter Riedemann: Early Anabaptist Leader." *MQR* 44 (1970) 38–39.

———. *The Theology of Anabaptism. An Interpretation.* SAMH. No. 15. Scottdale, PA: Herald, 1973.

Gäbler, Ulrich. *Huldrych Zwingli.* Edinburgh: T. & T. Clark, 1987.

George, Timothy. "The Presuppositions of Zwingli's Baptismal Theology." In *Prophet Pastor Protestant: The Work of Huldrych Zwingli after Five Hundred Years*, edited by E. J. Furcha and H. W. Pipkin, 71–87. Allison Park, PA: Pickwick, 1984.

Goertz, Hans-Jürgen. *The Anabaptists.* London, New York: Routledge, 1996.

Goncharenko, Simon Victor. *Wounds That Heal: The Importance of Church Discipline within Balthasar Hubmaier's Theology.* Eugene, OR: Pickwick, 2012.

Hall, Thor. "The Possibilities of Erasmian Influence on Denck and Hubmaier in Their View on the Freedom of the Will." *MQR* 35 (1961) 149–70.

Hilerbrand, H. J. "Anabaptism and History." *MQR* 45 (1971) 107–22.

Hosek, F. *Life of Balthasar Hubmaier, the founder of "New Christianity" in Moravia.* Texas Baptist History and Biographical Magazine, 1891.

Hutterian Brethren, editor. *The Chronicle of the Hutterian Brethren.* Vol. 1. New York: Plough, 1987.

Janz, Denis, et al. *Three Reformation Catechisms: Catholic, Anabaptist, Lutheran.* Texts and Studies in Religion 13. New York: Mellen, 1982.

Johnson, Todd E. "Initiation or Ordination? Balthasar Hubmaier's Rite of Baptism." *Studia Liturgica* 25 (1995) 68–85.

Keller, Ludwig. *Ein Apostel Der Wiedertäufer.* Leipzig: Hirzell, 1882.

———. *Geschichte Der Wiedertäufer.* Münster, 1880.

———. *Johann Von Staupitz Und Die Anfänge Der Reformation.* Leipzig, 1888.

Kelly, J. N. D. *Early Christian Doctrines.* 5th ed. London: Black, 1993.

Klaassen, Walter. "Speaking in Simplicity: Balthasar Hubmaier." *MQR* 40 (1966) 139–47.

Klassen, William. "Anabaptist Hermeneutics: The Letter and the Spirit." *MQR* 40 (1966) 83–96.

Kyle, R. "Semi-Pelagianism." In *EDT* 999–1000.

Leth, Carl M. "Balthasar Hubmaier's 'Catholic' Exegesis: Matthew 16:18–19 and the Power of the Keys." In *Biblical Interpretation in the Era of the Reformation*, edited by R. A. Muller and J. L. Thompson, 103–17. Grand Rapids: Eerdmans, 1996.

Bibliography

Littell, Franklin H. *The Anabaptist View of the Church*. 2nd ed. Boston: Starr King, 1958.
Lohse, Bernhard. *Martin Luther's Theology. Its Historical and Systematic Development*. Minneapolis: Fortress, 1999.
Loserth, Johann. *D. Balthasar Hubmaier Und Die Anfänge Der Wiedertaufe in Mähren*. Brünn: Verlag der histßstatist, 1893.
Lüdemann, H. *Refomation Und Täufertum in Ihren Verhaltnis Zum Christlichen Prinzep*. 1890.
Mabry, Eddie L. *Balthasar Hubmaier's Doctrine of the Church*. Lanham, MD: University Press of America, 1994.
———. *Balthasar Hubmaier's Understanding of Faith*. Lanham, MD: University Press of America, 1998.
MacGregor, Kirk R. *A Central European Synthesis of Radical and Magisterial Reform: The Sacramental Theology of Balthasar Hubmaier*. Lanham, MD: University Press of America, 2006.
———. "Hubmaier's Concord of Predestination with Free Will." *Direction* 35 (2006) 279–99.
Martin, Dennis D. "Catholic Spirituality and Anabaptist and Mennonite Discipleship." *MQR* 62 (1988) 5–25.
McClendon, James W., Jr. "Balthasar Hubmaier, Catholic Anabaptist." *MQR* 65 (1991) 20–33.
———. *Ethics*. Vol. 1 of *Systematic Theology*. Nashville: Abingdon, 1986.
McGrath, Alister E. *Christian Theology*. Oxford: Blackwell, 1997.
———. *Iustitia Dei. A History of the Christian Doctrine of Justification*. 2nd ed. Cambridge: Cambridge University Press, 1998.
———. *Justification by Faith*. Grand Rapids: Academie, 1990.
———. *Reformation Thought*. 3rd ed. Oxford: Blackwell, 2004.
———, editor. *The Christian Theology Reader*. Oxford: Blackwell, 1996.
Moore, Walter L. "Catholic Teacher and Anabaptist Pupil: The Relationship between John Eck and Balthasar Hubmaier." *ARG* 72 (1981) 68–97.
Muller, Richard A. *Dictionary of Latin and Greek Theological Terms*. Grand Rapids: Baker, 1985.
Murray, Stuart. *Biblical Interpretation in the Anabaptist Tradition*. Studies in the Believers Church Tradition. Kitchener: Pandora, 2000.
———. *Radical Christian Groups and Their Contemporary Relevance for the Church*. Cheltenham: Open Theological College, 1998.
Nam, Samuel Byung-Doo. "A Comparative Study of the Baptismal Understanding of Augustine, Luther, Zwingli, and Hubmaier." PhD diss., Southwestern Baptist Theological Seminary, 2002.
Neumann, G. J. "The Anabaptist Position on Baptism and the Lord's Supper." *MQR* 35 (1961) 140–48.
Oberman, Heiko A. *Masters of the Reformation*. Cambridge: Cambridge University Press, 1981.
Osterhaven, M. E. "Lord's Supper," in *EDT* 653–655.
Packull, Werner O. *Mysticism and the Early South German-Austrian Anabaptist Movement, 1525–1531*. SAMH. No. 19. Scottdale, PA: Herald, 1977.
Pearse, Meic. *The Great Restoration. The Religious Radicals of the 16th and 17th Centuries*. Lancaster: Paternoster, 1998.

Pelikan, Jaroslav. *Reformation of Church and Dogma 1300–1700*. Vol. 4 of *The Christian Tradition*. Chicago: University of Chicago Press, 1984.
Phipps, W. E. "The Heresiarch: Pelagius or Augustine?" *ART* 62 (1982) 124–33.
Pipkin, H. Wayne. "The Baptismal Theology of Balthasar Hubmaier." *MQR* 65 (1991) 34–53.
———. *Scholar, Pastor, Martyr: The Life and Ministry of Balthasar Hubmaier (ca. 1480–1528)*. Praha: IBTS of EBF, o.p.s., 2008.
Rempel, John D. *The Lord's Supper in Anabaptism. A Study in the Christology of Balthasar Hubmaier, Pilgram Marpeck, and Dirk Philips*. SAMH. No. 33. Waterloo, OT: Herald, 1993.
Richards, G. W. "Introduction on 'Commentary on True and False Religion.'" In *The Latin Works and the Correspondence of Huldreich Zwingli*, edited by S. M. Jackson, 1–42. Philadelphia: Heidelberg, 1929.
Ritschl, Albrecht. *Geschichte Der Pietismus*. Bonn: Adolp Marcus, 1880.
Rosemann, P. W. *Peter Lombard*. Oxford: Oxford University Press, 2004.
Rothenberger, J. R. *Caspar Schwenckfeld Von Ossig and the Ecumenical Ideal*. Pensburg, PA: Board of Publication of the Schwenckfelder Church, 1967.
Rupp, Gordon. *Patterns of Reformation*. London: Epworth, 1969.
Sachsse, Carl. *D. Balthasar Hubmaier Als Theologe*. Neue Studien Zur Geschichte Der Theologie Und Der Kirche 20. Berlin: Neudruck der Ausgabe, 1914.
———. *Dr Balthasar Hubmaiers Anschauungen von der Kirche, den Sakramenten und der Obrigkeit*. Bonn: Carl Georgi, Universitäts-Buchdruckerei, 1913.
Seebaß, Gottfried. "Das Zeichen Der Erwählten. Zum Verständnis Der Taufe Bei Hans Hut." In *Umstrittenes Täufertum, 1525–1975*, edited by H.-J. Goertz, 138–64. Göttingen: Vandenhoeck & Ruprecht, 1975.
Senn, Frank C. *Christian Liturgy*. Minneapolis: Fortress, 1997.
Snyder, C. Arnold. *Anabaptist History and Theology*. Scottdale, PA: Herald, 1997.
———. "The Birth and Evolution of Swiss Anabaptism (1520–1530)." *MQR* 80 (2006) 501–645.
———. "The Influence of the Schleitheim Articles on the Anabaptist Movement: An Historical Evaluation." *MQR* 63 (1989) 323–44.
———. "Modern Mennonite Reality and Anabaptist Spirituality: Balthasar Hubmaier's Catechism of 1526." *Conrad Grebel Review* 9 (1991) 37–51.
Staehelin, Ernst. *Briefe und Akten zum Leben Oekolampads*. Vol. 1. Leipzig: Nachfolger, 1927.
Stayer, James M., et al. *Anabaptists and the Sword*. 2nd ed. Lawrence, KS: Coronado, 1976.
———. "From Monogenesis to Polygenesis: The Historical Discussion of Anabaptist Origins." *MQR* 49 (1975) 83–121.
Steinmetz, David C. "The Baptism of John and the Baptism of Jesus." In *Continuity and Discontinuity in Church History: Essays Presented to George Huntston Williams on the Occasion of His 65th Birthday*, edited by F. F. Church and Timothy George, 169–81. Studies in the History of Christian Thought 19. Leiden: Brill, 1979.
———. "Scholasticism and Radical Reform: Norminalist Motifs in the Theology of Balthasar Hubmaier." *MQR* 45 (1971) 123–44.
———. *Luther in Context*. 2nd ed. Grand Rapids: Baker Academic, 2002.
Stephens, W. P. *The Theology of Huldrych Zwingli*. Oxford: Clarendon, 1986.

Bibliography

Vedder, Henry C. *Balthasar Hübmaier. The Leader of the Anabaptists.* Heroes of the Reformation 8. New York: Putnam's Sons, 1905.

Voth, G. L. "Anabaptist Liturgical Spirituality and the Supper of Christ." *Direction* 34 (2005) 3–14.

Walton, R. C. "The Institutionalization of the Reformation at Zurich." *Zwingliana* 13 (1972) 497–515.

Weaver, R. H. *Divine Grace and Human Agency: A Study of the Semi-Pelagian Controversy.* Marcon, GA: Mercer University Press, 1998.

Wenger, J. C. *Even Unto Death.* Richmond, VA: John Knox, 1961.

———. "Grace and Discipleship in Anabaptism." *MQR* 35 (1961) 50–68.

———. "The Schleitheim Confession of Faith." *MQR* 19 (1945) 248.

Williams, George Huntston. *The Radical Reformation.* 3rd ed. Sixteenth Century Essays & Studies 15. Kirksville, MO: Sixteenth Century Journal, 1992.

———. "Sanctification in the Testimony of Several So-Called Schwärmer." *MQR* 42 (1968) 5–25.

Windhorst, Christoph. "Anfänge Und Aspekte Der Theologie Hubmaiers." In *The Origins and Characteristics of Anabaptism*, edited by M. Lienhard, 148–68. The Hague: Nijhoff, 1977.

———. "Das Gedächtnis Des Leidens Christi Und Pflichtzeichen Brüderlicher Liebe, Zum Verständis Des Abendmahls Bei Balthasar Hubmaier." In *Umstrittenes Täufertum, 1525–1975*, edited by Hans-Jürgen Goertz, 111–37. Göttingen: Neue Forchungen, 1975.

———. *Täuferisches Taufverstädnis. Balthasar Hubmaiers Lehre Zwischen Traditioneller Und Reformatorischer Theologie.* Studies in Medieval and Reformation Thought 16. Leiden: Brill, 1976.

Wray, F. "Free Will with the Anabaptists." In *ME* 367–69.

Wright, David. F. "Pelagius the Twice-Born." *The Churchman* 88 (1972) 6–15.

Yoder, John. H. "Balthasar Hubmaier and the Beginnings of Swiss Anabaptism." *MQR* 33 (1959) 5–17.

Index

active, 34, 35, 45, 65–67, 73, 88, 119, 127, 143, 165, 182, 192
Adam, 41, 47–49, 51, 53–56, 61, 125, 126, 173
Anabaptism, 1, 6, 7, 9–13, 16, 17, 19, 23, 50, 127, 134, 142, 180
Anabaptist(s), ix, x, xi, 1–16, 18, 20, 22–26, 31, 43, 50, 71, 73, 74, 75, 84, 86, 95–98, 106, 108, 129, 131, 133, 134, 140, 147, 177, 186, 188, 189
angels, 65
anthropology, 1, 17, 21, 22
antinomianism, 28, 67
apocalyptic, 133
apologia, 6, 78, 108, 147
apostles, 83, 84, 93, 100
apostolic, 20, 74
Aquinas (Thomas), 152, 153
Aristotelian, 152, 157
ascension, 149, 155, 157–59, 166, 177, 189
ascetic(ism), 16, 126, 192
assurance, 34, 84, 104, 132, 163, 164, 190–92
astray, 83, 169
attribute, 37, 155, 166
Augsburg, 2, 7
Augustine, 54–60, 64, 77, 133
Augustinian, 19, 54, 59, 62, 133, 134, 137
authentic, 9–13, 24, 119
authority, 11, 37, 46, 77, 80, 82–84, 121–23, 143, 154, 175

ban, ix, xii, 121, 132, 150, 158, 162, 163, 174–77, 189, 194
baptism, ix, xii, 7, 8, 15, 18–20, 22, 23, 25, 26, 29, 30, 41, 44, 56, 68–70, 72, 74, 75, 69–145
  of believers, 1, 6, 8, 12, 71–74, 76–86, 88, 107, 119, 121, 133, 138, 146, 147, 150, 151, 162, 165, 186
  of blood, 78, 90, 108–10, 115, 116, 125–32, 143, 145, 187
  of Christ, 26, 98–106
  of infants, 1, 6, 71, 73, 74, 76, 80–84, 87–90, 95–100, 105–7, 133–142
  of John, 26, 98–106
  of the Spirit, 85, 107–17, 122, 127, 128, 131, 132, 143, 145, 171, 187
  threefold, 1, 78, 89, 90, 106–10, 116, 128, 131–33, 143, 145, 186, 187
  water, 29, 41, 78, 85, 86, 88–90, 96, 97, 100–103, 105, 108, 109, 111, 114–25, 131, 132, 138, 143, 145, 146, 150, 151, 161, 162, 171, 175–77, 186, 187, 194
baptist, 14, 63
belief, 34, 35, 44, 45, 64, 83, 88, 97, 119, 142, 169
believer(s), 7, 22, 40, 41, 42, 44, 57, 61, 65, 68, 71, 78, 79, 81, 82, 84, 85, 88, 89, 102, 104, 106, 108, 111, 116–25, 136, 138,

Index

believer(s) (*cont.*)
140, 141, 143–46, 148, 150,
159, 160–64, 168–79, 181,
184, 186–94
Bernard of Clairvaux, 21, 22, 25
Bible. *See* Scripture
biblical(ly), 4, 11, 20, 21, 43–46,
48, 51, 75, 77, 79–82, 84, 86,
103, 134, 136, 137, 141, 149,
150, 183, 186
Biel, G., 20, 26, 91, 93, 94, 102
bind, 123
birth, 2, 13, 41
body, 17, 21, 41–43, 45, 46, 48, 49,
51–53, 110, 124, 148–60,
162, 164–68, 170, 172, 174,
177, 178, 193, 194
bondage (of the will), 17, 31, 32,
38, 42–44, 59
Brandenburg-Ansbach, 42
Brethren, 9–13, 24
Bride, 122
brother(s/ly), 32, 72, 105, 120, 121,
125, 143, 148, 160, 161, 168,
174, 175
brotherhood, 9, 11, 73, 117

Calvin, J., 95, 169
captive, 41
catechism, 17, 40–42, 78, 79, 90,
108, 110, 147, 148, 150
Catholic (ism/tradition), ix, 2–4,
8, 14–16, 19, 20–22, 24–26,
31, 41, 70, 71, 73, 79, 91–93,
95, 97–99, 102, 103, 106,
107, 117–19, 122, 123, 133,
138, 139, 142, 143, 145–54,
156–59, 163–66, 169, 177,
178, 181, 186, 188, 189
choice, 18, 35–37, 39, 40, 61, 66,
189, 192
choose, 16, 18, 31, 38, 45–49,
53–57, 60, 61, 63, 67, 126,
141

Christian(ity), ix, xi, xii, 2–4, 6, 7,
10, 11, 13, 17, 19, 22, 23, 28,
29, 31–38, 40–44, 48, 49,
64, 71, 73, 78, 79, 81–85,
87, 88, 92, 98, 104, 105, 108,
114, 117, 118, 120, 122,
124, 125, 127, 129–36, 143,
144, 146–48, 153, 160–63,
169–71, 173–79, 189–95
Christolog(y/ical), ix, 1, 21, 43,
149–51, 155, 157–60, 166,
178, 189, 190
church, ix, xi, 3–9, 11, 14, 15, 19,
20, 22, 23, 28, 37, 41, 78,
81–83, 105, 109, 112, 117,
120, 121, 123, 127, 130, 132,
134–36, 138, 143, 146, 147,
149, 150, 159, 161, 162,
168, 174–77, 179–81, 187,
189–91, 193, 194
universal, 43, 122, 152
visible, 116, 119, 120–22
church fathers, 76, 77
circumcision, 92, 94, 135, 136
clergy, 4
communicatio idiomatum, 155, 166
communion. *See* Lord's Supper
community, 5, 82, 88, 104–6,
120–24, 129, 135, 136, 143,
144, 150, 161, 162, 174–78,
181, 186, 187, 189, 190,
192–94
congregation(al), 14, 68, 104, 116,
119, 120–22, 124, 128, 150,
160, 162, 169, 175–77
Constance, 5
connection, 8, 11, 15–17, 45, 61,
64, 68, 72, 120, 162, 163
consubstantiation, 21, 155, 156,
177
council, 5, 59, 77, 134, 152
conversion, 17, 40
covenant, 77, 97, 103, 106, 122,
131, 132, 134–36, 145, 161
Cyprian, 77

Danube, 8
death, xi, 7, 34, 41, 43, 47, 49–51, 53, 65, 78, 84, 99, 109, 120, 125–27, 148, 156, 160–71, 177–79, 187–91
destruction, 126
devil, 11, 51, 99
devotio moderna, 16
devotion, 7
Denck, H., 13, 15, 25, 131
dialogical personalism, 9, 30, 182–84
dichotomy, 18
discipleship, 9, 10, 20, 36, 98
discipline, 22, 123, 126, 128, 175
divinity, 154, 157
dynamic, ix, xii, 28, 29, 30, 32, 64, 67, 69, 142, 145, 162, 177, 181–85, 190–92, 194, 195

ecclesiology, 20–22, 82, 105
Eck, J., 2, 3, 8, 16, 25, 123
effort, 56, 59, 60, 127, 175, 189
election, 60, 112
enem(y/ies), 11, 48
entrance, 116, 119, 120, 175, 193
Erasmus, D., 3, 8, 15, 25, 35, 36, 37, 39, 40, 66, 123, 134, 181, 185
error, 2, 162, 175
Eucharist. *See* Lord's Supper
evangelical, 3, 7, 9, 12, 16
evil(doer), 18, 35, 41, 45–51, 53–55, 57–59, 61, 66, 110, 118, 126, 128, 129, 140, 141, 173, 176
ex opere operato, 93, 95, 102, 105, 138, 139, 186
exclusion, 175, 176, 177
excommunication, 105, 121, 123, 147, 150, 176–78
execut(e/ion), 7, 8
exegesis, 44, 51
external, 27, 42, 43, 64, 85, 92, 96, 97, 99, 102, 105, 111, 114, 116, 118, 125, 127, 128, 138, 142, 155, 186, 187

Faber, J., 80, 81
faith, ix, xi, xii, 1, 5–8, 17, 21, 23, 25, 28–35, 37–41, 43–45, 49, 54, 58, 61, 66–73, 78, 80, 82–89, 93, 94, 97, 98, 100, 103–6, 108, 110–25, 127–31, 135, 138–46, 151, 153, 154, 158–62, 164, 165, 167, 169, 170, 172, 175–77, 179, 181, 182, 184–88, 190–92, 194
fall(en), 16, 47–54, 56, 57, 59, 72, 73, 128, 139, 163
fanatic(s/al), 8, 11
fasting, 4
fellowship, 109, 120, 123, 124, 161, 165, 167, 168, 171, 172, 174, 176
Ferdinand II, 7
flesh, 41, 46–53, 59, 61, 62, 65, 108, 109, 114, 125, 126, 128, 136, 155, 157–60, 166, 168, 172, 173, 178, 187, 189
forbidden, 48, 53, 83, 119, 137
foreknowledge, 18, 39, 59
forgiveness, 41, 86, 93, 99, 100, 101, 103, 104, 106, 109, 116–20, 122–25, 135, 138, 143, 145, 164, 186, 187, 194
fraternal admonition, 121, 122, 147, 150, 163, 174–78, 189, 194
freedom, 5, 16, 39, 41, 42, 47, 48, 55, 58, 61, 83, 112,
of the will, 7, 15, 21, 29, 31–33, 35–37, 42–45, 48, 53–58, 60, 63, 66, 67, 146, 173, 181, 184, 185, 190
Freiburg, 2
Friedberg, 2, 73
Fromm, 33, 34
Frombmachung, 33, 34
future, 61, 62, 64, 65, 139, 140, 142, 170, 188, 191

205

Index

good, 15, 28, 34, 36, 37, 39, 41, 43, 45–51, 53–57, 59, 61, 62, 65, 66, 86, 99, 103, 114, 118, 125–28, 130, 136, 140, 153, 161, 167, 172–76, 179
gospel, 5, 34, 35, 83, 85, 86, 88, 112, 124, 128, 129, 131, 158, 164,
government, 4, 5, 13, 24, 74, 84, 119, 129, 130
grace, 15, 17, 20–22, 25, 31, 36, 37, 42, 49, 54–61, 65, 67, 85, 91, 92, 94, 95, 97, 98, 102, 112, 114–17, 140, 141, 151–53, 158, 165, 167, 168, 172–74, 179, 186, 188, 190, 191, 194
gratia gratis data, 15
Great Commission, 91
Grebel, C., 3, 4, 6, 11
Grebel circle, 13
guilt(y), 48, 73, 94, 101, 134

heretic(s), 5, 6, 8
Holy Spirit, 15, 43, 44, 49, 50, 72, 90, 99, 107–9, 111–16, 118, 120, 122, 126, 139, 173, 186, 187, 191
Hugh of St. Victor, 92
human, respons(e/ibility) 17, 21, 56, 58, 99, 116
humanism, 3, 16
Hut, H., 110, 131, 133
Hutterites, 9

I-It, 182–84, 186
I-Thou, 182, 183, 187
illumination, 50, 58, 109, 111, 113, 115, 116
images, 4, 71
incarnation, 155, 156
individual, xi, 15, 35, 37, 38, 46, 64, 65, 85, 87, 88, 104, 115, 121, 124, 126, 138, 168, 176, 180, 184, 189
Ingolstadt, 3, 73

institution, 72, 79, 83, 84, 92, 109, 118, 120, 138, 139, 148, 171
intellect(ual), 3, 16, 19, 20, 35, 154, 168
interpretation, 11, 19, 20, 23, 26, 27, 39, 48, 52, 53, 62, 63, 65, 66, 69, 70, 72, 74, 76, 79, 81, 82, 90, 91, 93–95, 97, 99, 102, 106, 124, 134, 136, 137, 147, 148, 150, 151, 156, 160, 170, 186

Jews, 3
just(ification/ify), ix, xi, xii, 1, 17, 19, 22, 28, 29, 31, 33, 34, 38, 39, 41, 47, 54, 55, 61, 70, 89, 92, 94–99, 105, 106, 108, 117, 127, 134, 135, 137, 142–144, 153, 181, 186, 191, 194

Karlstadt, A., 2, 147–49
Kreuzenstein castle, 7

Leonhard von Lichtenstein, 7
liturgy, 22, 121, 143, 149, 150, 167–69, 173
Lord's Supper, ix, xii, 1, 7, 8, 18–26, 29, 30, 41, 44, 65, 73, 135, 145–79, 182, 188–90, 194
Louis II, 7
Luther(an), 2, 4, 8, 11, 15, 16, 19, 21, 33–35, 37–40, 42, 44, 54, 70, 79, 81, 95, 117, 123, 126, 143, 149, 151, 153–59, 164, 166, 169, 177, 181, 185, 189

magistracy, 84
magisterial, ix, 11, 17, 21, 22, 24, 25, 26, 107, 150, 188
Mantz, F., 13
mass, 71, 73, 147–50, 152, 153, 162, 163, 169

206

medieval, 3, 9, 14, 15–17, 19–21, 26, 91, 92, 94, 95, 99, 101–3, 105, 106, 146, 147, 151, 181, 192
memorial(ism), 26, 41, 147–49, 156–58, 162–72, 177, 178, 188, 190
Mennonites, 8, 9, 11, 24
merit, 8, 15, 31, 55, 56, 58, 153
meritum de congruo (merit of congruity), 15
monk, 3
monogenesis, 8, 9, 11–13
Moravia, 7, 149
mortification, 109, 125, 126, 187
Müntzer(ite), 11, 111, 131, 132
mystical, 17, 43

nature, 22, 23, 31, 38, 39, 41, 42, 46–49, 51–53, 55–58, 69, 79, 88, 92, 95, 100, 102, 113, 125–28, 131, 152, 154–59, 166, 170, 173, 180, 183, 187, 190, 192
Nikolsburg, 7, 14, 146, 150
nominalism, 15

obedience, 51, 54, 62, 68, 118–20, 128, 130, 132, 135
object(ive), ix, 28, 64, 67, 69, 132, 137, 139, 142, 144, 153, 155, 160, 166, 182, 183, 185, 188, 195
obligation, 7, 29, 41, 67, 118, 148, 150, 162, 169, 171–73, 189, 190
Oecolampad, 72, 77, 78
oil, 127–29
omnipotence, 18, 156
Origen, 177

pacifism, 12
passive, 34, 66, 119, 144, 182

past (event), 61–65, 139, 140, 162, 165, 167–72, 178, 188, 190, 191
Peasant's War, 6
Pelagi(us/an/anism), 16, 17, 36, 54–57, 59, 60, 63, 64, 66, 67, 77, 137, 173
penance, 92
persecution, 50, 119, 125, 127–29, 131, 187
personal, 4, 7, 34, 37, 53, 64–66, 84, 87, 88, 106, 111, 115, 127, 144, 162, 171, 177, 182–86, 192
Peter Lombard, 20, 26, 91, 92, 93, 94, 102, 152
Philips, D., 21
physician, 99, 128
pilgrimages, 73
pledge (oath), 21, 22, 85, 98, 116, 120–22, 131, 135, 145, 149, 161–63, 168–73, 175, 178, 188–90
polygenesis, 8, 9, 12, 13
power of the keys, 116, 122–124
practice, 6, 16, 17, 22, 29, 68, 69, 72, 79, 82, 83, 85–87, 89, 94, 96, 97, 117–20, 122–25, 134–36, 138, 139, 141, 145–47, 150, 151, 153, 161, 162, 164, 169, 171, 174, 176, 178, 181, 186, 188, 192, 194
preaching, 3, 7, 28, 75, 85, 86, 87, 88, 99, 100, 103, 114, 115
precondition, 84, 87, 97, 160, 187
prerequisite, 87, 103, 110, 144, 146, 151, 160, 162, 165, 167, 188
predestination, 17, 18, 31, 35, 39, 44, 59, 60, 62, 192
present (tense), 21, 41, 61–65, 67, 131, 139, 140, 145, 155, 157, 163, 165, 167, 169, 170–72, 174, 178, 179, 183, 184, 188–91

Index

priesthood of all believers, 20, 81, 82
proclamation, 96, 148, 161, 164
Protestant(s/ism), xi, 8, 9, 14, 19, 28, 31, 142, 151
providence, 35, 38, 39, 45, 60, 63, 66, 67, 141
purgatory, 7, 73

radical(s), ix, 1, 4, 5, 8, 11–14, 17, 19, 21, 24, 26, 44, 79, 133, 134, 151, 188
rebaptism, 79, 93, 95–97
rebirth, 107, 113,
recognition, 34, 47, 53, 58, 86, 100, 106, 110, 114–16, 128, 131, 167, 168, 171, 172, 174, 175, 178, 179, 190, 191
reformation, xii, 1, 2, 4, 5, 8–11, 14, 16, 19, 21, 24, 28, 31–33, 39, 40, 54, 66, 67, 80–82, 119, 133, 136, 144, 151, 181, 188, 191, 192, 194
reformer(s), ix, x, xi, 4, 8, 11, 15, 17–19, 22–28, 31–34, 44, 45, 54, 58, 66, 67, 77, 79, 80, 82, 95, 107, 119, 133, 134, 142, 144, 150, 151, 153, 159, 188, 191
regeneration, 126
Regensburg, 3, 4, 73
relation(ship/al) 21, 23, 28–30, 39, 41, 51, 61, 65, 69, 78, 87, 93, 95, 100, 106, 107, 115, 124, 133–35, 137–40, 142, 145, 162, 165, 171, 175, 178, 181–86, 188, 190
 with God, 31, 38, 64, 114–16, 126, 127, 143, 144, 161, 166, 170, 173, 174, 176–78, 184, 187, 189, 191, 192
 with believers, 82, 104, 105, 120, 121, 124, 125, 142, 143, 161, 172, 174, 178, 186, 187, 192, 193

 with world, 129, 131, 143
remembrance, 148, 156, 160, 162, 164, 165, 167–69, 171, 190
remissionem peccatorum, 101, 138
repentance, 84, 92, 96, 99, 101, 103, 104, 106, 124, 143, 186
respond, 47, 67, 75, 98, 100, 103, 107
restoration, 47, 50, 58, 59, 65, 92, 113, 115, 117, 126, 128, 194
resurrection, 51, 72, 84, 91, 109, 114, 120, 126, 191
Reublin, W., 6, 72, 79
revolutionary, 11
Riedemann, P., 11
righteous(ness), 32, 33, 49, 99, 103, 128, 153
Roland of Bologna, 92
Rychard, W., 3
rule (of Christ), 100, 104, 105, 108, 115, 117, 119–21, 124, 125, 139, 143, 144, 150, 161, 162, 166, 175, 176, 182, 189–94

sacrament(s/al), 7, 14, 19, 21, 22, 26, 41, 43, 70, 91–96, 101–3, 105, 106, 109, 116, 118, 119, 122–24, 133–38, 140, 144–46, 152–55, 157, 159, 164, 167–70, 176, 186–88, 190, 194
salvation, ix–xi, xii, 2, 14–19, 22–24, 29–32, 35–39, 42, 54–61, 63–67, 69, 70, 81, 83, 85, 89, 93, 94, 96, 111, 112, 118, 119, 122, 124, 130, 134, 137–42, 144–46, 153, 164, 173, 177, 180, 181, 184–92, 194, 195
 by faith, 1, 25, 28, 29, 67, 71, 88, 181
 infant, 138, 140, 141
Samaritan, 127, 128
sanctification, 11, 92
Schaffhausen, 2, 5

Index

Schleitheim Conffession, 13, 84, 130
Scholastic(ism), 14–16, 18, 19, 95
Schwenckfelt, C., 43, 79
Second Zurich Disputation, 147, 148
semi-Pelagian(ism), 16, 17, 54, 59, 60, 63, 66, 67
separati(on/sm/st), 13, 26, 129, 131, 176, 187
sign(ify), 21, 41, 91, 92, 94, 97, 101, 103, 106, 114, 129, 133, 135, 136, 139, 145, 148, 156, 160, 161, 164, 170, 171, 178
sin(ful/ner), 33, 34, 36, 37, 41, 45, 48, 51, 55, 56, 59, 65, 74, 84, 86, 92–94, 97–104, 106, 109, 110, 116–28, 131, 133, 134, 136, 138–40, 143, 145, 162–64, 170, 174–78, 186, 187, 194
　　original sin, 56, 94, 133, 134, 135–38, 140, 141, 145, 181, 188
Simons, Menno, 19
sixteenth century, ix–xi, 1, 4, 8, 10, 12–15, 19, 20, 23, 33, 159, 180
sola fide(s), 18, 33, 70
sola scriptura, 80
soteriology(y/ical), ix, 1, 2, 8, 22, 23, 25, 28, 30, 32, 39, 45, 54, 57, 58, 60, 66–70, 89, 90, 119, 133, 137, 145, 181–83, 185–87, 190, 191, 195
soul, 17, 37, 41, 42, 45–53, 58, 59, 61, 62, 65, 66, 83, 112, 113, 115, 125, 126, 128, 132, 155, 157
spirit, 17, 41, 42, 43, 45–53, 59, 61, 62, 65, 76, 80, 126, 143, 155, 166
spiritual(ism/ist/ity), 7, 9, 19, 43, 44, 81, 92, 111, 113, 115, 126, 158, 159, 162, 166–68, 190
stake, 2, 7, 50
state, 5, 11, 134, 136
static, 28, 173, 182, 183, 192
Staupitz, J., 14
Strasbourg, 72
subject(ive), 64–67, 69, 116, 130, 131, 139, 142, 144, 160, 166, 171, 178, 181–85, 188, 190
suffer(ing), 41, 46, 47, 50, 51, 78, 108, 119, 120, 127–29, 131–33, 144, 147, 148, 156, 160, 161, 167, 168, 171, 177, 178, 183, 187, 190
sword, 5, 11, 13, 14, 50, 76, 130
synergism, 17, 30, 37

Tertullian, 77
testimony (public), 39, 76, 84, 88, 100, 103–6, 109, 116–21, 125, 128, 139, 161
transactional, ix, 28, 64, 67, 69, 137, 138, 141, 142, 144, 160, 178, 180–83, 185, 186, 188, 189, 191, 195
transgression, 48, 121, 132, 134
transubstantiation, 149, 151–56, 158, 164, 165, 166, 177
treatise(s), xii, 5–7, 33, 37, 42–45, 57, 60, 66, 73–78, 90, 96, 98, 99, 107, 108, 111, 130, 147–149, 162–64
trichotomi(c/sm), 17, 42, 45–47, 51–53, 66, 185
Trinitarian, 98
Trinity, 38, 93, 123, 159
tripartite, 1, 17
truth, 6, 7, 10, 28, 29, 34, 38, 45, 58, 62, 80–82, 112, 113, 171

Vienna, 2, 7
voluntas, 18, 36

Index

Waldshut, 2–7, 72, 146, 150
Wellenberg prision (Wasserturm), 6
will, ix–xiii, 1, 7, 8, 15–21, 23, 25, 28, 29, 31–69, 85, 88, 101, 104, 105, 112–14, 116, 120–22, 126–31, 139, 141–44, 146, 165, 168, 171–73, 175, 181, 182, 184, 185, 187, 190, 192, 193
witness, 50, 82, 104, 127, 132, 142
Word, 6, 10, 19, 38, 41, 43, 44, 49–51, 58, 65, 66, 72, 74, 76, 80–89, 100, 103, 109, 110–16, 120, 122, 125, 126, 132, 135, 139, 141, 142, 150, 154–58, 160, 164, 165, 176, 187
works, 15, 17, 22, 39, 43, 59, 86, 87, 99, 100, 110, 111, 118, 125, 127, 130, 141, 165, 173
wound(ed/s), 41, 48, 49, 52, 99, 127, 128
wrath, 41

Zurich, 4–7, 9, 10, 72, 75, 79, 81, 108, 134, 136
Zwingli(an), 4, 6, 8–10, 15, 19–21, 26, 29, 70, 73–81, 83, 85, 87–91, 95–99, 102, 105–8, 111–13, 123, 133–37, 139, 142, 145, 147, 148, 151, 156, 157, 159, 160, 163, 164, 166, 170, 177, 181, 186, 189, 190
Zwickau prophets, 111

www.ingramcontent.com/pod-product-compliance
Lightning Source LLC
Chambersburg PA
CBHW070253230426
43664CB00014B/2517